MODERNISM AND CULTURAL CONFLICT, 1880–1922

In *Modernism and Cultural Conflict*, Ann Ardis questions commonly held views of the radical nature of literary modernism. She positions the coterie of writers centered around Ezra Pound, T. S. Eliot, and James Joyce among a number of groups in Britain intent on redefining the cultural work of literature at the turn of the twentieth century. Ardis emphasizes the ways in which these modernists secured their cultural centrality by documenting their support of mainstream attitudes toward science, their retreat from a supposed valuing of scandalous sexuality in the wake of Oscar Wilde's trials in 1895, and the conservative cultural and sexual politics masked by their radical formalist poetics. Recovering key instances of opposition to modernist self-fashioning in British socialism and feminism of the period, Ardis considers how literary modernism's rise to aesthetic prominence paved the way for the institutionalization of English studies through the devaluation of other aesthetic practices.

ANN L. ARDIS is Professor of English and Director of the University Honors Program at the University of Delaware. She is the author of *New Women, New Novels: Feminism and Early Modernism* (1990) and co-editor (with Bonnie Kime Scott) of *Virginia Woolf Turning the Centuries: Selected Papers from the Ninth Annual Conference on Virginia Woolf* (2000) and (with Leslie Lewis) of *Women's Experience of Modernity, 1875–1945* (2002).

MODERNISM AND CULTURAL CONFLICT
1880–1922

ANN L. ARDIS

CAMBRIDGE
UNIVERSITY PRESS

PUBLISHED BY THE PRESS SYNDICATE OF THE UNIVERSITY OF CAMBRIDGE
The Pitt Building, Trumpington Street, Cambridge CB2 1RP, United Kingdom

CAMBRIDGE UNIVERSITY PRESS
The Edinburgh Building, Cambridge, CB2 2RU, UK
40 West 20th Street, New York, NY 10011-4211, USA
477 Williamstown Road, Port Melbourne, VIC 3207, Australia
Ruiz de Alarcón 13, 28014 Madrid, Spain
Dock House, The Waterfront, Cape Town 8001, South Africa

http://www.cambridge.org

First published 2002

Printed in the United Kingdom at the University Press, Cambridge

Typeface Baskerville Monotype 11 / 12.5 pt   *System* LATEX 2ε   [TB]

A catalogue record for this book is available from the British Library

Library of Congress Cataloging in Publication data

Ardis, Ann L., 1957–
Modernism and cultural conflict, 1880–1922 / Ann L. Ardis.
p.   cm.
Includes bibliographical references and index.
ISBN 0 521 81206 2
1. English literature – 20th century – History and criticism.   2. Modernism
(Literature) – Great Britain.   3. Culture conflict – Great Britain.
4. Culture conflict in literature.   1. Title.
PR478.M6 A74   2002
820.9′112 – dc21   2002067060

ISBN 0 521 81206 2 hardback

Phil (again)
Rachel and Alex

Contents

Acknowledgments

My intellectual debts are many, and are recognized in endnotes throughout. I take this opportunity to thank the institutions and foundations that helped to underwrite the research and writing of this book. The National Endowment for the Humanities provided a summer grant in 1994 for work on D. H. Lawrence and early cinema. The Office of the Vice Provost for Academic Programs and Planning at the University of Delaware funded Anne Thalheimer's cite-checking of the final manuscript, and Morris Library's staff facilitated both the purchase of the *New Age* microfilm for its collection and innumerable interlibrary loans for me. Cambridge University Press's readers provided invaluable suggestions on the final draft. Earlier versions of material in several chapters appeared as essays under the following titles: "Beatrice Webb's Romance with Ethnography," *Women's Studies* 18, 2/3 (Fall 1990), 1–15; "Shakespeare and Mrs. Grundy: Modernizing Literary Value in the 1890s," *Transforming Genres: New Approaches to British Fiction in the 1890s,* ed. Meri-Jane Rochelson and Nikki Lee Manos (New York: St. Martin's Press, 1994), pp. 1–20; "Delimiting Modernism and the Literary Field: D. H. Lawrence and *The Lost Girl,*" *Outside Modernism: In Pursuit of the English Novel, 1900–30,* ed. Nancy Paxton and Lynne Hapgood (London and New York: Palgrave Macmillan/St. Martin's, 2000), pp. 123–44; "Reading 'as a Modernist'/De-naturalizing Modernist Reading Protocols: Wyndham Lewis's *Tarr,*" *Rereading Modernism: New Directions in Feminist Criticism,* ed. Lisa Rado (New York and London: Garland Press, 1994), pp. 373–90; "Netta Syrett's Aestheticization of Everyday Life: Countering the 'Counterdiscourse' of Aestheticism," in *New Approaches to British Aestheticism,* ed. Talia Schaffer and Kathy Psomiades (Charlottesville: University of Virginia Press, 1999), pp. 233–50; and "Toward a Redefinition of Experimental Writing: Netta Syrett's Realism, 1908–1912," *Famous Last Words: Women Against Novelistic Endings,* ed. Alison Booth (Charlottesville: University of Virginia Press, 1993), pp. 259–79. For permission to reprint the revised material here, I would like to thank Taylor and Francis Ltd., Palgrave Macmillan, and the University of Virginia Press. For permission to use a detail of Wyndham Lewis's "The Dancers" (1912) on the front cover, I thank the estate of Mrs. G. A. Wyndham Lewis and the Manchester City Art Galleries.

Introduction: rethinking modernism, remapping the turn of the twentieth century

Rachel Vinrace, the heroine of Virginia Woolf's first novel, *The Voyage Out* (1915), reads "modern books, books in shiny yellow covers, books with a great deal of gilding on the back, which were tokens in her aunt's eyes of harsh wrangling and disputes about facts which had no such importance as the moderns claimed for them."[1] She reads Ibsen and George Meredith's *Diana of the Crossways* as well during her three-month stay in South America, but the narrator's physical and thematic characterization of this reading matter in Chapter Ten strongly suggests that she is reading *fin-de-siècle* British titles: Bodley Head publications such as John Lane's "Keynotes" fiction series, bound volumes of the *Savoy* with bold yellow covers and gilding on the covers and spines.[2] Such texts were touchstones in the British debates about New Women, New Hellenism, and the cultural work of literature in the 1880s and 90s. Yet Rachel is encouraged by everyone she knows to read *something else*.

Her aunt, for example, encourages her to read "Defoe, Maupassant, or some spacious chronicle of family life" (130), and Mrs. Dalloway gives her Jane Austen. Her uncle allows her unlimited access to his library, while St. John Hirst lends her his copy of Gibbon's *Decline and Fall of the Roman Empire*, hoping thereby to begin the process of making up for her lack of a public school education and Oxbridge training. Most telling for my purposes is Terence Hewet's advice the morning he interrupts her piano-playing to demand that she listen while he reads aloud his own notes "under the heading Women" (323). As her fiancé, and as an aspiring young novelist intent on writing a book about Silence, Hewet is annoyed with Rachel in this scene for refusing to endorse his revelations concerning "the secrets of her sex" (324). When she objects to his interruption, he responds by chiding her, not for her piano-playing but for her reading habits: "Rachel, you do read trash! . . . And you're behind the times too, my dear. No one dreams of reading this kind of thing now – antiquated problems plays, harrowing descriptions of life in the east end – oh, no, *we've exploded all that.* Read poetry, Rachel, poetry, poetry, poetry!" (325, emphasis added).

Who is "we" in this context? And why is Hewet so determined to extricate Rachel from the *fin de siècle?*[3]

Louise DeSalvo has suggested that *The Voyage Out*, which Woolf worked on from 1905 to 1913, "bristles with social commentary and impresses one with Woolf's engagement with the most significant problems of Edwardian and Georgian England." Specifically, DeSalvo notes that Woolf comments upon

the trade union movement, labor unrest, the suffrage movement, Balfour and Lloyd George, the Lords' rejection of the budget, the conflict between humanism and empire building, changes in religion, the Irish nationalist movement, protectionism, class, the education of women, the excitement over airplanes, the prospect of war with Germany, the Moroccan crisis, revolution in Portugal, and the issue of the Dreadnoughts. (xiv)

In light of Hewet's conversation with Rachel, however, a crucial omission from this catalogue of Edwardian and Georgian concerns is the "blasting and bombadiering" about aesthetics through which the London-based Anglo-American avant-garde began catapulting itself – and, not quite coincidentally, the discipline of English studies – to cultural prominence during the pre-war years.[4]

In other words, Hewet's "we" might well be the "men of 1914": the coterie of writers and artists centered around James Joyce, Ezra Pound, T. S. Eliot, and Wyndham Lewis who credentialed themselves, each other, and the literary field through reference to the scientific precision of poetic observation, the a-politicization of aesthetics, and the elevation of individual consciousness over social action/interaction.[5] On one side of the binary oppositions Hewet deploys so belligerently in this scene lie poetry, Hewet's own as yet unwritten *écriture feminine*, and his aesthetic alliance with St. John Hirst. On the other lie hack writers of study guides (Miss Allen), female readers who either read books they presume are "modern" but which Hewet doesn't countenance as such (Rachel Vinrace) or reject the privileging of art over social action (Evelyn Murgatroyd), and the "entire 'gay' circle associated with 1890s book design."[6]

We've exploded all that.

Hewet's phrase, "all that," encompasses quite a wide array of "modern" phenomena: "harrowing descriptions of life in the east end," problem plays and controversial 1890s fiction, late Victorian aestheticism, (radical) politics. His linked binaries not only create hierarchies within the contemporary social world (poetry versus the novel, high art versus "trash," aesthetics versus politics). They also operate temporally, severing "us" from all things "antiquated." Thus, from Hewet's perspective, Rachel's "modern books" are in fact not modern at all. She's "behind the times" in her reading habits. "No one dreams of reading th[at] kind of thing now" (325). No one, that is, who is one of "us." Carving chasms between the past and the present, and between (male) aesthetic experts and both (female) common readers and the homosocial literary subculture of the 1890s, Hewet positions the poetry he values as *the* aesthetic of modernity, proclaiming its symbolic capital in the process.[7]

He seeks as well Rachel's agreement with him on these matters. Rather than endorse his views, however, she retreats into what Woolf terms elsewhere the "primitive" "sensuality" of illness.[8] In unexpected tandem with Signora Mendoza, the South American prostitute who is asked to leave the hotel at Santa Marina shortly before Rachel falls ill, she withdraws from the social system at this point rather than be interpellated by it. Thus, in the novel's closing scene, we are left to view the world through the eyes of Mrs. Flushing and St. John Hirst. That is, we are left to view the world through the eyes of two modernists. Mrs. Flushing, *The Voyage Out*'s "wildly eccentric patroness of the avant-garde," is based on Lady Ottoline Morrell, as DeSalvo has suggested (xiii). St. John Hirst, modeled, as any number of critics have noted, after Lytton Strachey, espouses a Bloomsbury-ite's disdain for the grotesque fleshiness (read femaleness) of the material world. Having once explained very carefully to Rachel his repulsion for the female breast, St. John now, "[w]ithout any sense of disloyalty to Terence and Rachel," "ceas[es] to think about either of them" in the last scene of the novel (415), focusing instead on the abstract patterns of sounds and images that he builds as he sits in the hotel drawing room while Mrs. Flushing admires the afterglow of a tropical rainstorm: "The movements and the voices seemed to draw together from different parts of the room, and to combine themselves into a pattern before his eyes; he was content to sit silently watching the pattern build itself up, looking at what he hardly saw" (415).

And yet, even though *The Voyage Out* thus charts a voyage *into* a modernist world view, Woolf's text enables a reading of this particular historical "progress" against the grain. Recent criticism on the novel has focused elsewhere: on Rachel's voyage toward death, Woolf's critique of British imperialism, and the novel's relationship to travel writing and anthropology.[9] I choose instead to foreground these liminal details, the characterization of Rachel's books and Hewet's criticism of her reading habits, because they emblematize so beautifully the dynamics of modernist literary and cultural historiography that my own book seeks to denaturalize.[10] Woolf's fictional representation of the process by which, to borrow Raymond Williams's phrasing, "a highly selected version of the modern" comes to stand in "for the whole of modernity," provides a useful point of entry into the turn-of-the-century debates about literary domain that this book maps as it offers a "thick description" of the Joyce–Pound–Eliot nexus of literary modernism.[11]

The influence of contemporary cultural geographers extends far beyond the boundaries of geography as a discipline. "Mapping" is this project's central conceit because it so usefully glosses not only the social constructedness of literary history but also the extent to which a reading of literary history, like that of a landscape, employs vertical, horizontal, and temporal scales and comparisons. Much recent work on modernism emphasizes the plurality of modernisms and the countercurrents, disagreements, and contestations *within* modernisms. By contrast, following Bonnie Kime Scott's lead, I continue to find a use for the "men of 1914"'s self-labeling as an exclusive coterie – if only as a means of helping us understand their exclusionary moves and anxious territorialism. Following the lead of critics such as Rita Felski as well, rather than use modernism as a more expansive or inclusive category, I would prefer to retain the specificity of the term as a designation for texts that display "formally self-conscious, experimental, [and] antimimetic features... while simultaneously questioning the assumption that such texts are necessarily the most important or representative works of the modern period."[12] My effort to "recover"[13] a turn-of-the-twentieth-century cultural landscape in which modernism did not (yet) throw gigantic shadows thus situates this project in conversation with the work of any number of revisionary critics of modernism whose research has "disclosed... territories previously forgotten or unknown" in "the all too familiar terrain of Edwardian and Modernist literature"[14] and reclaimed texts that were "exiled by genre"[15] when the modernist avant-garde garnered institutional backing for mapping modernity through a series of "great divides."[16]

I use the term "when" here deliberately – and intend for my readers to hear a reference to Raymond Williams's important essay, "When Was Modernism?," in this phrasing. As Williams notes, dating modernism isn't simply a matter of identifying beginning and end dates for a particular kind of artistic experimentation. Instead, understanding the "when" of modernism entails understanding the "machinery of selective tradition": the long and complex process by means of which the work of an international set of late nineteenth- and early twentieth-century artists in self-imposed exile from bourgeois culture has been "comfortab[ly] integra[ted]" into the academy, into museum culture, and into an international capitalist economy of art.[17] Rethinking modernism in this manner "as a discursive and historical field" thus involves tracking reception as well as production and recognizing modernism as an "evolving product of a continuing struggle for certain kinds of symbolic power."[18]

I will have more to say in specific chapters about my indebtedness to other scholars whose work is invoked in the previous paragraph. The reference above to "great divides" invites further comment, however, as it registers my considerable debt to Andreas Huyssen's *After The Great Divide: Modernism, Mass Culture, Postmodernism* (1986) as well as my sense of its limitations as a model for this study.

Huyssen's work has been tremendously influential in modernist studies. Even focusing exclusively on Anglo-American modernism (in other words, ignoring for the moment Huyssen's own focus on German literature and critical theory), it is fair to say that his 1986 study initiated what amounts to a paradigm shift in the conceptualization of modernism's relationships, respectively, to mass culture and science. As David Chinitz has suggested, a "reappraisal of modernism as a whole" is being achieved through the pursuit of Huyssen's suggestion that mass culture has always been the hidden subtext of the modernist project.[19] As Susan Squier has argued, Huyssen was "one of the first to suggest that the modernist commitment to scientificity may originate in a masculine reaction-formation against feminized mass culture." "With the modernism/modernity/masculinity nexus called into question, we are now able to rethink the hitherto unexamined relations among modernism and science, which has itself been understood as an equally, and unproblematically, masculine territory."[20]

Without discounting the productiveness of Huyssen's thesis or his status as the author (in Foucault's sense) of a new discourse about literary modernism, I would suggest that the reappraisal of modernism Huyssen initiated has not yet gone far enough. Huyssen's brilliant study has shown us that high modernism was never as "modernist" about its uniform hostility to mass culture as its earliest academic promoters might have liked, and it has given us a means of understanding the feminization of all things "other" to a modernist world order. While I endorse without reservation Squier's commitment to rethinking the "hitherto unexamined relations between modernism and science," I would not credit Huyssen with having pursued this insight very far. Rather, when Huyssen describes the need to place modernism in a "larger socio-historical framework" (*After the Great Divide*, p. 4), I am struck by what is missing: modernism's defense of high art is *not* recognized as one component of a very complex network of binary oppositions distinguishing "Literature" from nonliterary writing, culture from science and nature, and "progressive" from "degenerate" evolutionary trends in human history. Modernism's relationship to mass culture is *not* framed in relationship to the pursuit of disciplinary specificity and integrity driving the (re)organization of the human and natural sciences at the turn of the twentieth century. The tendency to treat science as something beyond the pale, outside the cultural critic's horizon of interests is, I would venture to suggest, one of the most unfortunate legacies of the Frankfurt School in Huyssen's work.[21] Technology has a key role to play in his conceptualization of modernism and modern life, yet the model of cultural analysis he inherits from Adorno encourages a rather dismissive characterization of science as the epitome of the enlightenment project's problematic faith in rationality. Thus, as Susan Squier has noted, rather than conceptualizing science sociologically, Huyssen reproduces while rendering invisible the "divide between scientific practice and the feminized discursive fields of literature [and] poetry" (Squier, 303–4). As a consequence, *After the Great Divide* provides an exemplary instance of what has been described as the "perplexin[g] stabi[lity]" of modernist categories of literary analysis in the late twentieth century.[22]

We have not yet managed "to *rethink* or *rechart . . .* modernism in terms other than those [it] narrated/laid out for itself," Deborah Jacobs has argued (277). We continue "to read modernism from within its own politics and prejudices" – even sometimes, I would add, when we think we're doing something else (288). Rather than "contin[uing] to settle for the 'thin' definition of modernism" derived from "dominant modernist narratives," Jacobs urges us to imagine "a larger discursive and highly politicized field of inquiry – a field wherein the 'literary' [is recognized as] only one of many newly specialized discourses struggling for legitimation," in the early twentieth century (288, 289). Questioning whether "the privileges and powers of *the subject position* we've inherited from modernist intellectuals" (276, emphasis in the original) are challenged by certain kinds of recovery work, Jacobs invites modernist studies to attend to "the cultural politics of the move toward expertise itself, the elite positioning of 'high' modernist art in relation to its 'others,' [and] the self-interested privileging of experimentation with technique over other ways of 'making it new.'" She goes on to suggest that "a commitment to transforming the category 'the literary' (and 'art,' 'the artist,' etc.) – especially as defined and privileged in/through/by modernist discourse – is precisely what we need more of right now" (277). Although substantial new work in modernist studies rises to the challenge Jacobs posed so eloquently in 1994, her point still holds today.[23] Keeping in mind the concerns she and scholars such as Bruce Robbins and Thomas Strychacz have raised regarding late twentieth-century criticism's investments in the reproduction of modernist categories of literary analysis, this study will ask: how did modernism come to be perceived as *the* aesthetic of modernity? What *other* aesthetic and political agendas were either erased from cultural memory or thoroughly discredited as the literary avant-garde achieved cultural legitimacy and English studies charged itself with disciplinary credibility? How are the edges, the margins, and even the limitations of modernism revealed once we start paying attention to the ways this literary movement intersects with, borrows from, and reacts against other cultural enterprises?

My study thus contributes in three ways to "the new modernist studies."[24] It positions the "men of 1914" as one among a number of interest groups in Britain at the turn of the twentieth century intent on redefining the cultural work of literature. It emphasizes the backdrop of disciplinary (re)structuring in the context of which the Joyce–Pound–Eliot strand of modernism either secured its own cultural legitimacy or – as in the case of T. S. Eliot's redaction of Ezra Pound's cultural writings into "literary" fare – had disciplinary legitimacy thrust upon it. And it calls into question some very basic and commonly held views of this particular nexus of modernism's radicalness by documenting the following: its support of mainstream attitudes toward science (Chapter 1); its retreat from a supposed valuing of scandalous sexuality in the wake of Oscar Wilde's trials (Chapter 2); the conservative cultural and sexual politics masked by its radical formalist poetics (Chapter 3); and its opposition to key forms of resistance to middle-class values at the turn of the century such as "New Woman" feminism and Guild Socialism (Chapters 4 and 5).

In *Theory of the Avant-Garde*, Peter Bürger distinguished the historical avant-garde from modernism on the basis of the former's critique of the institutionalization of art in the nineteenth century and the latter's investment in its own monumentalization. In the past ten years, scholars have usefully complicated Bürger's distinction by showing how the historical avant-garde, at least in Britain, functioned as what I term here a *modernist*

avant-garde: an avant-garde as interested in creating as in defying institutional affiliations. Studies such as Kevin Dettmar and Stephen Watt's
Marketing Modernism, Michael Coyle's *Ezra Pound, Popular Genres, and the
Discourse of Culture,* Joseph Kelly's *Our Joyce,* Gail McDonald's *Learning To
Be Modern,* and Lawrence Rainey's *Institutions of Modernism* have detailed
the very complicated processes by means of which the aesthetics and
reading practices put forth by modernists and their earliest academic
supporters became the dogma of the new professionals of literary studies, thus guaranteeing an honored place for modernism in the academy
for decades to come.[25] Yet, as I hope to demonstrate in the chapters
that follow, the new modernist studies will continue to be informed by
modernist categories of analysis, and the "reappraisal of modernism as a
whole" that scholars such as David Chinitz have called for will remain in
fact quite limited, unless we are willing to more effectively de-naturalize
both modernist protocols of literary analysis and the modernist mapping
of turn-of-the-twentieth-century British literary and cultural history.

What follows, thus, is a set of case studies that invites us to rethink
the Joyce–Pound–Eliot paradigm of modernism's highly restrictive and
exclusionary mapping of culture and the literary field. I begin by looking at two figures who are, paradoxically, both liminal and central to
British modernism: Beatrice Potter Webb and Oscar Wilde. In Chapter
1 Pound's dismissive characterization of Webb and her husband Sidney in "The Serious Artist" (1913) provides an occasion to reflect on
the changing rhetorics of fiction, ethnography, and social science in the
1880s and 90s. Careful attention to the professional and disciplinary anxieties fueling both Pound's caricature of the Webbs as Fabian Socialists
who believed "that the arts had better not exist at all"[26] and his defense of "serious" art's scientific values reveals some perhaps surprising
similarities between these two seemingly antithetical figures. The female
social scientist who is accused of being "poetry-blind," "fiction-blind,
and drama-blind"[27] and the male modernist aesthete who proclaims the
"scientific" value of art's "data" are both, I argue, byproducts of the renegotiation of disciplinary boundaries that began in the closing decades of
the nineteenth century.

Chapter 2 considers a second strategy through which the London-
based modernist avant-garde sought to shore up literature's symbolic
capital in the face of the rising authority of the (social) sciences: the invention of a literary tradition in which "classic" works of art are deemed
to have universal, transhistorical aesthetic appeal. I seek here to understand how Oscar Wilde's status as an ambiguously gendered *fin-de-siècle*

father-figure to literary modernism is related to celebrations of William Shakespeare as a writer who provides access to ahistorical and universal human truths, and thus can function as the centerpiece of a newly invented national literary tradition.

Chapter 3 focuses on two writers, D. H. Lawrence and Wyndham Lewis, who in certain regards lie "outside" the specific nexus of literary modernism that this study recontextualizes historically. A close reading of Lawrence's *The Lost Girl* (1920) emphasizes the mapping of "modern" culture and the literary field that influential early academic advocates of literary modernism such as F. R. Leavis found so appealing in Lawrence's work, while consideration of a key scene in and early modernist reviews of Lewis's *Tarr* (1918) leads to discussion of the excess of hostility toward bourgeois culture, representational art, and women that powers both Lewis's own and his earliest reviewers' championing of modernist "experimental writing."

Taking a cue from the late Raymond Williams, Chapters 4 and 5 counterpose "alternative traditions" "taken from the neglected works left in the wide margins of the century" against the Joyce–Pound–Eliot vector of modernism's self-serving narratives of cultural centrality.[28] Chapter 4 surveys the work of an Edwardian middlebrow feminist novelist who "talks back" to the modernist avant-garde in order to demonstrate the latter's radical simplification of the scene of literary production in early twentieth-century Britain through its insistence upon a high/low mapping of culture. And Chapter 5 immerses us in the open, spirited, and frequently acrimonious debates about art and art's role in culture among modernists and Guild Socialists in the *New Age* under A. R. Orage's editorship. Although the *New Age* is frequently described as a modernist journal, in fact its editors and contributors point up, over and over again, the cranky narrowness and rather sectarian views of any number of influential modernists as they promote "a revival of the arts"[29] that was never satisfied by or contained by modernist experimentalism.

"We've exploded all that," announces Virginia Woolf's fictional wanna-be modernist, echoing the violent, pugilistic rhetoric of *real* modernist avant-gardists, dismissing "all that" "trash" reading from the Victorian *fin de siècle* he finds in Rachel Vinrace's study – and reminding *us* of the gendered dynamics of power at play in the production and dissemination of a modernist world-view. Refusing identification with Hewet's (or T. S. Eliot's, or Ezra Pound's) "we," this study seeks to tell a different story, a more complex and less teleologically directed story, about the competition among emergent aesthetic and political traditions animating British cultural life at the turn of the twentieth century. At the risk of being accused of obscuring some of the disagreements and contestations taking place *within* modernism(s), I am choosing instead to foreground one particular strand of modernism's dismissive treatments of *other* writing practices. The competition among emergent aesthetic and political traditions in turn-of-the-century Britain was not only fiercer than modernism's own histories of the period suggest. The dynamics among these competing factions – the quarreling as well as the voracious borrowing of ideas – will also require, I argue, a much more detailed and nuanced topographical mapping of the period than modernism's classic "narrative[s] of rupture" have ever provided.[30]

NOTES

1. Virginia Woolf, *The Voyage Out* (New York: Signet Classic, 1991), pp.130–1; Introduction by Louise DeSalvo. Subsequent references to this edition will be cited parenthetically in the text.

2. My thanks go to Margaret Stetz for helping me understand Woolf's physical description of Rachel's *fin-de-siècle* reading. As Stetz notes, "there is no precise correspondence" between what Rachel is reading and any specific 1890s publications. "What Woolf is instead *creating* – not describing – is a kind of composite, deliberately imprecise, notion of an ur-1890s book that alludes in a vague, poetic, and comprehensive way to Bodley Head publications, as well as to non-Bodley Head productions, such as the bound volumes of the *Savoy* (which do, in fact, have gilt lettering and designs on their covers and spines . . .). Hers is a summing up of a 'type' of book and of [1890s book production], with no exact referents." (Private correspondence with the author.)

3. "Extricate" is Hugh Kenner's phrasing, as used to describe his planning of *The Pound Era* to function "as an X-ray moving picture of how our epoch was extricated from the *fin de siècle*"[*The Pound Era* (Berkeley and Los Angeles: University of California Press, 1971), p. xi]. There is no student of literary modernism who *isn't* indebted to Kenner in one way or another, but I echo him here – and begin this study with Woolf, a writer he refers to only three times in *The Pound Era* – in order to sound this study's differences from his work. I shall have more to say below regarding my interest in sounding modernism's deep and complex entanglements in *fin-de-siècle* cultural debates rather than reproducing its moves to "extricate" itself from them.

4. "Blasting and bombadiering" is Wyndham Lewis's phrase, as used to title his collected essays, *Blasting and Bombadiering*, 2nd edition (Berkeley and Los Angeles: University of California Press, 1967 [1937]). Scholarship on the relationship between modernist aesthetics and the organization of English studies as a discipline that informs this study includes: Chris Baldick, *The*

Social Mission of English Criticism, 1848–1932 (Oxford University Press, 1983); Terry Eagleton, "The Rise of English Studies," *Literary Theory: An Introduction* (Minneapolis: University of Minnesota Press, 1983), pp. 17–53; Antony Easthope, *Literary into Cultural Studies* (London and New York: Routledge, 1991); Michael H. Levenson, *A Genealogy of Modernism: A Study of English Literary Doctrine 1909–1922* (Cambridge University Press, 1984); Gail McDonald, *Learning To Be Modern: Pound, Eliot, and the American University* (Oxford University Press, 1993); Bruce Robbins, *Intellectuals: Aesthetics, Politics, and Academics* (Minneapolis: University of Minnesota Press, 1990); Robbins, *Secular Vocations: Intellectuals, Professionalism, Culture* (London and New York: Verso, 1993); Thomas Strychacz, *Modernism, Mass Culture, and Professionalism* (Cambridge University Press, 1993); Raymond Williams, *The Politics of Modernism: Against the New Conformists* (London and New York: Verso, 1989).

5. "The men of 1914" is Wyndham Lewis's phrasing; see "War and Post War," *Blasting and Bombadiering*, pp. 249–51. For a useful discussion of this characterization of the original London-based modernist coterie, see Bonnie Kime Scott, *Refiguring Modernism: The Women of 1928* (Bloomington and Indianapolis: Indiana University Press, 1995), pp. xxxvii-xxxviii.

6. Margaret Diane Stetz, private correspondence with the author.

7. "Symbolic capital" is John Guillory's amendment of Pierre Bourdieu's terminology, as used in *Cultural Capital: The Problem of Literary Canon Formation* (University of Chicago Press, 1993). Guillory defines "linguistic capital" as the social standing one accrues by displaying "a socially credentialed and therefore valued speech, otherwise known as 'Standard English.'" Symbolic capital is the "kind of knowledge-capital whose possession can be displayed upon request and which thereby entitles its possessor to the cultural and material rewards of the well-educated person" (p. ix). Both together constitute what Bourdieu terms cultural capital.

8. Virginia Woolf, "On Being Ill," *Collected Essays of Virginia Woolf* (London: Hogarth Press, 1967), p. 194.

9. See, for example, Sheila Pardee, "Assuming Psyche's Task: Virginia Woolf Responds to James Frazer," in Ann Ardis and Bonnie Kime Scott (eds.), *Virginia Woolf: Turning the Centuries. Selected Papers from the Ninth Annual Conference on Virginia Woolf* (New York: Pace University Press, 2000), pp. 291–7; Lois J. Gilmore, "Virginia Woolf, Bloomsbury, and the Primitive," in Jeannette McVicker and Laura Davis (eds.), *Virginia Woolf and Communities* (New York: Pace University, 1999), pp. 127–35; Andrea Lewis, "The Visual Politics of Empire and Gender in Virginia Woolf's *The Voyage Out*," *Woolf Studies Annual*, 1 (1995): pp. 106–19; Kathy J. Phillips, *Virginia Woolf Against Empire* (Knoxville: University of Tennessee, 1994); Michelle Cliff, "Virginia Woolf and the Imperial Gaze: A Glance Askance," in Mark Hussey and Vara Neverow (eds.), *Virginia Woolf: Emerging Perspectives, Selected Papers from the Third Annual Conference on Virginia Woolf* (New York: Pace University Press, 1994), pp. 91–102; Suzette Henke, "De/Colonizing the Subject in Virginia Woolf's *The Voyage Out*: Rachel Vinrace as La Mysterique," in *Virginia Woolf: Emerging*

Perspectives, pp. 103–8; Laura Davis-Clapper, "Why Did Rachel Vinrace Die? Tracing the Clues from *Melymbrosia* to *The Voyage Out*," in Mark Hussey and Vara Neverow-Turk (eds.), *Virginia Woolf Miscellanies: Proceedings of the First Annual Conference on Virginia Woolf* (New York: Pace University Press, 1992), pp. 222–7;

10. For further explanation of the theoretical underpinnings of such attention to cultural "marginalia," see my discussion of Gayatri Spivak's "Explanation and Culture: Marginalia" in *New Women, New Novels: Feminism and Early Modernism* (New Brunswick: Rutgers University Press, 1990), pp. 5–9. My investigation of what Spivak would term the cultural "repression" orchestrated through classic modernist narratives of rupture from the Victorian period makes this current project, at least in this sense, a direct sequel to *New Women, New Novels*; however, this project's attention to issues of disciplinary organization takes it ultimately in a different direction.

11. Williams, *The Politics of Modernism*, p. 33. "Thick description" is Clifford Geertz's term, as borrowed from Gilbert Ryle; see "Thick Description: Toward an Interpretive Theory of Culture," *The Interpretation of Cultures* (New York: Basic Books, 1973), pp. 3–32.

12. Rita Felski, *The Gender of Modernity* (Cambridge and London: Harvard University Press), p. 25.

13. As the recent exchange between Mary Poovey, Margaret Homans, and Jill Campbell in the *Yale Journal of Criticism* suggests, "recovery" as a (feminist) historiographic enterprise raises thorny theoretical questions that speak to "our profession's current indecision about the role and nature of literary criticism" – and jeopardize "the foundational claims of our entire discipline" (Mary Poovey, "Recovering Ellen Pickering," *Yale Journal of Criticism*, 13, 2 [2000], 451). See also Homans, "A Response to Mary Poovey's 'Recovering Ellen Pickering,'" *Yale Journal of Criticism*, 13, 2 (2000), 453–60; Campbell, "A Response to Mary Poovey's 'Recovering Ellen Pickering,'" *Yale Journal of Criticism* 13, 2 (2000), 461–5; and Poovey, "A Response to Margaret Homans and Jill Campbell," *Yale Journal of Criticism* 13, 2 (2000), 467–8. While Poovey positions archival research on uncanonized women writers antithetically to work on disciplinary history in this fascinating and complex exchange, this study assumes a connection between both enterprises – assumes in fact that archival recovery work and disciplinary self-reflection are most productively pursued simultaneously.

14. Carola M. Kaplan and Anne B. Simpson (eds.), *Seeing Double: Revisioning Edwardian and Modernist Literature* (New York: St. Martin's Press, 1996), p. xx.

15. Celeste Schenck, "Exiled by Genre: Modernism, Canonicity, and the Politics of Exclusion," in Mary Lynn Broe and Angela Ingram (eds.), *Women's Writing in Exile* (Chapel Hill and London: University of North Carolina Press, 1989), pp. 225–50.

16. Andreas Huyssen, *After the Great Divide: Modernism, Mass Culture, Postmodernism* (Bloomington and Indianapolis: Indiana University Press, 1986).

17. Williams, *The Politics of Modernism*, pp. 32, 35.

18. Bridget Elliott and Jo-Ann Wallace (eds.), *Women Artists and Writers: Modernist (Im)positionings* (New York and London: Routledge, 1994), p. 1. For further discussions of these issues, see Hugh Witemeyer, *The Future of Modernism* (Ann Arbor: University of Michigan Press, 1997); Elazar Barkan and Ronald Bush (eds.), *Prehistories of the Future: The Primitivist Project and the Culture of Modernism* (Stanford: Stanford University Press, 1995); Charles Altieri, "Can Modernism Have a Future?," *Modernism/Modernity*, 7, 1 (January 2000), 127–43.

19. David Chinitz, "T. S. Eliot and the Cultural Divide," *PMLA*, 110, 2 (1995), 246.

20. Susan Squier, "Invisible Assistants or Lab Partners? Female Modernism and the Culture(s) of Modern Science," in Lisa Rado (ed.), *Rereading Modernism: New Directions in Feminist Criticism* (New York and London: Garland, 1994), pp. 301. Subsequent references to this source will be cited parenthetically in the text.

21. For a similarly inflected critique of T. J. Clark's monumental recent study of modernism, *Farewell to an Idea: Episodes from a History of Modernism*, see Karsten Harries's review in *Art Bulletin*, 83, 2 (2001), 358–64.

22. Deborah Jacobs, "Feminist Criticism/Cultural Studies/Modernist Texts: A Manifesto for the '90s," Rado, *Rereading Modernism*, p. 277. Subsequent references to this essay will be cited parenthetically in the text.

23. Strong examples of the kind of anti- or post-disciplinary work that Jacobs called for in 1994 include: T. Hugh Crawford, *Modernism, Medicine and William Carlos Williams* (Norman: University of Oklahoma Press, 1993); Timothy Armstrong, *Modernism, Technology, and the Body: A Cultural Study* (Cambridge and New York: Cambridge University Press, 1998); Lisa Rado (ed.), *Modernism, Gender and Culture: A Cultural Studies Approach* (New York: Garland, 1997); Micaela Di Leonardo, *Exotics at Home: Anthropology, Others, American Modernity* (University of Chicago Press, 1998); and Michael Szalay, *New Deal Modernism: American Literature and the Invention of the Welfare State* (Durham, N.C.: Duke University Press, 2000).

24. The term "the new modernist studies" was used first at the inaugural meeting of the Modernist Studies Association in October 1999 to distinguish current revisionary work on modernism from New Criticism's more purely celebratory presentation of modernism. Obviously, however, revisionary work on modernism predates the Modernist Studies Association's first meeting. This project is especially indebted both to feminist revisionary work on modernist dating back at least to the mid-1980s and to recent studies rethinking the relationship of modernism to the Victorian *fin de siècle*, including: Marie DiBattista (ed.), *High and Low Moderns: Literature and Culture, 1889–1939* (Oxford University Press, 1996); Felski, *The Gender of Modernity*; Jonathan Freedman, *Professions of Taste: Henry James, British Aestheticism, and Commodity Culture* (Stanford University Press, 1990); Cassandra Laity, *H. D. and the Victorian Fin-de-Siècle* (Cambridge University Press, 1996); Sally Ledger and Scott McCracken (eds.), *Cultural Politics at the Fin de Siècle* (Cambridge

University Press, 1995); Talia Schaffer, *The Forgotten Female Aesthetes: Literary Culture in Late-Victorian England* (Charlottesville and London: University Press of Virginia, 2000); and Talia Schaffer and Kathy Alexis Psomiades (eds.), *Women and British Aestheticism* (Charlottesville and London: University Press of Virginia, 1999).

25. Kevin J. H. Dettmar and Stephen Watt (eds.), *Marketing Modernism: Self-Promotion, Canonization, Rereading* (Ann Arbor: University of Michigan Press, 1996); Michael Coyle, *Ezra Pound, Popular Genres, and the Discourse of Culture* (Pennsylvania State University Press, 1995; Joseph Kelly, *Our Joyce: From Outcast to Icon* (Austin: University of Texas Press, 1998); Gail McDonald, *Learning to be Modern*; Lawrence Rainey, *Institutions of Modernism: Literary Elites and Public Culture* (New Haven, C.T.: Yale University Press, 1998). See also Ian Willison, Warwick Gould, and Warren Chernaik (eds.), *Modernist Writers and the Marketplace* (London: Macmillan; New York: St. Martin's Press, 1996).

26. Ezra Pound, "The Serious Artist," *The New Freewoman* 1, 9 (October 15, 1913), 161; as reprinted in Lea Baechler, A. Walton Litz, and James Longenbach (eds.), *Ezra Pound's Poetry and Prose: Contributions to Periodicals* (New York and London: Garland, 1991), p. 186.

27. Samuel Hynes, *The Edwardian Turn of Mind* (Princeton University Press, 1968), p. 126. Hynes's characterization of Webb will be discussed further in Chapter 1.

28. Williams, *The Politics of Modernism*, p. 35.

29. Arthur J. Penty, "Art and Plutocracy," *New Age*, 15, 1 (May 7, 1914), 10.

30. Tamar Katz, *Impressionist Subjects: Gender, Interiority, and Modernist Fiction in England* (Champagne-Urbana: University of Illinois Press, 2000), p. 7.

CHAPTER I

Beatrice Webb and the "serious" artist

It is curious that one should be asked to rewrite Sidney's Defense of Poesy in the year of grace 1913. During the intervening centuries, and before them, other centres of civilization had decided that good art was a blessing and that bad art was criminal, and they had spent some time and thought in trying to find means whereby to distinguish the true art from the sham. But in England now, in the age of Gosse as in the age of Gosson we are asked if the arts are moral. We are asked to define the relation of the arts to economics, we are asked what position the arts are to hold in the ideal republic. And it is obviously the opinion of many people less objectionable than the Sydney [sic] Webbs that the arts had better not exist at all.

Ezra Pound, "The Serious Artist" (1913)[1]

We've been sitting in the Park and listening to the Band and having a terrific argument about Shaw. Leonard says we owe a great deal to Shaw. I say that he only influenced the outer fringe of morality. Leonard says that the shop girls wouldn't be listening to the Band with their young men if it weren't for Shaw. I say the human heart is touched only by the poets. Leonard says rot, I say damn. Then we go home. Leonard says I'm narrow. I say he's stunted. But don't you agree with me that the Edwardians, from 1895 to 1914, made a pretty poor show. By the Edwardians, I mean Shaw, Wells, Galsworthy, the Webbs, Arnold Bennett. We Georgians have our work cut out for us, you see. There's not a single living writer (English) I respect: so you see, I have to read the Russians: but here I must stop. I just throw this out for you to think about, under the trees. How does one come by one's morality? Surely by reading the poets. And we've got no poets. Does that throw light on anything? Consider the Webbs – That woman has the impertinence to say that I'm a-moral: the truth being that if Mrs. Webb had been a good woman, Mrs. Woolf would have been a better. Orphans is what I say we are – we Georgians – but I must stop.

Virginia Woolf, letter to Janet Case, 21 May 1922 (528)[2]

> Never never never do I go there [to the Webbs' for lunch] again.
> I can't think how two small old people like that manage to destroy
> everything one likes and believes in.
>   Virginia Woolf, letter to Lady Robert Cecil, 19 February
>   1920 (422)[3]

Beatrice and Sidney Webb, founders of the London School of Economics
and the *New Statesman*, are not typically associated with Anglo-American
literary modernism. Nonetheless, they played an important, if under-
acknowledged, role in the articulation of modernist aesthetics. They are
featured prominently, for example, in the opening paragraph of Pound's
"The Serious Artist" (1913). Sidney Webb is "blasted" in the first issue
of Wyndham Lewis's short-lived modernist journal along with the likes
of Marie Corelli, Rabindranath Tagore, Annie Besant, and the Bishop
of London.[4] And Beatrice Potter Webb is singled out for attack by Virginia Woolf over and over again in letters and diary passages such as
the above. Why do the Webbs merit this kind of hostile attention, one
might ask? Why are they figured, again and again, as the antithesis of
the modernist literary project?

Answering these questions, I will argue in this chapter, entails both
acknowledging how unstable the literary field was in the 1910s and understanding how the modernist avant-garde positioned itself within a set
of gendered discourses about intellectuality, professionalism, and disciplinary (re)organization that dates back at least to the 1880s. This
chapter thus has a double historical focus. I read an exemplary modernist manifesto, Pound's "The Serious Artist," looking for evidence of
the disciplinary and professional anxieties fueling his characterizations
of science, medicine, and Fabian Socialism. But the discussion of this
classic modernist manifesto needs to be prefaced by consideration of a
moment in the late nineteenth century when new disciplinary regimes
and the professionalization of intellectual life more generally threatened
the epistemological authority of literary writing, and a young Beatrice
Potter decided *not* to be a novelist. Opting instead to write first for the *Pall
Mall Gazette* and the *Nineteenth Century*, then as a contributor to Charles
Booth's ethnographic study of London's East End, and finally as Sidney
Webb's collaborator in sociological treatises such as *The History of Trade
Unionism* (1894) and *Industrial Democracy* (1897), Webb describes in her di-
ary how she "puffs [herself] up into a professional," thereby claiming
the "scientific" authority of her social analysis.[5]

Writing twenty years after Webb's "conversion" to Fabian Socialism
and her adoption of the professional discourse of sociology, yet sharing

nonetheless her concerns (to be explored below) regarding what Suzanne Clark has termed "the gendering of intellectuality"[6] and the feminiza-tion of literature, literary modernists sought to (re)establish the cultural authority of literature on firmer ground in the 1910s. They did so by privileging poetry, appropriating the discursive authority of science, and thereby reconstituting the literary field as a "masculine" domain. Posi-tioning themselves antithetically to Fabian Socialists bent on creating the modern welfare state, they figured themselves as "serious," "scientific" artists with their fingers on the pulse of the modern world. This chapter reads these seemingly antithetical figures – the female social scientist who was allegedly "'poetry-blind,'" "fiction-blind and drama-blind"[7] and the male modernist aesthete/scientist – as mirror-image by-products of the renegotiation of disciplinary boundaries and the rise of a culture of professionalism that began in the closing decades of the nineteenth century and continued well into the twentieth century, fueling modernist rhetoric about the integrity of the literary field and the value of "serious" art.

"BUILDING CASTLES IN THE AIR": BEATRICE POTTER'S CRITIQUE OF THE NOVEL

In 1885 Beatrice Potter was twenty-seven. Her mother had been dead for three years, her father's health was declining, and Beatrice, the eighth of nine daughters, was splitting her time between tending her father and working in the East End managing the Katherine Buildings, a group of dwellings "designed and adapted to house the lowest class of the London poor."[8] London in the 1880s was "a place of opportunity" as well as dan-ger for women.[9] Jack the Ripper would begin haunting the public sphere and the public imagination in 1888, both crystallizing and mythologiz-ing a set of concerns about the negative consequences of middle-class women's entrance in the public sphere. But in the meantime, mixed-sex political and social clubs such as the Browning, Fabian, and Men and Women's Club welcomed women; women's clubs proliferated; and the establishment of new "heterosocial spaces"[10] such as public transport, museums, libraries, department stores, theatres, and music halls made it possible for middle-class women to travel alone through the city with-out risk to their sexual and class reputations. They took advantage of this opportunity to create new identities for themselves as all manner of professionals – charity workers, nurses, doctors, teachers, urban ethno-graphers, social investigators, journalists, photographers.

As Deborah Epstein Nord has noted, the 1880s was a "pivotal decade in the public lives of women," and the writing of women such as Eleanor Marx, Olive Schreiner, Margaret Harkness, and Amy Levy "reflects a certain precariousness or tentativeness in their social positions and, as a consequence, in their own notions of themselves."[11] This is certainly true in Beatrice Potter's case as well. She writes cheerily to her father in August 1885, for example, about her current schedule (days spent in the East End interviewing tenants in the Katherine Buildings, evenings in Chelsea at the home of her sister, Kate Courtney): "an interesting hard-working life, with *just a touch* of adventure! is so delightful, so long as one does not get stamped with that most damaging stamp 'Eccentricity.'" Yet she also insists that this letter is "not to be read publicly" to the whole family, for her sisters are not to know about her social charity work.[12] And her diary registers the depth of pain and turmoil she could not share with her father regarding the disastrous end of her romantic relationship with Joseph Chamberlain, leader of the Radical wing of the Liberal Party and President of the Board of Trade in Gladstone's Ministry in July 1885. Three years after their public rupture, she would still write, on the occasion of his marriage to a beautiful young socialite, "It is strange that a being who will henceforth be an utter stranger to my life should be able to inflict such intense pain." "[Work] and [work] alone, I have now to live for, day and night."[13]

In literary circles, George Moore's pamphlet, *Literature at Nurse; or, Circulating Morals*, made great waves in 1885. But Beatrice Potter's concerns lay elsewhere: at the outset of her self-described "working-womanhood" she had already determined *not* to associate herself with anything literary.[14] I want to examine here why Webb tried so hard to assume "the professional, 'scientific' stance of the male social investigator, suppressing her gender and sense of vulnerability";[15] why this sets her up for attack by literary modernists anxious about the cultural capital of their own writing; and finally how this antagonism between the *grande dame* of Fabian Socialism and the London literary avant-garde epitomizes the "gendering of intellectuality" at the turn of the century, opening a window on the stakes involved in the professionalization of literary study and "serious" art. First, though, it is necessary to understand why, in the 1880s, she could not afford to associate herself with the novel as a vehicle of social analysis.

In her diary and her autobiography, Potter offers unalloyed praise for the work of male eighteenth- and nineteenth-century novelists such as Balzac, Goethe, Fielding, Flaubert, and Thackeray. Balzac's "extraordinary power of analysis" attracts her to his work: until "psychology has advanced beyond the study of primitive man and of human characteristics in so far as they distinguish man from other animals," she predicts, it is novelists such as Balzac, the "great analytical students of human nature," whose work "will be found of use in any future of the mental life of humanity."[16] Reflecting in her autobiography on the extensive reading in psychology she did in the 1870s and 80s, Potter speaks very critically of the then newly established discipline:

Instead of the exact descriptions of the actual facts of individual minds, reacting to particular environments and developing in various directions, I seemed to find nothing but arbitrary definitions of mind in the abstract, which did not correspond with the mental life of any one person, and were, in fact, nothing but hypothetical abstractions from an idealized reflection of the working of the author's own mind... I regarded the manipulations of these psychological abstractions as yielding no more accurate information about the world around me than did the syllogisms of formal logic.

She goes on to explain that:

[f]or any detailed description of the complexity of human nature, of the variety and mixture of human motive, of the insurgence of instinct in the garb of reason, of the multifarious play of the social environment on the individual ego and of the individual ego on the social environment, I had to turn to novelists and poets, to Fielding and to Flaubert, to Balzac and Browning, to Thackeray and Goethe... Thrown back on books, books, and again books, I began to select these, not in order to satisfy curiosity and extend interest in life, but deliberately so as to forge an instrument of discovering about human nature in society.[17]

These very positive remarks differ significantly from Potter's comments about women novelists, who are consistently criticized for promoting the ideology of sentimentalism (though she herself doesn't use this term) – and discussed relatively rarely in any detail. In the earliest surviving fragment of her diary, which was probably written in 1868, Potter objects to the way young girls are brought up on a steady diet of romantic fiction. Lacking personal experience and practical opportunities, the young "girl of nine or ten" reads to escape from rather than engage with reality. Instead of reading to "gain knowledge," she "builds castles in the air"; her mind is "wasted on making up love scenes... where she is always the charming heroine without a fault." Herself a ten-year-old in 1868, Potter then confesses: "I have found it a serious stumbling-block to myself; whenever I get alone I always find myself building castles in the air of some kind; it is a habit that is so thoroughly immured in me that I cannot build a good resolution without making a castle in the air about it." Four years later, she echoes the earlier entry, this time striking an even harsher note of self-disgust at the intensity of her erotic ambitions, which preclude other interests:

to say the truth, I am very disgusted with myself; whenever I am in the company of any gentleman, I cannot help wishing and doing all I possibly can to attract his attention and admiration; the whole time I am thinking how I look, which attitude becomes me, and contriving every possible [way] to make myself more liked and admired than [my] sisters.[18]

Almost ten years later still, she determines to use her diary as a detoxification program, a medium for purging herself of "miserable egotistical feelings" and forcing herself "out of herself."[19]

Potter's sense of her own susceptibility to erotic fantasies begins to explain the harshness of her infrequent remarks about women novelists' work. *Jane Eyre*, she notes, is not "a pure book"; the "author's conception of love is a feverish, almost lustful passion."[20] Even George Eliot does not escape her condemnation. Eliot, she observes after finishing *Daniel Deronda*, has "an almost naïve belief in human nature which most English readers would call a morbid idealism." Though *Deronda* "interest[s her] deeply," Potter remains skeptical about the preference she assumes Eliot gives "to emotive over purely rational thought."[21] She views even more critically the simultaneous professionalization and feminization of the literary marketplace taking place among her own generation. While Eliot herself makes a crucial distinction between "silly lady novelists" and genuine artists, Potter offers the following sweeping generalization about the efforts of upper-middle-class women to establish themselves in the domain of letters shortly after her mother's death in 1882, as she is trying to decide how and where she will find employment outside her parents' home.[22]

In most of us there is a desire to express our thought, feelings, or impressions. Women generally choose music or drawing, but there is really no more pretension in writing, *so long as one does not humbug oneself as to the value of the stuff written . . .* Probably the hankering after novel-writing in the literary amateur springs from somewhat the same causes as the preference given by the same individual to the metaphysical and moral sciences. The study of metaphysics and novel-writing can be attempted without the drudgery of mastering a difficult and tedious groundwork.[23] [emphasis added]

Two things are key to the contrast Potter begins to develop here between the literary production of men and women. Most obviously, she credits only male writers with a sense of professional responsibility in presenting "accurate information about the world" in "truth-telling fictions."[24] Conversely, she finds lacking in women's fiction the element of objective analysis she values so highly in Balzac, for example. Women novelists, she implies, have not done "the difficult and tedious" work of mastering a given discipline. They write, but they "humbug" themselves as to the value of the "stuff" written. Such remarks seem to evidence Potter's unselfconscious acceptance of mid-Victorian gender ideology, as it informs not only the characterization of male and female "nature" but also the gendered ranking of different kinds of cultural discourses. Reason is male, emotion is female. Objectivity, systematic analysis, professionalism: all of these valued qualities are "male" also, and they are set off against amateurishness and subjective impressionism – the "stuff" that women do, and with which Potter is trying so hard *not* to identify.

At other points both earlier and later in her life, Potter will rebel against the effort involved in "put[ting] horrible facts, multitudinous details, exasperating qualifications into a readable form."[25] She will fantasize about indulging her "vulgar wish to write a novel," "to create characters and to move them to and fro among fictitious circumstances."[26] She will ponder wistfully the pleasure of having what she terms "a fling" with "pure Fiction."[27] The comments cited here, however, suggest that at the outset of her career she could not afford even the fantasy of such "feminine" indulgences. That is, she could not afford to "engender" herself as a woman writer: to mark her writing as female in that very public way. For this would not only expose her amateurishness, it would also discredit any attempt at producing the kind of systematic, objective social analysis she attributes to the work of male novelists.

Several significant oversights in Potter's characterization of the nineteenth-century literary tradition – or rather, her characterization of the parallel traditions of novel-writing by men and by women – need to be noted. Potter neglects to mention the contribution mid-Victorian women writers made to the "Condition of England" debate. Moreover, she fails to recognize either the sentimentalism of male writers or the way in which fiction by both men and women uses domestic and sentimental conventions for political and rhetorical purposes. In other words, she fails to recognize domestic novels as a form of political activism, not an indulgence in romantic "castle-building" for female authors and readers alike.[28] These important omissions in Webb's characterization of the early and mid-Victorian novelistic tradition go hand in hand with the notable lack of commentary in her diary and autobiography about efforts being made by her late nineteenth-century contemporaries, male and fe-male, to (re)politicize the domestic novel. In spite of the fact that she knew someone like Margaret Harkness quite well, for example (indeed, saw her on a daily basis while Harkness was writing *A City Girl*, as Deborah Epstein Nord has noted), there is remarkably little discussion in her diary of writers such as Harkness who were using the novel in the 1880s and 90s as a forum for criticizing, from any number of ideological perspec-tives, dominant bourgeois traditions. One thinks here not only of "New Woman" fiction that de-naturalizes the bourgeois marriage plot but also of "exposure" novels such as Walter Besant's *All Sorts and Conditions of Men* (1882), George Gissing's *Thyrza* (1887) and *The Nether World* (1889), and Arthur Morrison's *A Child of the Jago* (1896), which offered middle-class readers intimate views of life in the "lower depths." Whether informed by naturalistic principles of scientific experimentalism, inspired by Christian philanthropic meliorism, or written as sensational journalism, these nov-els confronted residents of London's West End with (their responsibilities toward) the people of the East End. Additionally, utopian socialist fictions published during this same period, such as William Morris's *News from Nowhere* and Robert Blatchford's *Merrie England* (1894) and *Julie* (1900), theorize alternatives to an Arnoldian politics of culture, while socialist-feminist novels such as Harkness's *A City Girl* (1887), *Out of Work* (1888), and *Captain Lobe* (1889), Jane Hume Clapperton's *Margaret Dunmore; or, A Socialist Home* (1888), Constance Howell's *A More Excellent Way* (1889), Isabella Ford's *Miss Blake of Monkshalton* (1890), Katharine Bruce Glasier's *Husband and Brother* (1894) and *Aimee Furniss, Scholar* (1896), and Gertrude Dix's *The Image-Breakers* (1900) attempt to "carve out a new literary space in which a genuinely transformative socialist-feminist politics could be explored."[29]

　　I offer this catalogue of *fin-de-siècle* titles and authors because Beatrice Potter doesn't. In spite of the fact that she was increasingly well-networked in (Fabian) socialist circles in the late 1880s, she seems to have remained oblivious to what scholars writing recently have char-acterized as an emerging socialist literary tradition – perhaps because of the heavily binarized, gendered ideology of literary production she demonstrates in her writings about eighteenth- and nineteenth-century fiction. Contemporary literary experiments with the formal and thematic range of the (bourgeois) novel do not seem to have interested her. Potter spent the years between her mother's death and her self-declaration as a Socialist in 1890 "re-construct[ing] her relationship to the working class and examin[ing] her own class identity."[30] But fiction, quite notably, was not, for her, a means of doing so. Unlike any of the writers mentioned above, she seems to have distrusted narrative as a ground for politics. This is true especially insofar as she assumes that readers and critics are going to perceive the political critique offered by a woman novelist as limited – limited because, of course, all women are presumed to have limited experience in the public sphere. In this respect, the feminization or domestication of the novel in the nineteenth century represented a liability for Potter. Rather than assimilating herself into this well-established tradition of women writers, she seems to have felt it necessary to experiment with other kinds of discourse.

Mikhail Bakhtin's work can be helpful here: the internally persuasive voice of the (female) novelist is not persuasive enough for Potter: it cannot compete effectively against the standards of empirical proof demanded by the newly professionalized social scientists at the end of the nineteenth century.[31] Susan Lanser's suggestion that we think "in more complex ways about [how] the dichotomy of gender" has been attached to public and private discourse pertains here as well.[32] Novelistic discourse is public, of course; but it is "female," for Potter: sentimental, egotistical, obsessed with "building castles in the air." Thus, she was to seek new discursive opportunities in order to engender her writing differently, to avoid marking her writing as female in a rhetorical context which she feared, perhaps erroneously, guaranteed its reception as amateurish and unprofessional. And she found them: first writing ethnographic studies of London's East End, then collaborating with Sidney Webb.

A ROMANCE WITH ETHNOGRAPHY

As James Clifford has argued, anthropology's newly found professional respectability and disciplinary legitimacy at the end of the nineteenth century was predicated upon the standardization of a new model of cross-cultural research, "participant-observation" ethnography.[33] Whereas mid-century ethnographic accounts of other cultures were written by missionaries, traders, and travelers – writers with long-term intimacy with a given culture, but no professional training in ethnography, *per se* – turn-of-the-century ethnographic fieldworkers were professionals who distinguished themselves from mere amateurs by their training in the latest analytic techniques and modes of scientific explanation. In other words, even though an earlier generation of cross-cultural travelers might have had better language skills and a longer history of contact with the population under study, the new ethnographers claimed superiority on the basis of their scientific methodology. The participant-observer model of ethnographic research was informed not only by "objective" scientific hypotheses that were nonetheless inflected with cultural biases but also by the narrative conventions of nineteenth-century literary realism. In effect, the new ethnographers compensated for their lack of long-term intimacy with a native culture by means of their ability to narrate events so as to maximize a reader's sense of "being there." Recent work on the history of anthropology has critiqued this model of ethnographic research, challenging the reputed objectivity of the ethnographer. My interest, by contrast, lies in suggesting what would have made the conventions of participant-observation ethnography appealing to a woman such as Beatrice Potter.

"Pages from a Work-Girl's Diary" is the fourth article Potter published in the 1880s. As the work of a writer with a growing reputation, it exemplifies her satisfaction with her newfound role as a "social investigator," the title by which she refers to herself in this essay. Simply to compare the title of this essay with the title of her first publication, "A Lady's View of the Unemployed," tells you something important about how anxious Potter was to carve out a new identity for herself at this point in her life.[34] By contrast to that earlier piece (excerpts of which will be discussed below), "Pages from a Work-Girl's Diary" is not suffused with apologies for the writer's limited knowledge of economics in general or of the particular issues relating to unemployment and sweated labor. The tone here is confident, and the painstakingly detailed descriptions of life in the East End seem guaranteed to appeal to the middle-class novel-reading audience of the *Nineteenth-Century*, guaranteed, that is, to satisfy the expectations of formal realism.[35] The essay opens with the following setting of the scene and introduction of main characters.

It is midday. The sun's rays beat fiercely on the crowded alleys of the Jewish settlement: the air is moist from the heavy rains. An unsavoury steam rises from the down-trodden slime of the East End streets and mixes with the stronger odours of the fried fish, the decomposing vegetables, and the second-hand meat which assert their presence to the eyes and nostrils of the passers-by.

For a brief interval the "whirr" of the sewing-machines and the muffled sound of the presser's iron have ceased. Machinists and pressers, well-clothed and decorated with heavy watch-chains; Jewish girls with flashy hats, full figures, and large bustles; furtive-eyed Polish immigrants with their pallid faces and crouching forms; and here and there poverty-stricken Christian women – all alike hurry to and from the midday meal; while the labour-masters, with their wives and daughters, sit or lounge round about the house-door, and exchange notes on the incompetency of "season hands", the low price of work, the blackmail of shop foremen, or else discuss the more agreeable topic of the last "deal" in Petticoat Lane and the last venture on race-horses.

Jostled on and off the pavement, I wander on and on, seeking work. Hour after hour I have paced the highways and byways of the London Ghetto. No bills up except for a "good tailoress," and at these places I dare not apply, for I feel myself an imposter, and as yet my conscience and my fingers are equally unhardened. Each step I take I am more faint-hearted and more weary in body and limb. At last, in sheer despair, I summon up my courage. In a window the usual bill, but seated on the doorstep a fat cheerful-looking daughter of Israel, who seems to invite application.

"Do you want a plain 'and," say I, aping ineffectually a work-woman's manner and accent, and attaining only supreme awkwardness.[36]

Potter herself described this essay, which was very well received by the readers of *Nineteenth Century*, and which increased immeasurably her credibility in the circle of East End ethnographers, as a "cheap triumph" because it was taken almost verbatim from her diary.[37] Both her notes about this writing and the debacle surrounding her 1887 Parliamentary testimony, however, attest to her sense of the difficulty in creating a public voice at this particular stage in her life. In June of 1888 she characterizes another essay she is currently writing as a "horribly stiff bit of work...I feel as if I were hammering it out of me, not writing it. Fear it won't be a success."[38] By contrast, "Pages from a Work-Girl's diary" is indeed easier: it is "a paper of a different sort"; "nothing but a bright description of an audacious adventure." Yet it is also "connected in [her] mind with a false step: the inaccuracy of [her] evidence before the Lords."[39]

Potter is alluding to her testimony before the House of Lords the previous April. Potter had, "through nervousness, exaggerated the number of days she had actually worked as a trouser-hand" in testifying before a committee investigating the system of sweated labor. Conservative newspapers such as the *Pall Mall Gazette* seized upon both the "detestable mis-statement of [her] evidence" and the unconventionality of her public appearance as a court witness.[40] Worse still, as Potter herself notes, Margaret Harkness, a "false friend," assumed the newspaper accounts to be true and "sprea[d] a report that [she] had been telling stories."[41] The following August, Potter writes in her diary of passing "horrible nights [in] self-torture: heart palpitating the night through, the mind one mass of whirling possibilities all of them of the nightmare type, the mouth parched," haunted by these memories of adverse publicity and wondering how her most recent work will be received by the public.[42] It is, then, with extreme relief that she notes on September 14, 1888:

"My 'Pages of a Work-Girl's Diary' has been very successful, and no unpleasant consequence has resulted from the publication of it."[43]

Insofar as Potter drew significantly upon her diary in writing the article published by *Nineteenth Century*, perhaps "Pages" is indeed a "cheap triumph." Consideration of the revisions Potter made to the diary entry in moving from a private to a public mode of discourse would suggest, however, how sensitive she was to the rhetorical pressures of this new genre of urban observation, how carefully she worked to construct a voice in this essay that is *not* that of "A Lady." Consider, for example, by way of contrast to the opening of the published essay, the beginning of the diary entry of April 11, 1888:

Settled at 56 Great Prescott St., to begin life as a working woman. With a very queer feeling I left the house in my old clothes and walked straight off to Princes Street and Wood Street, a nest of tailors. No bills up, except for "good tailoress", and at these places I daren't apply, feeling myself rather an imposter. I wandered on, until my heart sank within me, my legs and back began to ache, and I felt all the feelings of "out o' work". At last I summoned up courage and knocked at the door of a tailor wanting a "good tailoress". A fat and comfortable Jewess opened the door.

"Do you want a plain 'hand?' " said I, trying to effect a working-class accent.

"No," was the reply.[44]

In revising this passage for publication, Webb strips out all references to specific streets and addresses and adds the lengthy description of the East London street scene quoted earlier. By doing so, she not only preserves the anonymity of the people with whom she has come in contact (e.g., the family at 56 Great Prescott St. who has taken in a boarder, the Jewess who employs her); perhaps even more importantly, she also trades historical specificity for novelistic typicality. A Lukàcsian argument about the novel's figuration of historical typicality is also born out by the snippets of conversation and details of dress and manner she adds to flesh out characters who remain one-dimensional in the diary entry. She also supplements the diary account with descriptions of additional characters, presumably in an effort to portray the full range of social 'types' to be found in a tailoring shop: from the "woman of the slums" who supports her alcoholic husband, to the "genuine daughters of the people brim[ming] over with the frank enjoyment of low life," to the frail young lower-middle-class girl whose father has died, leaving her to support herself and her mother as best she can in a "respectable" trade (307, 311, 312). By thus rendering her account more novelistic, Potter supplements the "male" authority of the "social investigator" with the "female" strengths of novelist representation. Or perhaps Potter considered the published account both more novelistic *and* more scientific because it was freer from extraneous detail. Either way, the trick here is that she writes novelistically without writing a novel or a short story. She fictionalizes the diary account so as to shape it to the conventions of participant-observer ethnography, while at the same time avoiding the charge of "telling stories."

The objectivity of this analysis is, of course, something a twenty-first-century reader is likely to question – given the anti-semitism, the xenophobia, and the middle-class pathologization of dirt that informs Webb's representations of life in the East End. Yet objectivity is precisely what Webb is striving for; it is the "domain of expertise" she seeks in repackaging the diary observations to fit the narrative conventions of participant-observer ethnography.[45] A key narrative strategy in this regard, and a crucial difference between the diary and the published account, is the development of a distinction between the "I" who experiences these events and the "social investigator" who documents them. In her diary Potter uses the first person throughout; in the essay, by contrast, she very carefully distinguishes between the "I" who masquerades as a work-girl, and fears being discovered, and the "investigator," the social scientist intent on discovering something about sweated labor. The "I" in both versions registers the sights and smells and sounds of Stepney Green. The "I" registers as well her increasing faint-heartedness and the pain in her legs and back after walking from shop to shop, looking for a place where she can apply without feeling "an imposter." Meanwhile, the "investigator" analyzes the scene economically, asking questions about the financial exchanges that underlie the visible activity and making notes, like a laboratory scientist, of telling details: if coats, vests, and trousers are offered for sale in the shop window, but only vests and trousers are manufactured on the premises, then "where and at what price" are "coats made out?" When a small boy returns a pile of unfinished garments, and the mistress hands them over to the girls in the shop, saying, "'all this to be done extra before Friday – Perkins won't wait for no one!,'" the "investigator" notes "inwardly": "[t]he name of a wholesale shipping firm; so she works for export as well as for retail and pays same price for both." But this thought distracts the "work-girl" from her sewing enough so that she "pushes her needle into her thumb-nail, and in her agony digs her elbow into her neighbour's half-turned back, which causes a cannonade all around the table" and earns the "work-girl" severe looks from the mistress (308–9).

The balance Potter achieves here is notable. In this ethnographic study she sustains the kind of "objective" socio-political analysis which she feels fiction-writing precludes, at least for the woman writer, while she also sustains her reader's interest in the suspense plot she weaves. Will the work-girl's ineptness betray the investigator? That is, will Potter's life-long indifference to the middle-class feminine art of fine needlework sabotage the effectiveness of her impersonation of a work-girl, ruining her chance to make herself into something other than "A Lady"? To put this yet another way, will the body of the work-girl betray the mind of the investigator? The nonfictional discourse of ethnography offers Potter the protection of professionalism; it provides her with an opportunity, as she herself notes in her diary, "to carve out a career of disinterested re-search."[46] But it also allows Potter to make use of the narrative strategies of the fiction writer. The mode of discourse Potter chose as an alterna-tive to the novel in the 1880s is, then, a hybrid genre: the product of a marriage, so to speak, between the "male" discourse of political econ-omy and the "female" form of the novel. The narrative strategies of the novelist inform the scientific discourse of the ethnographer; but they are subsumed within a new rhetorical framework. Thus, Potter's narrative produces not a reader's sympathetic identification with a character but an "objective," dispassionate, authoritative account of sweated labor in the tailoring industry. What Potter refers to in several other essays she wrote during this period as "a more vivid realisation of the problem" yields "true charity": charity which is to be distinguished from either a Mrs. Gaskell's concern for the fallen Ruth or a Salvation Army worker's con-descension towards her settlement house tenants; charity which points to the need for "socialistic legislation"[47] to "enforce a higher standard of life among female, foreign, and unskilled English workers."[48] And all of this enables Potter to re-create herself: to transform the writer of "A Lady's View of the Unemployed" into a social investigator.

On March 24, 1883, Potter wrote the following in her diary:

What distresses me about my own little work is the small amount of material I have to work on, the *trivial subjectiveness of my thought*. That is what I am painfully conscious of when I meet really clever men. My work, if it can be dignified by that name, is so amateurish and yet I don't know that I have a right to pretend to anything better and more businesslike.

   All my duties lie in the practical direction; why should I, wretched little frog, try and *puff myself up into a professional*?[49] [emphasis added]

Such self-deprecation is pervasive in Potter's diary. But remarks like this should not be taken as evidence of her unselfconscious acceptance of

Victorian culture's gender stereotyping. Rather, they evidence Potter's extreme self-consciousness about her negotiations with her own culture, not merely the "foreign" cultures of London's East End. In *Writing Culture,* James Clifford describes the current trend in ethnography toward "a specification of discourses...who speaks? who writes? when and where? with or to whom? under what institutional and historical constraints?"[50] Diverging from the classic mode of participant-observer ethnography, contemporary ethnographers not only acknowledge but value the kind of subjectiveness Potter complains about in this diary entry. But if this passage suggests that she felt the need to purge subjectivity – which, for her, represents the mark of gender – from her public voice, it also shows her doing this quite self-consciously. In other words, Potter already has the kind of "distance from the conventions" of participant-observer ethnography Clifford maintains we have only acquired recently.[51] Recognizing both gender and genre as determinants of narrative meaning, Potter writes ethnography because novelistic discourse had become feminized in the nineteenth century. She assumes the rhetorical stance of objectivity in her ethnographic writing because that is the strategy of authority her readers value. But she is not seduced by the ideal of scientific objectivity. Rather, she "puffs [her]self up into a professional." She enacts for her readers' benefit the interplay of voices, of positional utterances, she sustains throughout her life.

THE SCIENCE OF "SERIOUS" ARTISTS

The irony in this context, of course, is that literary modernists have never credited Beatrice Potter Webb with anything like this kind of sensitivity (and vulnerability) to the changing rhetorics of fiction, ethnography, and social science. They hear only the confident, "male" voice of the Fabian Socialist, not the self-doubting voice of the diary writer. Thus, they figure her in either of two ways. In the first they figure her as an Edwardian harpy intent on convincing the world that "the arts had better not exist at all," as Pound puts it so bluntly in "The Serious Artist." In the second, as is the case in Woolf's "Mr. Bennett and Mrs. Brown," the 1924 essay that expands upon the generational mapping Woolf first sketches in the 1922 letter to Janet Case that was featured as an epigraph for this chapter, modernists obscure the political Edwardians entirely from view in arguing for "Georgian" writers' distinctiveness from their literary predecessors, their crucial status as "orphans":

I want to make out what we mean when we talk about 'character' in fiction; to say something about the question of reality which Mr Bennett raises; and to suggest some reasons why the younger novelists fail to create characters, if, as Mr Bennett asserts, it is true that fail they do. This will lead me, I am well aware, to make some very sweeping and some very vague assertions. For the question is an extremely difficult one. Think how little we know about character – think how little we know about art. But, to make a clearance before I begin, I will suggest that we range Edwardians and Georgians into two camps; Mr Wells, Mr Bennett, and Mr Galsworthy I will call Edwardians; Mr Forster, Mr Lawrence, Mr Strachey, Mr Joyce, and Mr Eliot I will call the Georgians.[52]

Yet we need to ask: in what ways are Webb's efforts to assume the professional authority of science an exact corollary to rather than the antithesis of the modernist literary project? That is, in what sense is Webb – in her need to establish cultural authority in an uncertain, even hostile public sphere – *another* modernist, not its demonized other? Paying careful attention to the professional and disciplinary anxieties fueling Pound's figuration of the Webbs and the "serious" artist enables a very different reading of this seeming antithesis.

We are so used to thinking of modernist writing as "literature" that it is easy to forget the fragility of all claims about the cultural capital of the arts when Pound, T. E. Hulme, Wyndham Lewis, and T. S. Eliot began proselytizing, in the early 1910s, on behalf of the "diverse synchrony of movements" that has come to be known as modernism.[53] In saying this, I do not mean to suggest that the literary field was stable at some earlier point in history and somehow lost this inherent integrity at the end of the nineteenth century – though certainly many modernists share with late Victorians such as Matthew Arnold an intensely nostalgic view of this kind of lost paradise. Instead, I simply want to emphasize here how literary modernists define and delimit the literary field through reference to what modernism is *not* – and how modernists' disciplinary and professional anxieties are revealed by insistent repetition of what it is.

By disciplinary and professional anxieties I mean the set of concerns glossed by Pound's final sentences in the opening paragraph of "The Serious Artist": "We are asked to define the relation of the arts to economics, we are asked what position the arts are to hold in the ideal republic. And it is obviously the opinion of many people less objectionable than the Sidney Webbs that the arts had better not exist at all." Pound's immediate concern here is with Fabian Socialism's inability to conceptualize superstructural phenomena such as the arts as anything but ancillary to the central operations of culture. As noted earlier, the public myth about the Webbs – sustained by if not originating among modernists such as Pound – was that they were oblivious to the arts. In reality, Sidney Webb's letters are almost as full of literary references as are Karl Marx's, and Beatrice Potter Webb was both deeply conflicted about the rhetorical constraints of sociological analysis and respectful of the social analysis provided in some if not all fiction.[54] In "The Serious Artist," however, the grossest of generalizations about the Webbs' indifference to literary matters suits Pound's purposes. Caricaturing leftist models of culture that focus exclusively on the economic base, Pound paints the Webbs in the broadest possible terms as antipathetic to the project of broad cultural "uplift" he establishes as the mission of literary modernism.[55]

Notably, the Webbs are not singled out for criticism here simply because their particular version of Fabian Socialism found no place for art in the ideal republic. Rather, they are also bludgeoned publicly because they epitomize the ethos of professionalism with which literary artists such as Pound were struggling to come to terms in the early twentieth century. To understand this second vector of signification in Pound's figuration of the Webbs, we need to hear the echoes of late nineteenth-century debates about the (re)organization of the natural and human sciences in this 1913 manifesto. We need to situate this particular manifesto, and literary modernism more generally, within the cross-currents of the *fin-de-siècle* disciplinary turf wars engaged in by Matthew Arnold, George Moore, Emile Zola, Oscar Wilde, and John Ruskin.

Consider, then, how Pound begins to lay out his case for the "serious" art and "serious" artists. "It is obvious," Pound writes,

that ethics are based on the nature of man, just as it is obvious that civics are based upon the nature of men when living together in groups.

It is obvious that the good of the greatest number cannot be attained until we know in some sort of what that good must consist. In other words, we must know what sort of animal man is, before we can contrive his maximum happiness, or before we can decide what percentage of that happiness he can have without causing too great a percentage of unhappiness to those about him.

The arts, literature, poesy, are a science, just as chemistry is a science. Their subject is man, mankind, and the individual. The subject of chemistry is matter considered as to its composition.

The arts give us a great percentage of the lasting and unassailable data regarding the nature of man, of immaterial man, of man considered as a thinking and sentient creature... [T]he arts give us our best data for determining what sort of creature man is. As our treatment of man must be determined by our knowledge or conception of what man is, the arts provide data for ethics. (186)

Although Pound notes in the opening sentence of "The Serious Artist" that he is rewriting Sidney's *Defense of Poetry* and although he does allude briefly to the Renaissance in the second paragraph of the essay, these passages in "The Serious Artist" more obviously revisit Matthew Arnold's 1882 essay, "Literature and Science." Arnold's essay was a response to T. H. Huxley's inaugural address at the opening of the Scientific College at Birmingham in 1880. Countering Huxley's claim that the "modern" university's curriculum should be centered on training in science, not the classics, and that anyone needing to earn his living should not waste his time learning Greek and Latin, Arnold argues for the evolutionary necessity of knowing Greek. Specifically, he takes issue with Huxley's overly narrow definition of literature as *belles-lettres*. Characterizing all "genuine humanism" as "scientific," he then criticizes work in the natural sciences for ignoring "the facts" of human nature; these "facts" include, most importantly for Arnold, "our instinct" for "beauty" and "conduct."[56] Chris Baldick has described Arnold's work as marking "a transformation in English criticism, from the defense of poetry to a bold offensive against poetry's potential competitors: religion, philosophy, and science. He also suggests that Arnold "quarantines" science, that is, reduces its threat to the cultural authority of humane letters by characterizing it as nothing more than a gathering of data in works such as *Schools and Universities on the Continent* (1868), "On Poetry" (1879), and "The Function of Criticism at the Present Time" (1865).[57] I would describe Arnold's intervention in the late Victorian debates about the relationship of the arts and sciences somewhat differently. Faced in the 1880s with the increasing institutional and educational status of science as well as an intensification of the more general questioning of claims to cultural authority beyond the sphere of natural knowledge, Arnold does not simply "quarantine" science. Rather, he coopts the authority of science for the humanist. Alluding to William Wordsworth's claim in the "Preface to *Lyrical Ballads*" that scientists are specialists while poets can speak to the common man, but rejecting Wordworth's characterization of science's mandarin culture, Arnold empowers the "scientific" humanist by charging him with the task of relating the results of modern science to the basic human "instincts" for beauty and conduct.

In his 1885 polemic, *Literature at Nurse; or, Circulating Morals*, George Moore reiterates Arnold's effort to shore up the cultural authority of "Literature" through reference to its scientificity. While his most obvious and immediate concern is with the circulating libraries' stranglehold on the literary marketplace, Moore's pamphlet, like Arnold's speech and essay, participates in a very broad debate about literature's place in the hierarchy of discourses about culture and the impact of an ever-expanding commercialism. As both writers suggest, the literary field was under attack in the 1880s. Internally, it was threatened by the circulating libraries' dissemination of popular novels that, as Moore suggests, "disgrace the intelligence of the English nation."[58] Externally, it was threatened by the increasingly secure intellectual and educational status of science post-1870. And Moore follows Arnold's lead in combating both by demanding that the circulating libraries' "liberate" literature so it can pursue "the spirit of scientific inquiry." The following passages capture the substance and the tone of his argument:

The strength, virility, and purpose, which our literature has always held,...is being gradually obliterated to suit the commercial vision of a narrow-minded tradesman... [I]n and out of his voluminous skirts run a motley and monstrous progeny, a puling brood of bastard bantlings, a race of Aztecs that disgrace the intelligence of the English nation. (18)

You are the great purveyor of the worthless, the false, and the commonplace... [a] fetter about the ankles of those who would press forward toward the light of truth... [Y]ou feel not the spirit of scientific inquiry that is bearing our age along... [Y]ou impede the free development of our literature. (16, 17)

Recent scholarship has shown how the articulation of a distinction between high and low culture at the turn of the twentieth century served as leverage in a variety of eugenically inflected arguments about national identity and the development of consumer culture.[59] In the first of these two passages, it is obvious enough how Moore's argument sustains an agenda of cultural eugenics: his savagely contemptuous characterization of Mudie as a grotesquely frumpish and ambiguously gendered Mrs. Grundy whose "puling brood of bastard bantlings" race in and out among "his voluminous skirts" links the health of English literature directly to the genetic health of the race and nation-state. What is worth lingering over in the second passage is Moore's invocation of science in his characterization of a hierarchy of literary and non-literary discourses about culture and nature: "You are the great purveyor of the worthless, the false, and the commonplace... [a] fetter about the ankles of *those who would press forward toward the light of truth... [Y]ou feel not the spirit of scientific inquiry that is bearing our age along*... [Y]ou impede the free development of our literature" (emphasis added). Significantly, the distinction between high and low art that Moore articulates through his grotesque feminization of Mudie associates "real" literature (what Pound will term "serious" art) with the "spirit of scientific inquiry that is bearing our age along." "Real" literature "presses forward" toward "truth"; it upholds the spirit of scientific inquiry rather than working at cross-purposes with it. Hence, Mudie's novels are both "worthless" and "false": worthless *because* they are false. In other words, the high/low culture divide that has received so much contemporary critical attention is one component – but only one component – of a very complex network of binary oppositions distinguishing "Literature" from popular culture, "the spirit of scientific inquiry" from "false" and "commonplace" ideas, and progressive from degenerate evolutionary trends in human history. Lying just barely over the horizon in Moore's essay is the total reorganization of intellectual life that was orchestrated at the turn of the century through the professionalization of science, the establishment of new disciplinary discourses, and the (re)organization of the modern university.

It is within this larger historical context, then, that Pound borrows the structure as well as much of the substance of Arnold's defense of scientific humanism in writing "The Serious Artist." Like Arnold, Pound begins his essay by characterizing the arts as a "theater of proof," a physical space in which the objects of science, in this case, "man considered as a thinking and sentient creature," are said to be viewed objectively.[60] Like Arnold, he will end his manifesto with a declension of perfect poetic lines, the grounds of the debate having shifting significantly in the interim, from consideration of "the arts, literature, [and] poesy" in general to a narrow focus on the individual poem's "precise," "scientific," "orderly" "bearing of true witness" to the "inner nature and conditions of man" (187). Like Arnold as well, Pound co-opts both the rhetoric and the cultural authority of science for the artist when he suggests that the arts "are a science, just as chemistry is a science" and that they "give us a great percentage of the lasting and unassailable data regarding the nature of man...As our treatment of man must be determined by our knowledge or conception of what man is, the arts provide data for ethics." This last phrase is most telling: like Arnold, Pound is less interested in "quarantining" science than he is in empowering the "serious" artist by describing his interests as essential to the continuation of the human race.

Where Pound's strategy of argumentation does differ from Arnold's, revealing most clearly the unique pressures of his own historical moment, is in his reliance upon a rhetoric of cultural hygiene and his obsessive return to comparisons with medicine. Pound refers to medicine nine times in the first two sections of "The Serious Artist," which were published together originally in a single issue of the *New Freewoman*. Medicine functions both as an exemplary instance of the scientific method and as a model for the kind of cultural work Pound claims the serious artist will accomplish. The arts, Pound insists,

> begin where the science of medicine leaves off or rather they overlap with that science. The borders of the two arts cross . . . If any science save the arts were able more precisely to determine what the individual does actually desire, then that science would be of more use in providing the data for ethics. In like manner, if any sciences save medicine and chemistry were more able to determine what things were compatible with physical wellbeing, then those sciences would be of more value for providing the data of hygiene. (186, 187)

On the one hand, it could be argued that Pound is simply echoing Emile Zola's appropriation of Claude Bernard's exposition of the scientific method in "The Experimental Novel" (1880). In Zola's work, the example of medical science justifies Zola's characterization of the naturalist novel's elevated status in the hierarchy of medical and scientific discourses. ("The experimental novel is a consequence of the scientific evolution of the century," Zola writes. "[I]t continues and completes physiology, which itself leans for support on chemistry and medicine; it substitutes for the study of the abstract and the metaphysical man the study of the natural man".[61]) On the other hand, there are new pressures of professionalization to be recognized in Pound's anxious and insistent characterization of the "serious" artist as a medical "specialist." This conceit takes up considerable space (more than five paragraphs) in this essay. Recent work on modernism has established "the profound identity between the structure of professional discourses and of modernist writing strategies"[62] and illustrated how important medicine's "emerging scientific hegemony" was to literary modernists such as William Carlos Williams in finding a voice "at a time when widely divergent voices competed for attention in the literary marketplace."[63] Careful consideration of the scientific analogies that give "Pound's literary criticism its characteristic tone"[64] suggests that literary modernists need not have been practicing physicians to believe in newly standardized laboratory practices and the scientific basis of medical education and practice. As T. Hugh Crawford has suggested, the "cultural power of science and technology can be measured by adoption of their vocabulary and epistemology by other discourses."[65] This is even more clearly evidenced in modernist manifestos such as "The Serious Artist" and T. S. Eliot's "Tradition and the Individual Talent" than it is in late-nineteenth-century texts such as "Literature and Science" and *Literature at Nurse*. Some historians of modernism emphasize the difference between late nineteenth-century "literary scientism's" modeling on mid-nineteenth-century observational methods in biology and clinical medicine and early modernism's "immaterial and energic scientism," which is "patterned after the force fields and energy transformations" of late nineteenth-century electromagnetic and atomic physics.[66] But Pound's prominent conceit comparing "serious" art with clinical medicine complicates and contradicts this neat and historically progressive modeling of a scientific paradigm shift. For what distinguishes Pound's from Arnold's and Moore's literary scientism is the emphasis placed on the professional's credentials, not the modeling of scientific method or the conceptualization of the physical world's operations.

In "The Decay of Lying," Oscar Wilde writes disparagingly of exactly this commitment to scientific professionalism in the arts. The literary naturalist, he notes, "has his tedious *document humain*, his miserable *coin de la création*, into which he peers with his microscope. He is to be found at the Librairie Nationale, or at the British Museum, shamelessly reading up on his subject."[67] Instead of endorsing the dominant characterization of art as a search for scientific truth, Wilde offers lying as the model of artistic activity. Notably, Pound never entirely abandons the central tenet of Wildean aestheticism: the celebration of art's "glorious uselessness" in "The Serious Artist," its existence as a goal in itself rather than as a means for attaining some other goal.[68] "[A]rt never asks anybody to do anything, or to think anything, or to be anything. It exists as the trees exist, you can admire, you can sit in the shade, you can pick bananas, you can cut firewood, you can do as you jolly well please," he insists. Significantly, however, he houses key precepts of Wildean aestheticism within a professional discourse of medicine that emphasizes both the service to society rendered by the "skilful physician" (read "serious artist") and the closed society of professionals to which the serious artist belongs:

The arts give us our data of psychology, of man as to his interiors, as to the ratio of his thought to his emotions, etc., etc., etc.

The touchstone of an art is its precision. This precision is of various and complicated sorts and only *the specialist* can determine whether certain works of art possess certain sorts of precision. I don't mean to say that any intelligent person cannot have more or less sound judgement as to whether a certain work of art is good or not. An intelligent person can usually tell whether or not a person is in good health. It is none the less sure that it takes a skilful physician to make certain diagnoses or to discern the lurking disease beneath the appearance of vigour.

It is not more possible to give in a few pages full instructions for knowing a masterpiece than it would be to give full instructions for all medical diagnosis. (188, emphasis added)

Segueing rather inexplicably here from a discussion of artistic production into a discussion of aesthetic evaluation, and in the process collapsing a distinction between creative and critical writing, Pound provides the "serious" artist with the equivalent of professional accreditation/scientific validation. Having in effect licensed the artist in this manner in the first two sections of the essay, Pound then proceeds to talk in more familiar "literary" ways about poetic technique in the final two sections of the essay, to be published, respectively, two and four weeks later.[69]

In his important recent book, *Ezra Pound, Popular Genres, and the Discourse of Culture*, Michael Coyle has argued that T. S. Eliot's packaging of Pound's critical writings in his definitive edition, *Ezra Pound: The Literary Essays* was a shrewd means of separating Pound's literary criticism from his political criticism in the public mind – and hence of isolating "those features of Pound's work that most resembled the emphases of postwar formalism, the professionally aggressive 'New Criticism' of John Crowe Ransom and others."[70] Focusing specifically on Eliot's determination, in the 1950s, to establish "the frontiers of literary criticism," he has shown how Eliot's anxiety about the "very advisability of criticism that mixes the analysis of poetic texts with social prescription" informs his selection for an anthology of Pound's "literary" criticism (19, 12). Not unlike either Henry James's redaction of his own work in the New York edition or Pound's editing and subsequent marketing of *The Waste Land*, Eliot's edition of Pound's essays is thus an "historical milestone in the institutionalization of modernism," Coyle suggests, because it provided readers with a generic frame – a categorization of "the literary" that is in fact much narrower than Pound's – through which to view "the sprawling and heterogeneous body of Pound's prose" (18). Eliot's conceptualization of "the literary," Coyle notes, "was consonant with the more 'advanced' critical thinking of his time, the so-called New Criticism; by contrast Pound's use of the term "the literary" was, in the middle decades of our century, almost anachronistic," a throwback to the Victorian sages' "organic" approach to cultural endeavor. "And yet Pound was not blind," Coyle goes on to argue; "he was simply dead set against the more professional and precise use for the term that Eliot and other critics were developing with such enthusiasm" (26).

Coyle's work on Pound is an exemplary instance of current work on the marketing and institutionalization of modernism that is providing the thicker historical contextualizations of modernism that distinguish the "new modernist studies." I would quibble, though, with Coyle's characterization of Eliot's packaging of Pound in one sense, as it bears upon this reading of "The Serious Artist." As I have tried to show here, Pound was as sensitive as other avant-gardists to the increasing hegemony of science and the increasingly bureaucratized culture of professionalism in the early twentieth century. He may indeed have been dead set against the more narrowly professional and precise use of the term "the literary" that Eliot and others would wield so effectively in the 1930s, 40s, and 50s to orchestrate the institutionalization of English studies. But in an essay such as "The Serious Artist" – at a stage in the history of the historical avant-garde when it was allegedly functioning most effectively in opposition to institutional networks of power[71] – he himself wields the rhetoric of "scientific" professionalism quite effectively to justify both the arts in general and "poetry" (as a metonymic stand-in for "literature") in particular. To put this yet another way, even though he wields a broader definition of literature than the one that emerged from the institutionalization of literary study, Pound is as interested in "accrediting" literature as Eliot and the New Critics would be.

Charles Altieri has recently taken issue with new work on modernism that "show[s] how deeply modernist art was engaged in the issues and themes developed by the sciences." His fear is that, "simply because we can find analogies or because the artists and writers make vague claims about matters like the fourth dimension, we will go on to use our knowledge of the science to force strong thematic analogies onto the work." If we rely too directly on these invocations of science, he argues, "we run the risk of underplaying the considerable uneasiness most of the modernists had about such dependencies."[72] True enough, but Altieri's subsequent invocation of Hegel takes us in the wrong direction, I think, and lands us (once again) in a Kantian landscape of aesthetics. What needs to be mapped instead is a turn-of-the-twentieth-century cultural landscape in which "literature" and "science" are both recognized as what Gillian Beer has termed "open fields":[73] fields whose claims to authority over their "quasi-objects" of study were developed through the fragile "networks of truth production"[74] they established and the cultural projects they worked to naturalize. What needs to be articulated as well is a critical methodology for English studies that acknowledges rather than suppresses this kind of disciplinary instability.

In "Feminist Criticism/Cultural Studies/Modernist Texts: A Manifesto for the 90s," Deborah Jacobs takes issue with "revisionary" work on modernism that nonetheless fails to "*rechart* or *rethink* the definition of modernism in terms other than those modernism narrated/laid out for itself" and calls for more "cross- or anti-disciplinary studies" of modernism "and its manifestations across discursive fields." "We could focus less," she writes,

> on what *separates* the literary modernist (male or female) from his/her culture (a long-encouraged emphasis) and more on what his/her projects might have *in common* with other early-twentieth-century specializing enterprises such as psychoanalysis, ethnography, or eugenics, projects that, like literary modernism, can also be described as enterprises that advanced themselves through the creation and exploitation of needs (markets?) for their allegedly superior abilities at making distinctions. (278)

On first view, Pound's characterization of the Webbs in the opening paragraph of "The Serious Artist" or Woolf's characterization of Beatrice in her letters would suggest that the Fabian Socialist who speaks with the "male" authority of the social scientist functions as the literary modernist's antithesis. As this chapter has shown, however, closer analysis – anti-disciplinary analysis – reveals why Beatrice Potter Webb needs to be recognized as *another modernist*, not simply as modernism's other.

Potter is as sensitive to the risks and responsibilities of self-fashioning as any of the modernists modeling the importance of masks, personae, or posing. She is as determined to distinguish between the body that suffers and the mind that creates as T. S. Eliot will be in "Tradition and the Individual Talent." And she is as dependent as Eliot or Pound on the rhetoric of scientific professionalism to affect that crucial dis-association. In other words, she shares a "repertoire of [cultural] forms" with the literary avant-gardists in spite of the fact that they often found it convenient to position themselves antithetically to her.[75] She operates, as they do, according to the logic of the modern, aggressively pursuing "distinction-making projects" while denying the proliferation of "monstrous hybrids"[76] – e.g., ethnographic *poseurs* and scientific artists – generated in this process.

What truly does distinguish the literary modernists from other early twentieth-century specializing enterprises is the former's claim that "serious" art is not exclusively a specialist's domain. Instead, it is a coterie culture that claims to have universal appeal: a culture that presumes to be cultureless because it is transhistorical; a specialization that assumes its pertinence to everyone because it both presents and appeals to what is "permanent" in human character. In this chapter I have tried to show how an exemplary modernist manifesto, "The Serious Artist," defines and delimits the literary field through references to what it is *not*. I have shown, as well, how the disciplinary and professional anxieties of the literary modernist are revealed through the liminalization of Fabian Socialists accused of being poetry-blind, fiction-blind, and drama-blind. Pursuing consideration of the modernist avant-garde's investments in the cultural authority of literary study takes us next to its complicated and contradictory relationship to yet another figure who is both liminal and central to its version of turn-of-the-twentieth-century cultural and literary history: Oscar Wilde.

NOTES

1. Pound, "The Serious Artist," *The New Freewoman*, 1, 9 (October 15, 1913), 161; as reprinted in Baechler, Litz, and Longenbach (eds.), *Ezra Pound's Poetry and Prose: Contributions to Periodicals*, p. 186. Subsequent references to this essay will be cited parenthetically in the text.
2. Virginia Woolf, letter to Janet Case, 21 May 1922, *The Letters of Virginia Woolf, Volume II: 1912–1922*, ed. Nigel Nicholson and Joanne Trautmann (New York and London: Harcourt Brace Jovanovich, 1976), p. 529.
3. Virginia Woolf, letter to Lady Robert Cecil, 19 February 1920, *The Letters of Virginia Woolf, Volume II*, ed. Nicholson and Trautmann, p. 422.
4. *Blast I* (June 29, 1914), 21.
5. Beatrice Potter Webb, *The Diary of Beatrice Webb, Volume I, 1873–1892: "Glitter Around and Darkness Within,"* ed. Norman and Jean MacKenzie (London: Virago, 1982), p. 79.
6. Suzanne Clark, *Sentimental Modernism: Women Writers and the Revolution of the Word* (Bloomington and Indianapolis: Indiana University Press, 1991), p. 3.
7. Samuel Hynes, *The Edwardian Turn of Mind*, p. 126. Hynes notes that "poetry-blind" is Webb's own self-characterization, and he volunteers the extension of this aporia to fiction and drama. See his chapter, "The Fabians: Mrs. Webb and Mr. Wells" (pp. 87–131), for an important historical overview of Fabian Socialism's relationship to the arts.
8. [B. Potter], "A Lady's View of the Unemployed at the East," *Pall Mall Gazette*, 18 February, 1886, p. 11.
9. Deborah Epstein Nord, *Walking the Victorian Streets: Women, Representation, and the City* (Ithaca: Cornell University Press, 1995), p. 182. See also Judith Walkowitz, *City of Dreadful Delight: Narratives of Sexual Danger in Late-Victorian London* (University of Chicago Press, 1992); and Nord, *The Apprenticeship of Beatrice Webb* (Amherst: University of Massachusetts Press, 1985).

10. Mary Ryan's phrasing, as used in *Women in Public: Between Banners and Ballots, 1825–1880* (Baltimore: Johns Hopkins University Press, 1990); see especially Chapter 2, "Gender and the Geography of the Public," pp. 58–94.

11. Nord, *Walking the Victorian Streets*, p. 182.

12. Norman MacKenzie (ed.), *The Letters of Sidney and Beatrice Webb*, (Cambridge University Press, 1978), p. 39.

13. Webb, 11 November 1888, *Diary of Beatrice Webb, Volume I*, ed. Norman and Jean MacKenzie, p. 267; 10 November 1888, *ibid.*, p. 265.

14. *Ibid.*, p. 177.

15. Nord, *Walking the Victorian Streets*, p. 184.

16. Webb, 10 September 1882, *Diary of Beatrice Webb I*, ed. MacKenzie, p. 58. An aside that will make more sense subsequently: T. S. Eliot expresses a similar discomfort with/contempt for psychology as a discipline in *Knowledge and Experience in the Philosophy of F. H. Bradley* (New York: Farrar, Straus and Co., 1964); see in particular, pp. 72–4.

17. Beatrice Webb, *My Apprenticeship* (London: Cambridge University Press, 1979), p. 138.

18. Webb, *Diary of Beatrice Webb, Volume I*, ed. MacKenzie, p. 11.

19. Webb, 14 May 1881 and 28 April 1881, *ibid.*, p. 42.

20. Webb, 11 July 1875, *ibid.*, p. 21.

21. Webb, 2 February 1881, *ibid.*, pp. 42, 41.

22. See George Eliot, "Silly Women Novelists," *Westminster Review*, 66 (October 1856), 442–61; as reprinted in David H. Richter (ed.), *Narrative/Theory* (New York: Longman, 1996), pp. 34–41.

23. Webb, 2 January 1883, *Diary of Beatrice Webb, Volume I*, ed. MacKenzie, p. 74.

24. Webb, *My Apprenticeship*, p. 138.

25. Webb, 1 February 1895, *Diary of Beatrice Webb, Volume II*, ed. Norman and Jean MacKenzie (London: Virago, 1984), pp. 66–7.

26. Webb, 30 September 1889, *Diary of Beatrice Webb, Volume I*, ed. MacKenzie, p. 298.

27. Webb, 1 February 1895, *Diary of Beatrice Webb, Volume II*, ed. MacKenzie, pp. 66–7.

28. For further discussion of nineteenth-century domestic fiction's politicization, see studies such as Deidre David, *Fictions of Resolution in Three Victorian Novels: North and South, Our Mutual Friend, Daniel Deronda* (New York: Columbia University Press, 1981) and Nancy Armstrong, *Desire and Domestic Fiction: A Political History of the Novel* (New York: Oxford University Press, 1987). I'd like to thank Pat Collier for his help in recasting this section of the argument.

29. Chris Waters, "New Women and Socialist-Feminist Fiction: The Novels of Isabella Ford and Katharine Bruce Glasier," in Angela Ingram and Daphne Patai (eds.), *Rediscovering Forgotten Radicals: British Women Writers, 1889–1939* (Chapel Hill and London: University of North Carolina Press, 1993), p. 40. For further discussion of a developing tradition of socialist fiction, see also Gustav Klaus (ed.), *The Literature of Labor: Two Hundred Years of Working-Class*

Writing (New York: St. Martin's Press, 1982); and Klaus (ed.), *The Socialist Novel in Britain: Toward the Recovery of a Tradition* (New York: St. Martin's Press, 1982).

30. Nord, *The Apprenticeship of Beatrice Webb*, p. 154. It is important to recognize the methodological conflicts driving wedges between Harkness and Potter, in spite of their strong friendship; Potter's characterizations of other women carving out professional lives for themselves – Annie Besant and Octavia Hill, for example – are also colored by a sense of competition and method-ological/ideological difference.

31. M. M. Bakhtin, *The Dialogic Imagination: Four Essays*, ed. Michael Holquist, trans. Caryl Emerson and Michael Holquist (Austin: University of Texas Press, 1981); "Discourse in the Novel," pp. 259–422.

32. Susan Lanser, "Towards a Feminist Narratology," *Style* 20 (1986), 354.

33. James Clifford, "On Ethnographic Authority," *Representations* 1 (1983), 124; see also *Writing Culture: The Poetics and Politics of Ethnography* (Berkeley: University of California Press, 1986).

34. [B. Potter], "A Lady's View of the Unemployed at the East," *Pall Mall Gazette*, 18 February 1886, 11.

35. Ian Watt's term, as used first in *The Rise of the Novel: Defoe, Richardson, and Fielding* (Berkeley: University of California Press, 1957).

36. Potter, "Pages from a Work-Girl's Diary," *Nineteenth Century* 24 (1888), 301–2. Subsequent references to this essay will be cited parenthetically in the text.

37. As noted by Norman and Jeanne MacKenzie (eds.), in *Diary of Beatrice Webb, Volume I*, p. 231.

38. Webb, 6 June 1888, *Diary of Beatrice Webb, Volume I*, ed. MacKenzie, pp. 252–3.

39. Webb, 21 August 1888, *ibid.*, p. 259.

40. Webb, *ibid.*, pp. 231, 250–2.

41. Webb, 25 May 1888, *ibid.*, p. 251.

42. Webb, 28 August 1888, *ibid.*, p. 259.

43. Webb, 14 September 1888, *ibid.*, pp. 259, 261.

44. Webb, *ibid.*, pp. 241–2.

45. John Tagg, *The Burden of Representation: Essays on Photographies and Histories* (Minneapolis: University of Minnesota Press, 1993), p. 11.

46. Webb, *Diary of Beatrice Webb, Volume I*, ed. MacKenzie, p. 234.

47. "Dock Life of East London," *Nineteenth Century* 22, 128 (October 1887), 499.

48. "East London Labour," *Nineteenth Century* 24, (August 1888), 183.

49. Webb, *Diary of Beatrice Webb, Volume I*, ed. MacKenzie, p. 79.

50. Clifford, *Writing Culture*, p. 13.

51. *Ibid.*, p. 35.

52. Virginia Woolf, "Mr Bennett and Mrs Brown," in S. P. Rosenbaum (ed.), *A Bloomsbury Group Reader* (Oxford and Cambridge, M.A.: Blackwell, 1993), p. 234. As Rosenbaum notes, Woolf read a paper entitled "Character in Fiction" to the Cambridge Heretics Society in May, 1924. She later revised her essay for T. S. Eliot's *Criterion* and then finally published it as a Hogarth

Press pamphlet under the title "Mr Bennett and Mrs Brown." The point I would emphasize here is that, in the process of revising and repackaging these ideas for different modernist markets, and in moving from private (the letter to Janet Casey in 1922) to public contexts, Woolf drops out all mention of the *political* Edwardians, Shaw and the Webbs.

53. Vicky Mahaffey, "Heirs of Yeats: Eire as Female Poets Reinscribe Her," in Elazar Barkan and Ronald Bush (eds.), *Prehistories of the Future: The Primitivist Project and the Culture of Modernism* (Stanford University Press, 1995), p. 100.

54. For a detailed discussion of the Webbs' broad range of literary references, see Wolf Lepenies, *Between Literature and Science: The Rise of Sociology*, trans. R. J. Hollingdale (Cambridge University Press, 1988), pp. 117–23.

55. "Cultural uplift" is a term that has its origin in turn-of-the-century African-American writings about the role of the "talented tenth." I use it here to underscore the commitment to cultural and literary eugenics among white British modernists as well, though certainly it is important to note how hostile both Eliot and Pound can both be, at times, to this kind of characterization of programs for social improvement (particularly socialist programs for social improvement).

56. Matthew Arnold, "Literature and Science" (1882); as reprinted in Miriam Allott and Robert H. Super (eds.), *Matthew Arnold* (Oxford University Press, 1986), p. 459, 471.

57. Chris Baldick, *The Social Mission of English Criticism, 1848–1932*, pp. 19, 41.

58. George Moore, *Literature at Nurse; or, Circulating Morals* (London: Vizetelly, 1885), p. 18. Subsequent references to this pamphlet will be made parenthetically in the text.

59. See Sara Blair, *Henry James and the Writing of Race and Nation* (Cambridge University Press, 1996); Gail Bederman, *Manliness and Civilization: A Cultural History of Gender and Race in the United States, 1880–1917* (University of Chicago Press, 1995); Laura Anne Doyle, *Bordering on the Body: The Racial Matrix of Modern Fiction and Culture* (New York: Oxford University Press, 1994).

60. T. Hugh Crawford, "Imaging the Human Body: Quasi Objects, Quasi Texts, and the Theater of Proof," *PMLA* 111, 1 (January 1996), 67.

61. Zola, "The Experimental Novel" [1880], *The Experimental Novel and Other Essays*, trans. Belle M. Sherman; as excerpted and reprinted in Richard Ellmann and Charles Feidelson, Jr. (eds.), *The Modern Tradition: Backgrounds of Modern Literature* (New York: Oxford University Press, 1965), p. 279.

62. Strychacz, *Modernism, Mass Culture, and Professionalism*, p. 26.

63. Crawford, *Modernism, Medicine, and William Carlos Williams*, pp. 9, 4.

64. Ian F. A. Bell, *Critic as Scientist: The Modernist Poetics of Ezra Pound* (London and New York: Methuen, 1981), p. 1. Bell notes Pound's influence on Eliot in this regard as well.

65. Crawford, *Modernism, Medicine, and William Carlos Williams*, p. 4.

66. Bruce Clarke, *Dora Marsden and Early Modernism: Gender, Individualism, Science* (Ann Arbor: University of Michigan Press, 1996), p. 5.

67. Wilde, "The Decay of Lying" [1889], *The Works of Oscar Wilde*, ed. G. F. Maine (London: 1948); as excerpted and reprinted in *The Modern Tradition*, p. 18.
68. Eagleton, "The 'Rise' of English Studies," *Literary Theory: An Introduction*, p. 21.
69. Pound, "The Serious Artist. III. – Emotion and Poesy," *New Freewoman* 1, 10 (1 November 1913), 194–5; Pound, "The Serious Artist. IV," *New Freewoman* 1, 11 (15 November 1913), 213–14.
70. Coyle, *Ezra Pound, Popular Genres, and the Discourse of Culture*, p. 17. Subsequent references to this study will be cited parenthetically in the text.
71. For arguments regarding the consolidation and institutionalization of "modernism" only *after* World War I, see Levenson, *A Genealogy of Modernism*; and Marjorie Perloff, *The Futurist Moment: Avant-garde, Avant Guerre, and the Language of Rupture* (University of Chicago Press, 1986).
72. Charles Altieri, "The Concept of Force as Modernist Response to the Authority of Science," *Modernism/Modernity* 5, 2 (April 1998), 77, 78.
73. Gillian Beer, *Open Fields: Science in Cultural Encounter* (Oxford: Clarendon Press, 1996).
74. Crawford, "Imaging the Human Body," p. 67.
75. Clifford Geertz, *The Interpretation of Cultures: Selected Essays* (New York: Basic Books, 1973), p. 453.
76. Bruno Latour's phrasing, as used throughout *We Have Never Been Modern*, trans. Catherine Porter (Cambridge, M.A.: Harvard University Press, 1993).

CHAPTER 2

Inventing literary tradition, ghosting Oscar Wilde and the Victorian fin de siècle

The best thing for everybody now is to forget all about Oscar Wilde, his perpetual posings, his aesthetical teachings and his theatrical productions. Let him go into silence, and be heard from no more.

Echo (1895)[1]

Curiously enough, in light of literary modernists' demonization of the Webbs for the latters' presumed indifference to the arts, Beatrice Potter Webb keeps perfect company with the likes of T. S. Eliot, Ezra Pound, and Virginia Woolf in observing the silence about Oscar Wilde advocated by the *Echo* in 1895 – and preserving it for twenty-odd years.[2] In one sense, Webb's failure to mention Wilde even once in any of her writings is entirely in keeping with her complete silence on contemporary socialist writings about art, as noted in Chapter 1. Still, it is hard to imagine now how and why a woman with her commitment to diary- and letter-writing could have failed to register any response whatsoever to one of the key events of her time. Webb's silence roars.

Of course, silence, as Foucault has taught us to understand, is "less the absolute limit of discourse" than "an element which functions alongside the things said."

There is no binary division to be made between what one says and what one does not say; we must try to determine the different ways of not saying such things, how those who can and cannot speak are distributed, which type of discourse is authorized, or which form of discretion is required in either case. There is not one but many silences, and they are an integral part of the strategies that underlie and permeate discourses.[3]

Recognizing thus that Webb's motivations for silence might have been quite different from those of any of the literary modernists to be discussed below, it is nonetheless worth noting how frequently the *Echo*'s injunction to silence is honored by the latter as well. Wilde's significance for Willa Cather, Katherine Mansfield, and Radclyffe Hall as lesbian writers attempting to find antecedents for their own sexual dissidence has been noted recently, and Joyce's interest in Wilde has been well documented for many years.[4] But the silences on the subject of Oscar Wilde observed by other major early twentieth-century writers associated with the London-based avant-garde might well give us pause.

The first two volumes of Virginia Woolf's letters, for example, include no reference to Wilde. In 1931, she will write "candid[ly] and caustic[ally]" about Edmund Gosse's attempts to distance himself from Wilde during and after his trials in the spring of 1895, and she will respond in 1939 with great warmth to Elizabeth Robins's suggestion that she review her autobiography, *Both Sides of the Curtain* (1940), noting with enthusiasm that she will "perhaps encounter Oscar Wilde" in its pages. But she offers no commentary until then on the most momentous literary and social scandal of her adolescence.[5] Ezra Pound's treatment of *fin-de-siècle* decadence in "Hugh Selwyn Mauberley" has been discussed in detail by numerous critics; still, it is worth noting that, aside from a single reference in a 1915 letter, he also never mentions Wilde in his letters. Nor does he respond to Dorothy Shakespear's comments about performances of plays by Wilde she saw in 1911 and 1913.[6] T. S. Eliot is almost equally silent, referring to Wilde only once in his private writings, as will be discussed further below.

In a little-known and uncollected essay for *Vogue* entitled "A Preface to Modern Literature" (1923), Eliot does suggest, however, that modern literature emerges out of the "vast background of death" epitomized by Wilde's trials in 1895. "To give a fair view of the present, as it appears to a contemporary," he writes, "it is necessary to begin with the dreariest part of the subject, the vast background of death against which the solitary figures of the future are relieved. It is necessary to begin about the date of the trial of Oscar Wilde."[7] Prominent early twentieth-century literary critics who are not typically associated with literary modernism, such as Arthur Ransome, also claim his influence even over men "who would indignantly deny that their work was in any way dictated by [him]." In the opening pages of his 1912 biography of Wilde, Ransome, for example, insists upon the following:

Whether or not [Wilde's] writings are perfectly successful or not, they altered in some degree the course of literature in his time, and are still an active power when the wind has long blown away the dust of newspaper criticism with which they were received. It is already clear that Wilde has had an historical importance too easily underestimated. His indirect influence is incalculable, for his attitude in writing gave literature new standards of valuation.[8]

In stark contrast to both the silences of many public intellectuals at the turn of the century and these isolated attempts to grant Wilde centrality in a genealogy of modern writing are the aggressively hostile denunciations of all things "effeminate" that figure so prominently in literary modernism's efforts to create chasms between the art it values and the Victorian *fin de siècle*. Pound's characterization of the 1890s as "soft and muzzy"; *Blast*'s association of Wilde with Futurism's sensational sentimentalism, and its contempt for both the gentleman and the outcast bohemian; W. B. Yeats's retrospective rejection of his own *fin-de-siècle* "womanish introspection"; T. E. Hulme's, Eliot's, Pound's, and Richard Aldington's gendered rhetoric of aesthetic evaluation, which contrasts the "hard," "virile," "strong" writers they appreciate with the effete, effeminate, and/or female writers who don't, for one reason or another, make the modernist grade: all of these well-known examples of literary modernism's vilification of either Wilde in particular or *fin-de-siècle* aestheticism more generally stand out in striking contrast to both the silences and the assertions of Wilde's absolute centrality noted above.[9]

The extremes compel further inquiry. As many scholars of modernism have noted, the creation of a usable past was a key means of both coming to terms with and keeping at bay the pressures and the alleged chaos of the modern world at the turn of the twentieth century. This chapter seeks to understand Wilde's "ghosting" from modernist mappings of literary history. "Ghosting" is Terry Castle's term, as used to describe the literary history of lesbianism as a history of de-realization, spectralization.[10] In very similar terms and for very similar reasons, Oscar Wilde, I will suggest, haunts the modernist imaginary as an ambiguously gendered father-figure whose paternity is dangerous to claim. The plethora of excellent studies on Wilde published in the past ten years makes it easy to assume Wilde's symbolic importance to the art and culture of our *fin-de-siècle* as well as his. But queer theory's recent and highly celebratory rehabilitation of Wilde should not allow us to overlook or minimize the cultural backlash sparked by Wilde's trials. It may indeed be difficult for twenty-first-century readers to understand why late nineteenth-century society's "reaction to Wilde was so hostile, and, moreover, why it remained so for several generations after his death."[11] Doing so, however, goes a long way toward explaining how Wilde's trials "helped to establish the terms within which transgressive works of literature were read in Britain, and in the United States, in the early twentieth century."[12] Moreover, it also helps us make sense of the conservatism – specifically, the retreat from any supposed valuing of scandalous sexuality in the wake of Wilde's trials – fueling the modernist avant-garde's invention of literary tradition as what T. S. Eliot would term a transcendent "ideal order" in the early twentieth century.[13]

To understand fully Wilde's treatment by modernists such as Joyce and early modernist reviewers of Joyce such as Eliot and Ezra Pound, though, it is necessary, I would also like to suggest, to understand Wilde's symbolic antithesis to the *other* writer who played such a key role in turn-of-the-century debates about the cultural work of literature and literary studies: William Shakespeare. Therefore, this chapter leads off with consideration of three very distinctive figurations of Shakespeare in the 1890s, all of which have crucial bearing upon early arguments for the organization of English language and literature studies as an academic discipline, and all of which thus function as an important historical backdrop for the treatment of Wilde and Shakespeare in *Ulysses'* National Library scene and in influential early readings of Joyce by Eliot and Pound that will be the focus of discussion in the chapter's two final sections.

1890: SHAKESPEARE *VS.* MRS. GRUNDY

In its highly publicized symposium on "Candour in English Fiction" in 1890, the *New Review* featured essays by Eliza Lynn Linton and Thomas Hardy that invoke Shakespeare quite prominently in an effort to discredit their immediate literary predecessors' concessions to Mrs. Grundy, the mythical mid-Victorian defender of bourgeois morality. This symposium is certainly neither the first nor the only public forum in which the deadening effect of censorship on the British novel was debated in the Victorian *fin-de-siècle*.[14] The surprise here is that Linton, who is remembered to history mainly as one of the harshest critics of the New Woman and New Woman fiction,[15] and Hardy are *on the same side*, arguing the same case against Mrs. Grundy's censorship. And doing so by wielding Shakespeare's name.

Consider first Eliza Lynn Linton's argument. Linton's essay begins by comparing the contemporary British novelist with European and American counterparts and objecting to the former's very limited choice of subject matter.

Of all the writers of fiction in Europe or America the English are the most restricted in their choice of subjects. The result is shown in the pitiable poverty of the ordinary novel, the wearisome repetition of the same themes, and the consequent popularity of romances which, not pretending to deal with life as it is, at the least leave no sense of disappointment in their portrayal or of superficiality in their handling... [T]he subjects lying to the hand of the British novelist are woefully limited, and the permissible area of the conflict between humanity and society is daily diminishing.[16]

One can hear in this opening salvo a strong echo of George Moore's complaints in *Literature at Nurse; or, Circulating Morals* about the restrictiveness of romance conventions. Unlike Moore, however, Linton blames not the circulating libraries but "the British Matron" for the British novelist's inability to compete with European and American peers. The "British Matron," she argues,

is the true censor of the Press, and exerts over fiction the repressive power she has tried to exert over Art. Things as they are – human nature as it is – the conflict always going on between law and passion, the individual and society – she will not have spoken of...[N]o one must touch the very fringes of uncertificated love under pain of the greater and the lesser excommunication... If a writer, disdaining the unwritten law, leaps the barriers set up by Mrs. Grundy and ventures into the forbidden Garden of Roses, he is boycotted by all respected libraries and the severer kind of booksellers. (10, 11)

Linton presents herself in this essay as a strong advocate of the English novel's liberation from bourgeois domestic ideology. According to Linton, to write about "human nature as it is" or "uncertificated love" and the "conflict always going on between law and passion" is to risk more than the censure of critics. It means risking being denied access to readers, risking being shut out of the literary marketplace altogether. Note too what is implied by Linton's suggestion that "the permissible area of the conflict between humanity and society is daily diminishing." In Linton's view, Mrs. Grundy is increasing her stranglehold on the English market for fiction; rather than contributing to the healthy evolution of the novel as a form of art, she is constraining its development more and more significantly, and at a pace that must be measured not in years or in months but in days. The result: the production of fiction that is "fit" reading only for adolescents, fiction that does not meet the standards set either by contemporary European and American novelists or by British writers of previous centuries.

At this point in her argument Linton invokes Shakespeare:

Had the law which is in favour at the present day been the law of times past we should have lost some of our finest works; and the world would have been so much the poorer in consequence. But would any sane person propose to banish Fielding and Swift and Smollett and Richardson from our libraries, and Bowdlerise all our editions of Shakespeare, and purify the Bible from passages which once were simple everyday facts, that no one was ashamed to discuss, and now are nameless indecencies impossible to be even alluded to, because these are not the fit kind of reading for boys and girls in their teens? (11)

Linton answers this question in her closing remarks, which recast a local problem, an issue of concern in literary circles, as a very serious affront to the national honor:

The result of our present system of uncandid reticence . . . – the working response made to the demand of the British Matron for fairy tales, not facts – is that, with a few notable exceptions, our fictitious literature is the weakest of all at this present time, the most insincere, the most jejune, the least impressive, and the least tragic. It is wholly wanting in dignity, in grandeur, in the essential spirit of immortality. Written for the inclusion of the Young Person among its readers, it does not go beyond the schoolgirl standard . . . Thus we have the queer anomaly of a strong-headed and masculine nation cherishing a feeble, futile, milk-and-water literature – of a truthful and straightforward race accepting the most transparent humbug as pictures of human life. (14)

The challenge posed in Linton's final taunt is clear: if the British are to remain a "truthful and straightforward" race, they must stop emasculating literature; they must throw off the censorship of Mrs. Grundy and produce a literature that has "dignity" and "grandeur," a literature that reflects the "strong-headed" virility of the nation-state.[17]

Although we no longer think of Linton and Hardy as artists with a common aesthetic agenda, their arguments in the 1890 *New Review* symposium are strikingly similar. Like Linton, Hardy believes that the "great bulk of English fiction of the present day is characterized by its lack of sincerity," its inability to portray life "honest[ly]," its obsession with "the regulation finish that 'they married and were happy ever after.'"[18] Like Linton, he employs cyclical metaphors of progress and degeneration as he tries to envision alternatives to this "literature of quackery" (15):

Things move in cycles; dormant principles renew themselves, and exhausted principles are thrust by. There is a revival of artistic instincts towards great dramatic motives – setting forth that 'collision between the individual and the general' – formerly worked out with such force by the Periclean and Elizabethan dramatists, to name no other. (16).

Still more prominently than Linton, Hardy then showcases Shakespeare in positing a "revival of artistic instincts" that will allow the contemporary novelist to present "sexual relationship as it is," not Victorian "conventions concerning budding womanhood" (16, 20, 20). What makes his essay particularly noteworthy in the present context is the way he uses Shakespeare to map an evolutionary progress in literature that will not be endstopped by the circulating libraries' "censorship of prudery" (18).

Hardy begins by claiming that "conscientious fiction alone...can excite a reflective and abiding interest in the minds of thoughtful readers...who are weary of puerile inventions and famishing for accuracy" (16). He then establishes a precedent for this kind of conscientiousness: "This is the interest which was excited in the minds of the Athenians by their immortal tragedies, and in the minds of Londoners at the first performance of the finer plays of three hundred years ago" (16). Subsequently, he de-emphasizes the comparison with Greek drama, focusing more exclusively on Shakespeare in the final pages of the essay. Ultimately, Shakespeare alone, not ancient Greek or Elizabethan dramatists, represents the "true artist" (19) who can set an example for contemporary British writers who are frustrated with the current censorship practices in the publishing world:

To say that few of the old dramatic masterpieces, if newly published as a novel (the form which, experts tell us, they would have taken in modern conditions), would be tolerated in English magazines and libraries is a ludicrous understatement. Fancy a brazen young Shakespeare of our time – *Othello, Hamlet,* or *Anthony and Cleopatra* never having yet appeared – sending up one of those creations in narrative form to the editor of a London magazine, with the author's compliments, and his hope that the story will be found acceptable to the editor's pages; suppose him, further, to have the temerity to ask for the candid remarks of the accomplished editor upon his manuscript. One can imagine the answer that young William would get from his mad supposition of such fitness from any one of the gentlemen who so correctly conduct that branch of the periodical Press. (19)

At least three things are significant about Linton's and Hardy's invocations of Shakespeare in the *New Review*'s symposium: the extent to which they differ from mid-Victorian invocations of Shakespeare; their use in modeling a different future for the novel as a genre; and the rhetoric of repression driving these revisionary (and therefore enabling) maps of literary history. In *Woman and the Demon*, Nina Auerbach explains how Shakespeare was "assimilat[ed] to [the Victorian] age's religion of womanhood." Focusing on representative Victorian texts such as Anna Jameson's *Shakespeare's Heroines: Characteristics of Women, Moral, Poetical, and Historical* (1832) and Mary Cowden Clarke's *The Girlhood of*

Shakespeare's Heroines (1850), she argues that mid-Victorian writers valued Shakespeare's representation of women as "'incorruptibly just and pure.'"[19] In stark contrast, Linton and Hardy figure a "brazen" young artist who epitomizes their own objections to the "charlatanry" of Victorian sexual repression. Notably, what these late Victorians value about Shakespeare are his representations of "uncertificated love" (Linton's phrasing), of "sexual relationship as it is" (Hardy's), not his deference to the mid-Victorian ideal of female passionlessness. In other words, Shakespeare is useful to them not only because his work represents a standard of aesthetic value, *the* timeless standard of literary greatness, but also because he deals more "candidly" with sexuality than could a contemporary British novelist.

For Linton and Hardy, as for the literary modernists to be discussed subsequently, literary history is "not some consistent or continuous inheritance but something...construct[ed]."[20] These *fin-de-siècle* writers are interested in reappraising Shakespeare because he offers them (to use Linton's sexualized idiom) such a potent alternative to the emasculated tradition of nineteenth-century novelistic realism. Thus, while mid-Victorians remake Shakespeare as a good Victorian, Linton and Hardy envision a return to the Renaissance and a crossing of genres – the contemporary novel's cross-pollination with the "great dramatic motives" of Shakespearean tragedy – that will end the British novelist's tutelage to Mrs. Grundy.

Notably, these arguments about "candour in English fiction" and the remapping of English literary history are powered by what Foucault terms a repressive hypothesis. In *The History of Sexuality I*, Foucault notes how modern societies exploit sex as "*the* secret" even as they dedicate themselves "to speaking about it *ad infinitum*." What sustains any speaker's "eagerness to speak of sex in terms of repression," he argues, "is . . . [the] opportunity to speak out against the powers that be, to utter truths and promise bliss, to link together enlightenment, liberation, and manifold pleasures."[21] Foucault's argument about the way sex is sited as a secret truth to be discovered through discourse can help us understand the rhetorical force of the references to Shakespeare in the 1890 *New Review* symposium on "Candour in English Fiction." Because Shakespeare is characterized by both Linton and Hardy as a writer who knows "the truth" about human sexuality; and because Linton and Hardy associate their own work with his when they invoke his name, the latter license *themselves* to speak about "sexual relationship as it is" through their references to the Elizabethan dramatist. As in the draft of the title page to *Tess of the D'Urbervilles* – on which the line from *The Two Gentlemen of Verona*, "Poor wounded name! My bosom as a bed shall lodge thee," and the name "W. Shakespeare" appear in script nearly as large as that with which Hardy wrote his own name[22] – the reproduction of Shakespeare in the 1890 *New Review* symposium serves to legitimize a new, and presumably more truthful (i.e., Truthful), discourse about sexuality in the English "novel of the future."

1895: COMBATING CULTURAL "DEGENERATION" WITH "THE CLASSICS"

Although the circulating libraries still monopolized the literary marketplace in England in 1890, the next five years brought many changes in the publishing industry. Changes in international copyright law; the increasing effectiveness of literary agents in brokering contracts; attempts to expand the influence of the Society of Authors (a professional union for writers); publishers' increased use of advertising; changes in the format of the popular press; and the establishment of new venues for publication (both journals and publishing firms): these innovations in the publishing industry altered considerably the relations among authors, readers, and publishers.[23] Together with the rhetoric regarding the "liberation" of the novel from Mrs. Grundy's censorship, these changes contributed to the common perception of a revolution in the literary marketplace in the early 1890s. This perception is exemplified in the lead essay for the first issue of the *Athenaeum* in 1894. In their annual "Year in Review" headnote, the editors describe the British literary "scene" in 1893 in the following manner:

The year 1893, in its literary aspect, has been a year given over almost entirely to the younger writers, who have discovered one another throughout its course with unanimous and touching enthusiasm. The older men have been silent, while the juniors have enjoyed the distinction of limited editions and the luxury of large sales... [A]long with the short story ("poisonous honey stol'n from France") has come a new license in dealing imaginatively with life, almost permitting the Englishman to contend with the writers of other nations on their own ground; permitting him, that is to say, to represent life as it really is.

... Not so very many years ago Mr. George Moore was the only novelist in England who insisted on the novelist's right to be true to life, even when life is unpleasant and immoral; and he was attacked on all sides. Now every literary lady is "realistic," and everybody says, "How clever! how charming!"[24]

These editors repeat almost verbatim Linton and Hardy's 1890 charge about the British novelist's right to be "candid." Notably, though, what the latter had established in 1890 as an objective for the "novel of the future," the *Athenaeum* now presents as a *fait accompli*. If, however, a novelist can now be "true to life" and still be published, the *Athenaeum* seems at best ambivalent about this increased license in the literary marketplace: proud of the English novel's new competitiveness on the international market, intrigued by these young writers' supportiveness of each other's work, admiring of their financial success, but also concerned about what is perceived as the feminization of the market – and hence the proliferation of "clever" hackwork.

The intrusion of gender into this discussion makes it important to note more carefully how the *Athenaeum* has amended Linton and Hardy's arguments. Recall Linton's phrasing: "if a writer, disdaining the unwritten law, leaps the barriers set up by Mrs. Grundy and ventures into the forbidden Garden of Roses, he is boycotted by all respected libraries and the severer kind of booksellers." And Hardy's: "Fancy a brazen young Shakespeare of our time…sending up one of [his plays] in narrative form to the editor of a London magazine…One can imagine the answer that young William would get from…any one of the gentlemen who so correctly conduct that branch of the periodical press." Note how the dynamic between writers and publishers has been re-gendered in 1893 by the *Athenaeum* editors: a generation of "older men" sits on the sidelines watching their male "juniors" "deal imaginatively with life," while "every literary lady" is winning the public's accolades for her "clever" and "charming" realism. The phrasing of that last sentence is pointedly condescending, and suggests that what elicits the editors' ambivalence toward the current state of affairs in the literary marketplace is not contemporary writers' "candour" *per se*. Rather, it is *women's* efforts to break with nineteenth-century conventions regarding the representation of sexuality, and the public's endorsement of such efforts through the sales of their books, that provokes this ambivalent response to the "new" English realism.

In this "Year in Review" essay for 1893, the *Athenaeum* editors stop just short of accusing women writers outright of going too far in the pursuit of "candour." During the next several years, however, other critics will be quick to link the feminization of the literary marketplace in the 1890s with the "degeneration" of both literary standards and the culture at large. Whereas Linton and Hardy used the rhetoric of social Darwinism to justify their experimentation with novelistic conventions in 1890, critics writing later in the decade reject the metaphors of literary and social liberation, predicting instead a darker future for both the novel and English society. The following comments are from three book reviews published in the spring and early summer of 1895.

"Women's pictures, women's plays, women's books. What is it that makes them temporarily so successful, and eternally so wanting?," A. G. P. Sykes complains in "The Evolution of the Sex," in the *Westminster Review*. Sykes goes on to note that, in spite of the good that women have done by enlarging their sphere, "it seems a pity to have such good work marred by the mischievous, foolish, and ignorant style of fiction which continues to be poured into the market by women, and, since pure imitativeness always asserts its sway for the time being, by men also." He ends his article with a damning characterization of the present situation in the English publishing industry: "[A] wave of unwholesome, unsavoury matter has spread itself over literature generally... To achieve success, cry many, a [novel] must be seasoned with naughtiness, and seasoned so very thoroughly that the most blunted taste can perceive it."[25]

In "Tommyrotics," which appeared in the June 1895 issue of *Blackwood's*, Hugh E. M. Stutfield blames not only women writers but also male aesthetes and decadents for the recent "degeneration" of British literature and culture. Although most of his article focuses on "the woman of the new Ibsenite neuropathic school," his carefully curt references to both Wilde's trials and the homosexual subculture of the 1890s indicate that he views the latter as something still "more unlovely," pathological, and politically dangerous: "Recent events, which shall be nameless, must surely have opened the eyes even of those who have hitherto been blind to the true inwardness [read homoeroticism, sexual "invertedness"] of modern aesthetic Hellenism, and perhaps the less said on this subject now the better."[26] Unlike Max Nordau, whose lead he is following in other respects in this essay, Stutfield finds some hope in the fact that "the 'so-called Philistines'" are still a majority in British culture (844). He never backs down from his damning assessment of "the crazy and offensive drivel being poured forth over Europe – drivel which is not only written, but widely read and admired, and which the new woman and her male coadjutors are now trying to popularize in England" (843). But he nonetheless ends his essay on a hopeful note: "we may still hope that humanity will recover itself before it is ripe for Dr. Nordau's hospital or lunatic asylum" (843).

John Stokes has described this kind of argument by collocation as the habit of "lumping things together."[27] This habit of thought, which is so characteristic of the mid-1890s, allows political radicals, aesthetes, decadents, and New Women to be blamed indiscriminately for what one skeptical reviewer terms the "socio-literary portents" of "anarchy" in British culture.[28] My point here is not to discredit these apocalyptic assessments of literary and cultural degeneration but to show how they are countered by arguments regarding the production of a great national literature in the wake of the scandal surrounding Wilde's trials.

Writing for the *Athenaeum* several months before *Blackwood's* published "Tommyrotics," an anonymous reviewer of George Egerton's second book of short stories, *Discords*, seems as determined as Hugh Stutfield to check "the present outburst of sexual hysterics."[29] Yet, this *Athenaeum* reviewer is more confident than either Sykes or Stutfield that catastrophe can be averted. *Discords*, which was published in John Lane's "Keynotes Series" in 1894, is dismissed with confidence:

As we have said before, and shall, when necessary, say again, books of this class, published as they are, forsooth, in the name of art, are neither more nor less than deliberate outrages. They have, not unnaturally, a commercial success, and for the moment they are belauded by a long-suffering public; but there are not wanting signs that the present outburst of sexual hysterics (for which, to their disgrace, women have been chiefly responsible) has spent its fury, and will give place before long to the recognized masters of English fiction. (375)

Several things distinguish this review from Sykes's and Stutfield's. Whereas the latter's writing epitomizes the very hysteria both claim to be diagnosing in other authors, the tone of the *Discords* review is serene. Confident of his ability to distinguish between "books of this class" and the works of "recognized masters" (who remain unnamed), this reviewer is assured about his own position as a custodian of Culture, as is evidenced by the casual reference to past occasions upon which "we" have felt obliged to comment upon contemporary writers' "outrages." Moreover, he seems convinced that the present state of affairs is a temporary aberration: a storm to be weathered, not a hole in the ozone causing permanent, irreversible changes in the English literary stratosphere at the turn of the century.

An advertisement for William Heinemann's new series in literary criticism, which appeared in the July 27, 1895 issue of the *Athenaeum* – almost two months to the day after Wilde's conviction – indirectly echoes this review of *Discords* in several interesting ways. Noting first that the aim of this new series is to "mark a slight reaction against a recent tendency in literary criticism," the advertisement goes on to explain why this redirection of interests is necessary: "MR HEINEMANN believes that the moment has come when we are in danger of obscuring the central features of literature, and the beauty of the greatest writing in each country, by an exaggerated attention to points which are rather scientific than literary."[30] In this new series, which is to be edited by Edmund Gosse, "Honourable M. A. of Trinity College, Cambridge," Heinemann promises (echoing Matthew Arnold) that "literature will be interpreted as the most perfect utterance of the ripest thought by the finest minds, and to the classics of each country rather than its oddities and rather than to its obsolete features will particular attention be directed." Although these short "Histories of Literature will, it is supposed, prove serviceable in advanced classes and for college use,... that is not their primary object," the ad goes on to suggest. Rather, "authors of eminence, who are accustomed to write for the general public" are being solicited to write each of these volumes, which are intended "to present at once an accurate survey for scholars and delightful entertainment for the ordinary reader. If these books find a welcome for the public, it is proposed to extend their scope to all the recognized literatures of the world" (117).[31]

Like the review of *Discords*, this advertisement adopts what Barbara Herrnstein Smith terms a "magisterial mode of literary evaluation."[32] The distinction between literary "classics" and "oddities" is wielded with confidence, and reinforced by careful notation of the editors' scholarly degrees in the bottom third of the advertisement.

It should also be noted, though, that although this ad presents Gosse's association with Trinity College, Cambridge in a completely positive manner, the *Athenaeum*'s readers would probably still remember John Churton Collins's attack on Gosse's academic credentials and slipshod scholarship in the *Quarterly Review* in 1886. Stefan Collini describes Collins's scathing review of *From Shakespeare to Pope* as one of the most notorious "public squabbles" about the purpose and value of academic credentialing in late-nineteenth-century Britain. He also notes that "although the attack damaged Gosse's reputation somewhat," Collins came off still worse:

> though specialization was certainly making its inroads into the shared culture of the Victorian educated class, it still had some way to go, and the ambivalence toward excessive scholarly zeal manifested on this occasion may have reflected a deeper unease about the price to be paid for allowing the specialists to divide the kingdom of culture among themselves.[33]

In this larger context, then, Heinemann's advertisement seems both to brandish academic titles *and* to reassure the "ordinary reader" about these scholars' interest in bridging the gap between the academic and the non-academic reading public. What makes this advertisement particularly noteworthy is not the defense of the "classics" *per se* but the shift of policy that generates that defense. Along with John Lane, Grant Richards, and others, William Heinemann made his first money as a publisher in the early 1890s marketing novels that Mudie's and Mrs. Grundy would have considered too "candid" for the Young Person. Departing from the tried-and-true format of the three-decker novel, many new firms in the early 1890s (e.g., not only Heinemann's but also John Lane, T. Fisher Unwin, and Ward, Lock & Bowden) issued single-volume novels, which they could sell directly to readers for as little as six shillings each. The novels in Heinemann's "Pioneer Series," John Lane's "Keynotes Series," and T. Fisher Unwin's "Pseudonym" and "Antonym" series did not come already stamped with polite society's seal of approval. Instead, as one of their contemporaries noted in 1934, these publishers flirted with scandal – and made a tidy profit – by selling novels about contemporary controversies such as "the cause of revolting women, an equal moral law for both sexes, social purity, [and] the Contagious Diseases Acts."[34] At least until Oscar Wilde's trials in 1895 tipped the balance back in favor of Grundyism, these publishers were more than willing to affront bourgeois morality in the early 1890s by selling "racy," "mischievous," and "bold" (to borrow the language of their advertisements) works of fiction by previously unpublished writers such as "Sarah Grand" [Frances Elizabeth McFall], "George Egerton" [Mary Chavelita Bright], and "C. E. Raimond" [Elizabeth Robins].

Given the uproar surrounding Wilde's trials in April through June of 1895, it perhaps should come as no surprise that William Heinemann might want to dissociate his publishing company from the very social controversies it had paraded in front of the public's eye earlier in the decade. Promoting this new "Series of Short Histories of the Ancient and Modern Literatures of the World" and highlighting its listings in international literature is a smart move financially. For Heinemann's thus minimizes the risk of being sued by inviting the public to forget its previous associations with Wilde, John Lane, the *Yellow Book*, and all other things "yellow" in *fin-de-siècle* Britain. Instead, Heinemann's now smooths Mrs. Grundy's ruffled feathers by aggressively marketing "the classics."

Consider again, then this time in fuller detail, the final sentence in the second paragraph of this advertisement:

Without expressing any feeling but that of respect for the men who with infinite industry and the exercise of untiring research have added to our exact knowledge of the more curious and obscure parts of the subject [literature], or for those who have sought to combine its study more and more with that of language,

MR. HEINEMANN believes that the moment has come when we are in danger of obscuring the central features of literature, and the beauty of the greatest writing of each country, by an exaggerated attention to points which are rather *scientific* than literary. (117, emphasis added)

Given the publication date of this advertisement, the closing reference to points "scientific" rather than "literary" can be read at least two ways. On the one hand, the first half of the sentence refers to (then current) arguments about the curriculum for English literature and language studies in institutions of higher education. Heinemann's is positioning itself in support of those who favored an emphasis on literary rather than philological studies; taking a critical view of the sort of "Germanic" scholarship that is chiefly focused on categorizing rather than appreciating literature, the ad introduces this new series by reclaiming literary interpretation as something for the general reader, not something requiring the specialist or the professional critic or a "trained" audience.[35] On the other hand, however, when this advertisement promises that the volumes in this series will feature "the classics of each country rather than its oddities and . . . obsolete features," the latter phrasing can also be understood as an indirect reference to the "oddities" and "obscure features" of human sexual behavior documented in novels such as *The Heavenly Twins*, Sarah Grand's exposé of syphilis, and Heinemann's most scandalous bestseller in 1894.

In other words, when this advertisement proposes a new critical series on international classics, Heinemann's is in effect dissociating itself, at least somewhat, from the "candid" fiction it marketed so successfully in the early 1890s, fiction noted more often for its "scientific" detailing of sexual practices than for the beauty of its language. This is not to say that Heinemann's stopped publishing "degenerate" literature after Wilde's trials in 1895: Sarah Grand's *The Beth-Book* was published under the imprimature of the Pioneer Series in 1897, as was Stephen Crane's *Maggie, Girl of the Streets* in 1896, for example; and the firm continued to publish Gosse's translations of Ibsen through the rest of the decade. What I am suggesting, however, is that promoting this new series in July of 1895 allowed Heinemann's to bolster its already substantial reputation as an international publishing house while at the same time inviting Mrs. Grundy *not* to associate the firm with the scandals currently wracking British society. Granted, this case isn't as clear-cut as John Lane's reversal of policy during Wilde's trials; as many have noted, Lane quite abruptly dropped not only Wilde but also writers such as "George Egerton" as public response to the trials intensified.[36] Still, Heinemann's new series is a much safer commercial venture than the Pioneer Series. The feathers of a few academics may be ruffled by the firm's entrance into the controversy regarding literary versus philological studies; but the literature under discussion, we are assured, is not suspect in any way. Rather, it bears the imprimature of immortal greatness.

When this advertisement ends by promising that "French, Ancient Greek, English, Italian, Modern Scandinavian, and Japanese literature" will be represented equally in this new series and then teases readers with sample titles, "the classics" – a designation that would have invoked Shakespeare prominently for most readers – have thus taken on a new function in the British literary world of the 1890s. Rather than serving to legitimize rebellions against Grundyesque convention, rather than epitomizing the freedom to treat "uncertificated love" (Linton's phrasing) or "sexual relationship as it is" (Hardy's), Shakespeare will now function as a shorthand notation for the kind of timeless and atemporal literary artifact that will rise above all the "socio-literary portents" of sexual and political "anarchy" of the 1890s. To borrow Jean Howard and Marion O'Connor's phrasing, Shakespeare begins to serve (again) as a "cultural Esperanto" who transcends material, historical differences and offers "abiding truths of human existence."[37]

I'm anticipating later events somewhat in saying this, anticipating the arguments made, for example, in both of the critical studies of Shakespeare that will be published in this series after 1895: Georg Brandes's *William Shakespeare* (1898) and Gosse's critical history, *English Literature: An Illustrated Record* (1903). Significantly, although Shakespeare isn't mentioned explicitly in the July 1895 advertisement, he is featured in both of these studies as Britain's most important literary figure. Celebrating "the human spirit concealed and revealed in a great artist's work,"[38] weaving a story about a great man's life into the tapestry of a national literary tradition, these critics argue that Shakespeare represents Britain's highest literary achievement because he is an artist who can tell us not only "what Englishmen were like at the beginning of the seventeenth century" but also "what all men are like in all countries and at all times."[39]

Annie Combes and others have written recently about the increased interest in inventing and consolidating a national cultural identity in Britain at the turn of the twentieth century. Combes herself focuses on the production of museum exhibits; scholars such as Brian Doyle have shown how "a new patriotism" was fostered through the pursuit of English literature and language studies at the turn of the century in a movement to transform the curriculum that culminated with the publication of the

Newbolt Report in 1921.[40] The shift in the rhetorical deployment of Shakespeare during the 1890s that has been the focus of discussion in the first two sections of this chapter needs to be recognized as part of this much larger story about educational and cultural politics in Britain at the turn of the century. But I also need to complicate matters still further at this point by introducing a third influential troping of Shakespeare in the 1890s, consideration of which will reveal the relationship between these *fin-de-siècle* arguments about Shakespeare, "the classics," and the cultural work of English literature and language studies and the modernist avant-garde's ghosting of Oscar Wilde (and the Victorian *fin de siècle*) through its promotion of a universal, transhistorical aesthetic.

SHAKESPEARE THE NEW HELLENIST

In addition to being figured as an artist who could, alternately, "liberate" the Victorian novel from Mrs. Grundy or "rescue" English literature and culture from the *fin-de-siècle* degeneration epitomized, for some, in Wilde's trials, Shakespeare was also known in the 1890s as a New Hellenist: a man of intense "bi-social"[41] attachments; a man who loved Willie Hughes *and* the dark lady of the Sonnets. This third *fin-de-siècle* figuration of Shakespeare plays an important, though occluded, role in the production of literary value as something universal, transhistorical, and apolitical after 1895 that I have just been describing. Shakespeare the New Hellenist serves, in effect, as the unacknowledged antithesis of the Shakespeare celebrated in Heinemann's new series in literary studies who transcends the "differences of material existence" "to get at the abiding truths of human existence."[42] Shakespeare the New Hellenist is a figure who must be refuted or erased by anyone – academics attempting to legitimize English literature and language studies at the turn of the century or poet-impresarios blasting and bombadiering on behalf of the historical avant-garde in the 1910s and 20s – seeking a usable past in an "English" literary tradition. Before attempting, however, to make a case for the connection between literary modernists' interest in *not* being associated with Hellenic (read Shakespearean or Wildean) sexual dissidence and their investment in abstract figuration and aesthetic universality and ahistoricity, it is necessary to consider in some detail the *fin-de-siècle* history of New Hellenism.

During the great age of English university reform in the mid-Victorian period, as Linda Dowling and others have noted, Hellenism, the systematic study of Greek history, literature, and philosophy, served as a crucial means of both liberalizing political discourse and establishing the basis for a "homosexual counterdiscourse able to justify male love in ideal or transcendental terms."[43] On the one hand, the revisionary Greek ideal lying at the center of Oxford Hellenism was "the purest model of Victorian liberalism itself," promising to "restore and reinvigorate a nation fractured by the effects of laissez-faire capitalism and enervated by the approach of mass democracy." On the other hand, Oxford Hellenism also "provide[d] the means of sweeping away the entire accumulation of negative associations with male love which had remained strong through the beginning of the nineteenth century" (Dowling, 79, 31, 79).

We have seen Thomas Hardy link Shakespeare's name with that of Greek tragedy before pursuing an exclusive focus on Shakespeare in the final pages of his essay for the 1890 *New Review* symposium on "Candour in English Fiction." Notably, though, Hardy drops the parallel initially posited between Shakespearean and Greek drama almost immediately. The "brazen young Shakespeare" he goes on to figure as a champion of candour in English fiction is *not* the man who loved Willie Hughes, as Wilde's Cyril Graham will claim. This other, "Greek," Shakespeare was never assimilated into the Victorian age's public cult of true womanhood and manhood. He circulated solely between men in the exclusive, and exclusively academic, world of Victorian Oxford. "[T]riumphantly proclaiming" male love to be "the very fountain of civic health in a polity that [was] urged to take as its cultural model the ancient city-state of Athens," key figures in the Oxford reform movement such as Walter Pater and John Addington Symonds sought to realize the Platonic doctrine of eros, whereby an older man, "moved to love by the visible beauty of a younger man, and desirous of winning immortality through that love, undertakes the younger man's education in virtue and wisdom" (Dowling, 79, 81). As mediated through the Oxford Greats school, the conventions of Greek *paiderastia* provided Victorian Oxford with a model for cultural renewal as well as for the renewal of the individual: homoerotic friendship was to be a vital factor in the new culture, and a mode of self-conscious individual development. But as Edward Carson's attempt to use "The Portrait of Mr. W. H." in Wilde's trials as evidence against its author might also suggest, the dominant culture's sense of conflict between its own ideals and ideas and those of academic Hellenism increased exponentially as the century wore on.[44]

Critics have charted with great care Wilde's changing relationship with Walter Pater and discussed the significance of Wilde's years at Oxford.[45] They have also rehearsed in greater detail than is necessary here the various events between 1870 and 1900 that thrust "the sexual ambivalence within Oxford Hellenism, so plausibly depicted by Pater as the very engine of past and future cultural regeneration," into "a scandalous visibility upon the national stage" (Dowling, 104). These include the scandal surrounding the publication of Pater's *Renaissance* (1873), W. H. Mallock's parody of Pater in the *New Republic* (1877), and Symonds's work with Havelock Ellis in the 1880s. Wilde had long since left Oxford when "The Portrait of Mr. W. H." was published in *Blackwood's Edinburgh Magazine* in 1889; nevertheless, his arguments on three subjects – Shakespeare's love for Willie Hughes, the importance of the sonnets in Shakespeare's development as a dramatist, and the methods of literary scholarship – place him as squarely in that tradition of academic homosociality as his defense of "pure," "perfect," and "intellectual" male love in the final days of his last trial. The longer version of this work, which was not published until 1921, makes this lineage quite explicit.[46] But even the briefer 1889 version, with all of what Dowling terms its "unspecific amplitude of implication" (127), wears its Hellenism on its sleeve. Thus, as Alan Sinfield has noted, it "arous[es] suspicions about Wilde's sexuality in some quarters" in spite of its wonderfully playful and self-reflexive framing and reframing of the correlations between aestheticism, same-sex desire, effeminacy, and the interpellation of identity.[47]

Cassandra Laity has very usefully glossed male modernists' reluctance to be identified or associated with two *fin-de-siècle* figures, the Romantic androgyne and the decadent *femme fatale*, in *H. D. and the Victorian Fin-de-Siècle*. And she has pointed out how the hostile and hyper-heterosexualized rhetoric of their manifestos and prose writings about Romanticism and aestheticism is contradicted by their representations, in creative works, of polymorphously gendered figures. The following letter by T. S. Eliot to Scofield Thayer in 1916 on the occasion of the latter's marriage exemplifies precisely this two-faced modernist presentation of itself in relation to *fin-de-siècle* Hellenism. As this passage clearly suggests, particularly through the allusion to *Picture of Dorian Gray* buried in its core ("Only the soul can cure the senses, and only the senses can cure the soul"), not only was Eliot familiar with what Stephen Dedalus refers to in *Ulysses* as the "manner of Oxenford"; he was also willing to traffic in this homoerotic rhetoric in a private context if not in a public forum.

Can it be that a year ago you and I were charming the eyes (and ears) of Charflappers from one virginal punt, I by my voracity for bread and butter and you by Sidneian showers of discourse upon Art, Life, Sex and Philosophy? Yes! I recognize the Scofield of Magdelen, the connoisseur of puberty and lilies, in the Scofield of Washington Square, about to wed the Madonna of the mantlepiece, whose praises from your lips I have not forgotten. –So you have hit upon the Fountain of Eternal Youth, not in Florida, but Troy. 'Only the soul can cure the senses, and only the senses can cure the soul.' And the century of sonnets? And have I not St. Praxed's ear to pray horses for you, and brown Greek manuscripts? . . . to pray that domestic felicity may not extinguish the amateur, to pray that possession of beauty may not quench that ardour of curiosity and that passionate detachment which your friends admired and your admirers envied.

And I hope that within an interior of dim light drifting through heavy curtains, by a Buhl table holding a Greek figurine, and a volume of Faust bound in green and powdered with gold, with a bust of Dante, and perhaps a screen by Korin, a drawing by Watteau – a room heavy with the scent of lilies, you will enshrine such a treasure as that with which you credited me – a wife who is not wifely.[48]

In *Learning To Be Modern*, Gail McDonald has written powerfully about Eliot's work in the context of debates within the American academy at the turn of the twentieth century. But Eliot's reference to Magdelen College in the above should remind us of his early association with the *English* academy as well. Long before the association of literary modernism with Cambridge was made through F. R. Leavis in the 1930s, Eliot was familiar with Oxford connoisseurship of the arts, Oxford academic Hellenism, Oxford homosociality. I will come back to this passage again later in order to consider its relationship to the hyper-phallic rhetoric with which Eliot and others will promote their version of literary modernism. I turn now, however, to Joyce's treatment of Wilde and Wilde's Shakespeare in "Scylla and Charybdis" and to several of Eliot's and Pound's best-known efforts to teach early twentieth-century readers how to appreciate the work of the modernist avant-garde in order to establish a connection between their attempts to standardize a modernist method of reading and the academic treatments of Shakespeare discussed earlier in this chapter.

Shakespeare is omnipresent in modernism, of course, even if literary modernists' treatment of Shakespeare is not always or necessarily celebratory.[49] *Portrait of the Artist as a Young Man*, *Finnegan's Wake*, Woolf's *A Room of One's Own*, *Jacob's Room*, Wyndham Lewis's critical biography of Shakespeare, Eliot's critical and creative writings: all offer fertile ground for further inquiry in this regard. I choose to focus exclusively here on the scene in the National Library in *Ulysses* not only because Joyce alludes overtly to the turn-of-the-century controversies over Shakespeare discussed earlier in this chapter but also because *Ulysses* played such a crucial role in the marketing of high modernism that the contrast between Joyce's representations of Wilde's Hellenic Shakespeare and readings of Joyce's "masterpiece" by his earliest modernist critics and promoters is of particular interest.

Stephen Dedalus's painfully awkward attitude toward his own homosociality as well as that of Wilde and Wilde's Shakespeare has surfaced only relatively recently in critical discussions of Joyce's work.[50] Although Stephen dwells at greater length on Shakespeare's difficult heterosexual relationships, he shares not only Wilde's confusion of himself with Shakespeare in "Portrait of W. H.," but also his appreciation for the way in which, through art, we create ourselves through our imaginative identifications with the histories we repeat and transform. Even though Stephen keeps turning the discussion away from the topic of the Bard's presumed homosexuality during the scene in the National Library, it remains on his mind. In this regard, although he is a public advocate for a sexualized theory of creativity rooted in "thwarted heterosexuality," he "appears to practice another kind in private," as David Weir notes.[51] The reference to a long and complex homosocial tradition of artistic excellence in Stephen's allusion to "blond ephebe," as noted by Joseph Kestner, suggests as well that Stephen fears his exclusion from this tradition at least as much as its association with pederasty.[52]

In his 1957 study, *Joyce and Shakespeare*, which is still cited as the definitive work on Joyce's treatment of turn-of-the-century Shakespearean scholarship in *Ulysses*, William Schutte notes that Stephen makes extensive use of three turn-of-the-century sources: Frank Harris's series of articles for the *Saturday Review* in 1899; Georg Brandes's *William Shakespeare* (1898); and Sydney Lee's *A Life of William Shakespeare* (1898).[53] To a contemporary reader, what is perhaps most striking about Schutte's New Critical account of the "two major camps" of Shakespeare criticism during the latter part of the nineteenth century is his erasure of the homosexual Shakespeare from the historical and scholarly record. In describing the debate between "journalists" (Harris) who insist upon the artist's revelation of his individuality through his writing, and "scholars" (Lee) who refuse to ground literary interpretation in biographical analysis, Schutte neglects to mention how this debate hovers around the issue of Shakespeare's hetero- and homosexuality.

Although Harris, for example, claims to approach Shakespeare's work with an interest in showing "how Shakespeare painted himself at full-length, not once, but twenty times, at as many different periods of his life,"[54] he also rejects the argument that "the sonnets were the key to Shakespeare's heart," suggesting instead that "[t]he author whose personality is rich and complex enough to create and vitalize a dozen characters, reveals himself more fully in his creations than he can in his proper person" (199). Harris's characterization of a distinction between personal and artistic self-revelation is directly related to his defense of Shakespeare's heterosexuality:

"[I]f I were asked... why I take the trouble to re-create a man now three centuries dead, it is, first of all, of course, because he is worth it – the most complex and passionate personality in the world, whether of life or letters – because, too, there are certain lessons which the English learn from Shakespeare more quickly and easily than from any living man, and a little *because I want to get rid of Shakespeare by assimilating all that was fine in him, while giving all that was common and vicious in him as spoil to oblivion*" (xvii, emphasis added).

Unlike Georg Brandes, as we shall see, Harris frontloads the controversy in nineteenth-century Shakespeare criticism about the Bard's sexuality: "Hallam, 'the judicious,'" Harris writes, "held that 'it would have been better for Shakespeare's reputation if the sonnets had never been written,' and even Heine, led away by the consensus of opinion, accepted the condemnation, and regretted 'the miserable degradation of humanity' to be found in the sonnets" (227). "I take no interest in whitewashing Shakespeare," he goes on immediately to suggest: "I am intent on painting him as he lived and loved, and if I found him as vicious as Villon, or as cruel as a stoat, I would set it all down as faithfully as I would give proof of his generosity or his gentleness" (227). What Harris's survey of the biographical record and close readings of the sonnets ultimately reveals, though, is Shakespeare's confirmed heterosexuality. Thus, for example, he concludes his discussion of the first eighteen sonnets by suggesting that "Shakespeare makes use of the passion he has felt for a woman to give reality to the expression of his affection for the youth. No better proof can be imagined that he never loved the youth with passion" (233). When the "sonnet-story is finished[, t]he youth vanishes; no reader can find a trace of him, or even an allusion to him. But the woman [Mary Fitton] comes to be the centre ... of tragedy after tragedy" (247). And he will answer Hallam and Heine in the following way in his concluding remarks:

Hallam and Heine, and all the cry of critics, are mistaken in this matter. Lord Herbert's youth and boldness and beauty, hoped great things from his favour and patronage; but after the betrayal, he judged him inexorably as a mean traitor, 'a stealer' who had betrayed 'a twofold trust'; and later, cursed him for his ingratitude, and went about with wild thoughts of bloody revenge . . .

It is bad enough to show that Shakespeare, the sweetest spirit and finest mind in all literature, should have degraded himself to pretend such an affection for the profligate Herbert as has given occasion for misconstruction. It is bad enough, I say, to know that Shakespeare could play flunkey to this extent; but after all, that is the worst that can be urged against him, and it is so much better than men have been led to believe that there may be a certain relief in the knowledge. (248)

Like Harris, Georg Brandes is anxious to qualify the relevance of biographical data to literary interpretation. He concedes in his intro-duction that Shakespeare's sonnets "bring us more directly in touch with his personality than any of his other works"; but he quickly goes on to suggest that "to determine the value of the Sonnets as autobio-graphical documents requires not only historical knowledge but critical instinct and tact, since it is by no means self-evident that the poet is, in a literal sense, speaking in his own name."[55] Like Wilde, Brandes com-pares Shakespeare's with Michelangelo's sonnets in a chapter entitled "Platonism – Shakespeare's and Michael Angelo's Sonnets – the Tech-nique of the Sonnets." Unlike Wilde, however, Brandes insists upon the historical noncontiguity of the present and the past, while also erasing from the recent record not only the nineteenth-century interpretive tradi-tion leading from Hallam to Heine to Wilde but also the various turn-of-the-century scandals concerning same-sex relationships that resulted in the production of a "modern" distinction between homo- and heterosex-uality: "[T]he affection with which the young Lord inspired Shakespeare – the passionate attachment, leading even to jealousy of other poets ad-mired by the young nobleman – had not only a vividness but an erotic *fervour such as we never find in our own age manifested between man and man*," he claims (295, emphasis added). And he concludes this chapter, almost with relief, by referring first, and quite vaguely, to Shakespeare's "alleged relation to some woman, or implication in some amorous adventure," then providing a brief formal analysis of the entire sonnet sequence (298).

It is Sydney Lee, however – the author of the *Dictionary of National Biography* entry on Shakespeare – who most effectively ghosts the ho-mosexual Shakespeare from the record. His 1898 *William Shakespeare*, he claims, shall supply "an exhaustive and well-arranged statement of the facts of Shakespeare's career, achievement, and reputation," thereby "reduc[ing] conjecture to the smallest dimensions consistent with coher-ence."[56] This determination to produce the definitive biography does not mean that Lee is committed to reading Shakespeare's plays and poems autobiographically. Instead, he will reject such an approach out of hand: "To seek in [Shakespeare's] biography for a chain of events which should be calculated to stir in his own soul all or any of the tempestuous passions that animate his greatest plays is to under-estimate and to misapprehend the resistless might of his creative genius" (249). Promising in his introduction that his treatment of the sonnets will pursue "an original line of investigation" (vii), Lee puts to rest "all claims of the sonnets to rank as autobiographical documents" by first dismissing any investigation into the identity of "W. H." as misinterpretation of Elizabethan publishing transactions (92) and then documenting Shakespeare's immersion in a Renaissance tradition of sonneteering. "Genuine emotion or the writer's personal experience very rarely inspired the Elizabethan sonnet, and Shakespeare's sonnets proved no exception to the general rule," he concludes in the last of four chapters on the sonnets:

A personal note may have escaped him involuntarily in the sonnets in which he gives voice to a sense of melancholy and self-remorse, but his dramatic instinct never slept, and there is no proof that he is doing more in those sonnets than produce dramatically the illusion of a personal confession. (159)

BIRTHING MODERNISM, GHOSTING SHAKESPEARE
THE NEW HELLENIST AND OSCAR WILDE

To turn from Lee's 1898 biography of Shakespeare to T. S. Eliot's literary criticism of the late 1910s and 20s is to find a perhaps surprising amount of overlap in critical values. Like Harris, Brandes, *and* Lee, Eliot insists upon distinguishing "the man who suffers" from the "mind that creates."[57] Like Lee, he praises Shakespeare's ability to "transmute his personal and private agonies into something rich and strange, something universal and impersonal."[58] In other words, like Lee, what he values in a poet is his "historical sense": his sense "not only of the pastness of the past, but of its presence." "This historical sense, which is a sense of the timeless and of the temporal together, is what makes a writer traditional. And it is at the same time what makes a writer most acutely conscious of his place in time, of his own contemporaneity."[59]

Even as I would stress the extensive overlap between Eliot's and these turn-of-the-century scholars' and journalists' efforts to characterize art's impersonality and ahistoricity, I would also note the deliberate erasure of homosociality in Eliot's essay.

When Eliot theorizes the artist's imaginative identification with the past in "Tradition and the Individual Talent," the slippage between a man's identification with and desire for another man that is modeled in "Portrait of Mr. W. H." – and reiterated in both "Scylla and Charybdis" and Eliot's private correspondence with Scofield Thayer – will be erased through Eliot's highly abstract figuration of "the artist" and "the whole of the literature of Europe from Homer." Eliot will also allude to the artist's capacity to rise above mere procreative humanity in his 1916 letter to Schofield Thayer through his reference to wives who are not "wifely" and the "ardour of curiosity and that passionate detachment" which Thayer's Oxford "friends admired and your admirers envied." But in public writings such as "Tradition and the Individual Talent" he entirely dehumanizes the process of artistic creation. In other words, he offers what Eve Sedgewick has termed an "alibi of abstraction"[60] when he argues that the "more perfect" the artist, the "more completely separate in him will be the man who suffers and the mind which creates," the more impersonal will be his consciousness of the past. And thus, the more likely that his art will approach "the condition of science," he writes, reiterating a valorization of science's perfect objectivity we have already seen in Pound's "The Serious Artist."[61]

In essays such as *"Dubliners* and Mr. James Joyce" (1914) and *"Ulysses"* (1922), Pound adopts the same strategy, praising Joyce for his "clear hard prose" and his capacity to "deal with subjective things" without succumbing to "sloppiness" and "softness."[62] Although recent scholarship finds ample evidence of Joyce's interest in Wilde and the New Hellenism, as well as a great deal of ambivalence about homoeroticism and homosociality in *Portrait, Ulysses,* and *Finnegan's Wake,* Pound's *Dubliners* and *Ulysses* do not speak to and of any such matters. In other words, as has also been suggested of "Hugh Selwyn Mauberley," in writing about *Dubliners* and *Ulysses* Pound effectively "routed out"[63] the ambiguously gendered aesthete in favor of a more "virile" persona for the artist when he claims that Joyce presents subjective phenomena "with such clarity of outline that he might be dealing with locomotives or with builders' specifications" ("Dubliners," 399).

This same interest in both depersonalizing and universalizing art and the artist informs Pound's characterization of Joyce's Irishness, as Joseph Kelly has demonstrated in *Our Joyce.* Conceding that Joyce is Irish, Pound is eager to suggest that he does not "flop about" with Celtic imaginings. Instead, he "defines": "he accepts an international standard of prose writing and lives up to it." Which means that, even though he "gives us Dublin as it presumably is," in fact what he gives us is

> things as they are, not only for Dublin, but for every city. Erase the local names and a few specifically local allusions, and a few historic events of the past, and substitute a few different local names, allusions, and events, and these stories could be retold of any town ... Good writing, good presentation, can be specifically local, but it must not depend on locality. ("Dubliners," 400–401)

Echoing Eliot's language in "Tradition and the Individual Talent" about when and why art approaches the "condition of science," Pound concludes his 1922 essay for the *Dial* on *Ulysses* by insisting that a *"great literary masterwork is made for minds quite as serious as those engaged in the science of medicine"* ("Ulysses," 408, emphasis in original). Proclaiming the cultural centrality of literature in terms of its importance as a linguistic resource, he then takes one final poke at Wildean aestheticism. In sharp contrast to his re-wrapping of aestheticism's defense of art's "uselessness" in the rhetoric of science in "The Serious Artist," Pound here jettisons Wildean aestheticism while sustaining both the defense of "serious" literature and the analogy with the science of medicine discussed earlier in the 1913 manifesto:

> The public utility of accurate language ... can be attained only from literature ... I am not offering this fact as a sop to aesthetes who want all authors to be fundamentally useless. We are governed by words, the laws are graven in words, and literature is the sole means of keeping those words living and accurate.[64]

* * * * * * * * *

Scholars have documented with great care the multiplicity of Eliot's unacknowledged debts to Wilde and noted that Joyce's work "was intended to bring something like a new hellenism about."[65] If one thinks, however, of Eliot's and Pound's efforts, in their critical writings, to teach early twentieth-century readers how to appreciate the impersonality of "significant" emotion, the universality of aesthetic value, and the poet's sense of the presentness of the past, it is obvious that – in spite of their reproduction of key aspects of the New Hellenists' project of cultural rejuvenation – they are deeply invested in *not* identifying their own agenda with that of late Victorian New Hellenism. Yet their efforts are energized by what Richard Dellamora has termed the "crises of sexual identity and male privilege" of the 1890s to a degree that they themselves could not acknowledge.[66] Their arguments about (modernist) art's capacity to transcend history bear more fossilized traces of historically specific *fin-de-siècle* debates about cultural degeneration, effeminacy, and "tommyrotics" than they could afford to articulate – in their critical writings, if not in their creative work – as they were establishing the symbolic capital of "serious" art in the 1910s and early 20s.

NOTES

1. As quoted by Regenia Gagnier, *Idylls of the Marketplace: Oscar Wilde and the Victorian Public* (Stanford University Press, 1986), p. 29.
2. By contrast, as Thomas Beer notes, Wilde is mentioned in "at least nine hundred known sermons between 1895 and 1900" (*The Mauve Decade* [New York: Alfred A. Knopf, 1941], p. 99).
3. Michel Foucault, *The History of Sexuality I: An Introduction* (New York: Vintage Books, 1980), p. 27.
4. For further discussion of Wilde's significance for Mansfield, see Laity, *H. D. and the Victorian Fin de Siècle*, pp. 13–17; for Wilde's significance for both Cather and Mansfield, see Richard Dellamora, "Traversing the Feminine in *Salomé*," in Thaïs Morgan (ed.), *Victorian Sages and Cultural Discourses: Renegotiating Gender and Power* (New Brunswick: Rutgers University Press, 1990), pp. 246–64.
5. To Vita Sackville West, she writes on Thursday 9 April 1931: "Lord, what a letter to Robbie Ross. How cold cautious and clammy – like the writhing of a fat worm, red, shiny – and disgusting: yet Harold likes him – Gosse, I mean." (*The Letters of Virginia Woolf IV, 1929–31*, ed. Nigel Nicholson and Joanne Trautmann [New York: Harcourt Brace Jovanovich, 1975], p. 306.) Her letter to Elizabeth Robins is dated Sunday 4 June 1939 (*Letters of Virginia Woolf VI, 1936–41*, ed. Nigel Nicholson and Joanne Trautmann [New York: Harcourt Brace Jovanovich, 1975], p. 334).
6. Omar Pound and A. Walter Litz (eds.), *Ezra Pound and Dorothy Shakespear: Their Letters 1909–1914* (New York: New Directions, 1984); September 1911, p. 52, and 31 August 1913, p. 247. The reference in 1913 is the more interesting: Shakespear contrasts the performance of *Dorian Gray* she saw at the Vaudeville Theatre the night before with her reading of *Kim* in bed afterwards, noting her marked preference for Kipling. The "psychic part [of *Dorian Gray*] is so crude," she complains. "I am – perhaps you have helped me to know it – of another generation" (p. 247).
7. T. S. Eliot, "A Preface to Modern Literature," *Vanity Fair* 21 (1923), 44. Richard Shusterman refers to this as a "fugitive piece of journalistic criticism" and notes that this is as close as Eliot gets "(albeit very vaguely)" to admitting his own debt to Wilde; see "Wilde and Eliot," *T. S. Eliot Annual* 1 (1990), 144.
8. Arthur Ransome, *Oscar Wilde: A Critical Study* [1912] (New York: Haskell House, 1971), pp. 20–1. See also Frank Harris, *Oscar Wilde: His Life and Confessions* (New York: Brentano, 1916).

9. See Laity, *Modernism and the Victorian Fin de Siècle*, pp. 9–18, for an important discussion of these efforts to "detona[te] the Decadent past" (p. 14).

10. Terry Castle, *The Apparitional Lesbian: Female Homosexuality and Modern Culture* (New York: Columbia University Press, 1993).

11. Michael S. Foldy, *The Trials of Oscar Wilde: Deviance, Morality, and Late-Victorian Society* (New Haven, C.T.: Yale University Press, 1997), p. xi.

12. Adam Parkes, *Modernism and the Theater of Censorship* (New York: Oxford University Press, 1996), p. 6.

13. T. S. Eliot, "Tradition and the Individual Order," *Selected Essays* (New York: Harcourt, Brace & World, 1964 [1932]), p. 5.

14. George Moore's tirade against Mudie's, *Literature at Nurse; or, Circulating Morals* is probably the most notorious of these. But see also Rider Haggard, "About Fiction," *Contemporary Review* 51 (1887), 172–80; Florence Layard, "What Women Write and Read," *National and English Review* 10 (1887–88), 376–81; Elizabeth Lynn Linton, "Literature: Then and Now," *Fortnightly Review* 52 (1890), 517–31; Edward Salmon, "What Girls Read," *Nineteenth Century* 20 (1886), 515–29; and the preface to Olive Schreiner's *Story of an African Farm* (London: Chapman Hall, 1883).

15. Linton's trilogy of articles on "Wild Women" for the *Nineteenth Century* in 1891 and 1892 epitomizes conservative middle-class women's antagonism toward those who rebelled against Victorian domestic ideology by either pursuing work in the public sphere or having sexual relations ("free unions") outside marriage. See "The Wild Women as Politicians," *Nineteenth Century* 30 (1891), 79–88; "The Wild Women as Social Insurgents," *Nineteenth Century* 30 (1891), 596–605; and "Partisans of the Wild Women," *Nineteenth Century* 31 (1892), 455–64. In her 1890 essay, "Literature Then and Now," drawing upon the same nationalistic rhetoric she employs in "Candour in English Fiction," Linton chastises novelists who assert the right to be "candid" in their representations of "free unions," monogamous sexual relationships outside marriage. "In this day of universal disintegration and the supremacy of fads, there are so many who would sacrifice the good of the country – the integrity of empire – to some impracticable theory that looks like godly justice on paper and would be cruelly wrong in practice" (*Fortnightly Review* 53 [1890], 529–30). For further discussion of Linton's self-appointed role as the custodian of English culture in the 1890s, see Nancy Fix Anderson, *Woman Against Women in Victorian England* (Bloomington: Indiana University Press, 1987); and Ardis, *New Women, New Novels*, pp. 20–8, 46–7.

16. Eliza Lynn Linton, "Candour in English Fiction," *New Review* 2 (1890), 10. Subsequent references to this essay will be cited parenthetically in the text.

17. It is worth noting here the slippage between the terms "English" and "British" in Linton's essay. Linton's primary focus is the *English* publishing industry; but the rhetoric of *literary* as well as political nationalism welds the larger British "nation-state" together as a single entity.

18. Thomas Hardy, "Candour in English Fiction," *New Review* 2 (1890), 15, 17. Subsequent references to this essay will be cited parenthetically in the

text. "Sincerity" is a phrase in this essay that immediately brings to mind Oscar Wilde's prominent use of this same term a year earlier in "The Decay of Lying." Rather curiously, Hardy does not reference Wilde's critique of nineteenth-century novelists' blue-book faithfulness to reality in this essay; instead, as is also the case in Linton's essay for the *New Review*, the focus here is exclusively on Victorian novelists' *failure* to be sincere or to represent with any kind of accuracy basic realities of life, because of the conventions of the marriage plot.

19. Nina Auerbach, *Woman and the Demon* (Cambridge and London: Harvard University Press, 1982), pp. 213, 210 (quoting John Ruskin).
20. Levenson, *A Genealogy of Modernism*, p. 204.
21. Michel Foucault, *The History of Sexuality – Volume I: An Introduction*, trans. Robert Hurley (New York: Vintage, 1980), pp. 35, 7.
22. See the reproduction of this page in draft in Thomas Hardy, *Tess of the D'Urbervilles*, ed. Scott Elledge (New York and London: W. W. Norton and Co., 1991), p. xvi. My thanks go to Deborah Jacobs for first pointing this out to me.
23. Nigel Cross, *The Common Writer: Life in Nineteenth-Century New Grub Street* (Cambridge University Press, 1985); Wendell Harris, "John Lane's Keynotes Series and the Fiction of the 1890s," *PMLA* 83 (1968), 1407–13; Katherine Lyon Mix, *A Study in Yellow: The Yellow Book and Its Contributors* (Lawrence: University of Kansas Press, 1960); James Nelson, *Early Nineties: A View from the Bodley Head* (Cambridge, M.A.: Harvard University Press, 1971); Peter Keating, *The Haunted Study: A Social History of the English Novel 1875–1914* (London: Secker and Warburg, 1989); Peter D. McDonald, *British Literary Culture and Publishing Practice 1880–1914* (Cambridge University Press, 1997); Margaret D. Stetz, "'Life's Half-Profits': Writers and Their Readers in Fiction of the 1890s," Lawrence Lockridge, John Maynard, and Donald Stone (eds.), *Nineteenth-Century Lives* (Cambridge University Press, 1989), pp.169–87; John Stokes, *In the Nineties* (University of Chicago Press, 1989); Allon White, *The Uses of Obscurity: The Fiction of Early Modernism* (New York: Routledge and Kegan Paul, 1981), pp. 30–54.
24. "The Year in Review," *Athenaeum* (6 January, 1894), 17–18.
25. A. G. P. Sykes, "The Evolution of the Sex," *Westminster Review* 143 (1895), 397, 398, 398.
26. Hugh Stutfield, "Tommyrotics," *Blackwood's* 157 (1895), 833. Stutfield borrows the term "degeneration" from Max Nordau's famous study, which was published first in English in February 1895. Subsequent references to Stutfield's essay will be cited parenthetically in the text.
27. John Stokes, *In the Nineties*, p. 14 (quoting *Punch*, 11 May 1895).
28. "Socio-Literary Portents," *Speaker* 19 (1894), 684–5.
29. "*Discords*," *Athenaeum* (March 23, 1895), 375. Subsequent references to this essay will be cited parenthetically in the text.
30. *Athenaeum* (July 27, 1895), 117. Subsequent references to this advertisement will be cited parenthetically in the text.

31. It is worth noting in passing that, at its highest peak of empire, at the time of the most active orientalist studies in Britain, Indian literature is not mentioned in this list of "recognized literatures" and world "classics." In *Masks of Conquest*, Gauri Viswanathan has argued that the English curriculum was first established in India (and only after that in Britain) as a way to test it, correct it. (Viswanathan, *Masks of Conquest: Literary Studies and British Rule in India* [New York: Columbia University Press, 1989].) This testing was efficient because English literature was made to function as a moral example to India; all that was to be represented of the best morality was put into the production of "English studies," and English literature bore the burden of this teaching by example and model in India. Viswanathan also notes that Indian literature itself was considered complex enough for British consumption but not fit material for Indians themselves, as it was likely to be read by them in indecent, inappropriate ways. That is, being "immoral" and "impure," it needed an intellectual filter which British readers had and Indian readers lacked. Perhaps then, Indian literature is *not* mentioned in Heinemann's allegedly complete catalogue of world literatures because it might have been considered "improper" according to Heinemann's agenda. In spite of its wide dissemination and translation to and for British audiences at the turn of the twentieth century, Indian literature is not built into this sales pitch for the "classics" to an audience of "ordinary" English readers because it might undermine the project of cultural purification and nation-building Heinemann launches here with this new literary series. I want to thank Alpana Sharma for helping me understand this dynamic.

32. Barbara Herrnstein Smith, "Contingencies of Value," *Critical Inquiry* 10 (1983), 23.

33. Stefan Collini, *Public Moralists: Political Thought and Intellectual Life in Britain, 1850–1930* (Oxford: Clarendon Press, 1991), pp. 223, 222, 223.

34. Grant Richards, *Author Hunting, by an Old Literary Sportsman* (New York: McCann, 1934), p. 143. Richards's remarks are made specifically about William Heinemann, but they pertain equally well to Lane's Bodley Head and T. Fisher Unwin.

35. For further discussion of these turn-of-the-century arguments about literary study, the academy, and the public sphere, see Brian Doyle, "The Invention of English," in Robert Colls and Philip Dodd (eds.), *Englishness: Politics and Culture 1880–1920* (London: Croom Helm, 1986), pp. 89–115; Brian Doyle, *English and Englishness* (London and New York: Routledge, 1989); Janet Batsleer, Tony Davies, Rebecca O'Rourke, and Chris Weedon (eds.), *Rewriting English: Cultural Politics of Gender and Class* (London and New York: Methuen, 1985), pp. 13–40; Stephen Ball, Alex Kenny and David Gardener, "Literacy, Politics, and the Teaching of English," in Ivor Goodson and Peter Medway (eds.), *Bringing English to Order: The History and Politics of a School Subject* (New York, London, and Philadelphia: Faber Press, 1990), pp. 47–86; and Robin Morgan, "The Englishness of English Teaching," in Goodson and Medway (eds.), *Bringing English to Order*, pp. 187–241.

36. See Regenia Gagnier, *Idylls of the Marketplace*, p. 141; Katherine Lyon Mix, *A Study in Yellow: The Yellow Book and Its Contributors*, pp. 140–7; James Nelson, *Early Nineties: A View from the Bodley Head*, p. 211; Margaret D. Stetz and Mark Samuels Lasner, *England in the 1890s: Literary Publishing at the Bodley Head* (Washington, D.C.: Georgetown University Press, 1990), p. 40.

37. Jean Howard and Marion O'Connor, *Shakespeare Reproduced: The Text in History and Ideology* (New York: Methuen, 1987), p. 4.

38. Georg Brandes, *William Shakespeare* (London: William Heinemann, 1898), p. 1.

39. Stephen Ball, Alex Kenny and David Gardner, "Literacy, Politics, and the Teaching of English," p. 52.

40. Annie E. Combes, "Museums and the Formation of National and Cultural Identities," *Oxford Art Journal* 11, 2 (1988), 57–68; see also her book-length study, *Reinventing Africa: Museums, Material Culture, and Popular Imagination in Late Victorian and Edwardian England* (New Haven, C.T.: Yale University Press, 1994).

41. Margaret Stetz's term, "The Bi-Social Oscar Wilde and 'Modern' Women," *Nineteenth-Century Literature* 55, 4 (March 2001), 515–37.

42. Howard and O'Connor, *Shakespeare Reproduced*, p. 4.

43. Linda Dowling, *Hellenism and Homosexuality in Victorian Oxford* (Ithaca: Cornell University Press, 1994), p. xiii. Subsequent references to this study will be cited parenthetically in the text.

44. As Robert J. G. Lange notes, a short version of this novella was published first in *Blackwood's* in July 1880; the longer version was not completed until the summer of 1891, possibly even later. In February 1895, plans for its publication by the Bodley Head were still unsettled, and the manuscript was in Wilde's possession on April 5 when he was arrested and his Tite Street home was sacked. In May 1921, a 1000-copy limited edition was published in the U.S. by Kennerly, and Vyvan Holland was arraigned for printing ten copies by Duckworth to reserve British copyright. See Lange, "The Provenance of Oscar Wilde's 'The Portrait of Mr. W. H.': An Oversight?," *Notes and Queries* 42, 2 (June 1995), 202–3.

45. See, for example, Denis Donoghue, "The Oxford of Pater, Hopkins, and Wilde," in George C. Sandulescu (ed.), *Rediscovering Oscar Wilde* (Gerrards Cross: Smythe, 1994), pp. 94–117; Alan Sinfield, *The Wilde Century: Effeminacy, Oscar Wilde, and the Queer Movement* (New York: Columbia University Press, 1994); Josephine M. Guy, *The British Avant-Garde: The Theory and Politics of Tradition* (New York: Harvester Wheatsheaf, 1991); and John Paul Riquelme, "Shalom/Solomon/Salomé: Modernism and Wilde's Aesthetic Politics," *The Centennial Review* 39, 3 (Fall 1995), 575–610.

46. See, for example, its reference to Arthur Hallam's suggestion of regret "that the Sonnets had ever been written," having seen in them "something dangerous, something unlawful even." Its presentation of Symonds and Swinburne as critical authorities on Renaissance neo-Platonism, and its

characterization of Shakespeare's attempts to "pierc[e] through the veil of flesh" in search of "the divine idea it imprisoned" (Oscar Wilde, *The Portrait of Mr. W. H.* [New York: Mitchell Kennerley, 1921], pp. 66, 63) also distinguish it from the 1889 version.

47. Sinfield, *The Wilde Century*, p. 19.
48. T. S. Eliot, letter to Scofield Thayer, 7 May 1916; Valerie Eliot (ed.), *The Letters of T. S. Eliot* (London: Faber and Faber, 1988), pp. 137–8.
49. It is germane to the following discussion to note, for example, just how ambivalent both Eliot and Pound are toward Shakespeare: Eliot tended to exalt Tourneur and other minor Elizabethans, and his most famous essay on Shakespeare argues that *Hamlet* is a failure; Pound tended to omit Shakespeare almost entirely from his cultural curriculum (though not from his son's name). For a valuable discussion of Eliot's treatment of Shakespeare, see Steve Ellis, *The English Eliot: Design, Language and Landscape in* Four Quartets (London and New York: Routledge, 1991).
50. Although Joyce's interest in Wilde was established long ago, the homoeroticism and homosexuality of Stephen Dedalus and other Joycean characters is a relatively new and recent focus of interest in Joyce studies; see, for example, the "Queer Joyce" issue of the *James Joyce Quarterly*, especially: Joseph Valente, "Thrilled By His Touch: Homosexual Passion and the Will to Artistry in *Portrait of the Artist as a Young Man*," *James Joyce Quarterly* 31, 3 (Spring 1994), 167–88; David Weir, "A Womb of His Own: Joyce's Sexual Aesthetic," *James Joyce Quarterly* 31, 3 (1994), 207–31; and Joseph Kestner, "Youth by the Sea: The Ephebe in *Portrait of the Artist* and *Ulysses*," *James Joyce Quarterly* 31,3 (1994), 233–76.
51. Weir, "A Womb of His Own," pp. 220, 228.
52. Kestner, "Youth by the Sea," p. 233.
53. William Schutte, *Joyce and Shakespeare: A Study in the Meaning of Ulysses* (New Haven, CT: Yale University Press, 1957), p. 153.
54. Frank Harris, *The Man Shakespeare and his Tragic Life-Story* (New York: Harris, 1921), pp. ix–x. Subsequent references to this study will be cited parenthetically in the text.
55. Georg Brandes, *William Shakespeare: A Critical Study* (London: Heinemann, 1902), p. 4. Subsequent references to this study will be cited parenthetically in the text.
56. Lee, *A Life of William Shakespeare* (London: Macmillan, 1898), p. vi. Subsequent references to this study will be cited parenthetically in the text.
57. T. S. Eliot, "Tradition and the Individual Talent," *Selected Essays of T. S. Eliot* (New York: Harcourt, Brace & World, 1964), p. 8.
58. T. S. Eliot, "Shakespeare and the Stoicism of Seneca," *Selected Essays of T. S. Eliot*, p. 117.
59. Eliot, "Tradition," p. 4.
60. Eve Kosofsky Sedgwick, *Epistemology of the Closet* (Berkeley: University of California Press, 1990), p. 169. Sedgwick describes modernist formalism as an interest in abjecting not the figuration of just *any* body, the figuration

of figurality itself, but, rather, that represented in a very particular body, the desired male body. Sedgewick goes further than I would in attributing the modernist drive to formalist abstraction entirely to this purpose. As I will argue in Chapter 3 and as I have already shown in Chapter 1, this is powered as much by anxiety about the increasing authority of science and the feminization and massification of culture as it is by an interest in abjecting homosocial desire.

61. Eliot, "Tradition," p. 7.
62. Ezra Pound, "Dubliners and Mr James Joyce," *The Literary Essays of Ezra Pound*, pp. 399, 400. Subsequent references to this essay will be cited parenthetically in the text.
63. Laity, *H. D. and the Victorian Fin de Siècle*, p. 399.
64. Pound, "*Ulysses*," *Literary Essays of Ezra Pound*, pp. 408, 409.
65. Richard Ellmann, "The Uses of Decadence: Wilde, Yeats, Joyce," in Ceri Crossley and Ian Small (eds.), *Studies in Anglo-French Cultural Relations: Imagining France* (London: Macmillan, 1988), 32.
66. Richard Dellamora, *Masculine Desire: The Sexual Politics of Victorian Aestheticism* (Chapel Hill: University of North Carolina Press, 1990), p. 217.

CHAPTER 3

The Lost Girl, Tarr, *and the "moment" of modernism*

After Modernism is canonized . . . by the post-war settlements and its accompanying, complicit academic endorsements, there is then the presumption that since Modernism is *here* in this specific phase or period, there is nothing beyond it. The marginal or rejected artists become classics of organized teaching and of travelling exhibitions in the great galleries of the metropolitan cities. "Modernism" is confined to this highly selective field and denied to everything else in an act of pure ideology.

Raymond Williams, *The Politics of Modernism*[1]

[T]he moment of modernism is the moment of its construction as a rigorously exclusionary category of value in the twentieth-century academy, as *the* canonical form of early twentieth-century literature; a moment in which one particular form of aesthetic practice, a practice committed to particular kinds of formal and linguistic experimentation, was privileged above others; a moment in which a restricted group of texts and authors was removed from the complex social and cultural specificities of history and located in that transcendent ideal order of the literary tradition described (or invented) by Eliot in 'Tradition and the Individual Talent'; a moment in which a particular 'discipline of reading' was established by the 'intellectual hegemony of Eliot, Leavis, Richards, and the New Critics.' In this latter sense, the moment of modernism is a prolonged one in which a hegemonic view of literary history and value is first produced and then reproduced by a literary academy committed to working constantly over the same relatively small group of texts.

Lyn Pykett, *Engendering Fictions: The English Novel in the Twentieth Century*[2]

For various reasons D. H. Lawrence and Wyndham Lewis do not fit the Joyce–Pound–Eliot paradigm of modernism that this study has been recontextualizing historically. Lawrence has never been classified uncontentiously as a modernist either by early twentieth-century or by more recent literary scholars; moreover he himself was determined to disassociate himself from his modernist contemporaries because of their investment in what he considered a life-denying notion of aesthetic autonomy. And while Lewis was certainly a member of the men of 1914's original London coterie, his work has never been successfully packaged as modern "classics" and marketed for consumption as "our Lewis" either in school or university curricula, as Joseph Kelly has shown to be the case with James Joyce.[3] Nevertheless, I want to consider in this chapter the roles that both writers played in what scholars such as Raymond Williams and Lyn Pykett have termed "the moment of modernism." Specifically, I want to suggest that two of their novels, *The Lost Girl* (1920) and *Tarr* (1918; 1928), can help us understand their role in the long and complex process of institutionalizing and standardizing a modernist "discipline of reading" both literary texts and culture.

Some might argue that Williams and Pykett overstate their case: that their characterization of modernism's "hegemonic view of literary history and value" – and my endorsement of it here in framing this chapter – exaggerates and homogenizes a multiplicity of modernist literary movements, creating a falsely monolithic view of modernism that bears no relation to the complexities of its material and institutional history. While it is important to recognize modernism's multiple modalities and the complexity of its institutional history, I would also argue that it is equally important to recognize the ways in which its most basic categories of analysis were stitched into the very fabric of English studies as a discipline as the latter established its professional credibility in the 1920s, 1930s, and 1940s. If modernism's legacies to the discipline still remain somewhat invisible to us even today, perhaps this is because they remain so familiar. Recent characterizations of modernism's "prolonged" moment, as Pykett puts it, are therefore useful for my purposes insofar as they call attention to what Williams has termed the "machinery of selective tradition": the apparatus of reviews, academic endorsements, curricular revision, etc., that enables a "highly selected version of the modern" to stand in for "the whole of modernity."[4]

What I *won't* be doing in this chapter is providing the kind of richly material history of modernism's contribution to the inauguration of English studies that scholars such as Chris Baldick, Michael Coyle, Terry Eagleton, Michael Levenson, Gail McDonald, and Thomas Strychacz have offered in studies such as *The Social Mission of English Criticism*, *Ezra Pound, Popular Genres, and the Discourse of Culture*, "The Rise of English Studies," *A Genealogy of Modernism*, *Learning To Be Modern*, and *Modernism, Mass Culture, and Professionalism*. Rather, their work, and that of scholars such as Pykett, Antony Easthope, and Bruce Robbins provides a crucial backdrop to my treatment here of two texts that have, curiously (tellingly), remained more or less "outside" both modernism and English studies.[5] Elsewhere in this study the discussion in any given chapter has ranged and will range broadly across a multiplicity of texts. The focus here is deliberately narrow. In "The Rise of English Studies," Terry Eagleton has described how a modernist practice of close reading, which "was to be triumphantly consummated in the American New Criticicism," encourages "the illusion that any piece of language, 'literary' or not, can be adequately studied or even understood in isolation."[6] As the domain of expertise in English studies has expanded to include cultural studies in recent years, the modernist practice of close reading has been re-purposed, has become a means of understanding texts *in* contexts, contexts *as* texts. The close readings of *The Lost Girl* and *Tarr* that follow thus invite us to think more self-consciously about the interpretive paradigms we have inherited from modernism and to historicize our own critical practices, even as we historicize those of the London-based modernist avant-garde.

IN DEFENSE OF "LITERARY" LITERACY: D. H. LAWRENCE AND *THE LOST GIRL*

The Lost Girl has had the dubious distinction of being the lost text in Lawrence's canon, even though it is the only book for which Lawrence received a major award during his lifetime, and even though its publication in 1920 "opened the way for...publication [or republication] of nearly all Lawrence's books."[7] As a highly self-reflexive meditation on the rapidly changing scene of aesthetic production in Britain at the turn of the twentieth century, it is a key transition work in Lawrence's career, enacting a defense of the literary field that sets the stage for all of his later work. Because *The Lost Girl*'s critique of modernity, which is enacted *through* his defense of the 'literary,' would prove immensely attractive to academics in the 1930s such as F. R. Leavis, who paved the way for the institutionalization of English studies through their advocacy of modernist aesthetics, a close reading of it can help us appreciate this larger process as well. This discussion thus has two goals. First, I want to demonstrate how a modernist delimitation of the literary field is consolidated in *The Lost Girl* through Lawrence's treatment of three forms of expressive culture vying for cultural authority in early twentieth-century Britain: cinema, music hall theater, and the novel. And second, I want to show how Lawrence's defense of "literary" literacy together with his devaluation of *other* aesthetic practices, enabled his co-optation by a Leavisite/New Critical paradigm of modernism, in spite of his genuine antipathy to key tenets of a modernist aesthetic platform.

The year 1920 was a particularly difficult moment in Lawrence's career. *The Rainbow* had been suppressed by court order in England since November 1915, and *Women in Love* had not yet been privately published when, in November of 1919, Lawrence began rewriting the manuscript that was eventually published as *The Lost Girl*.[8] Additionally, in December of 1919 Lawrence broke off ties with his English literary agent, J. B. Pinker, and began handling his publishing arrangements himself. As John Worthen has noted, Lawrence was eager to use *The Lost Girl* as a bargaining chip in his negotiations with Martin Secker, his English publisher, over the publication of *Women in Love* and *The Rainbow*. Anxious to allay Secker's fears about repeating "the *Rainbow* fiasco"[9] as well as to secure a much-needed income, Lawrence describes *The Lost Girl* as a "perfect selling novel"[10] that would offset the risks Secker would be taking in publishing *Women in Love* and *The Rainbow*. Similarly, writing to Thomas Seltzer, his American publisher, Lawrence emphasizes *The Lost Girl*'s commercial viability rather than its aesthetic merit: "*Women in Love* is best, next to *The Rainbow*. I am doing Mixed Marriage [one of the many early titles of *The Lost Girl*] – it should be more popular – one withdraws awhile from battle."[11]

In these letters to publishers, Lawrence makes a distinction between writing produced in the service of his muse (e.g., *The Rainbow* and *Women in Love*) and that which is publishable. Significantly, however, either that opposition ceases to operate or *The Lost Girl* is characterized as "true" art, not work for hire, in other letters to Secker and in letters to friends. In June of 1920, for example, Lawrence describes the novel to Secker as a "queer book... Being out here [i.e., in Italy], I find it quite good – a bit wonderful, really."[12] Writing to Compton Mackenzie in May of 1920, he confesses that he is "terrified of my Alvina, who marries a Cicio." He goes on to note: "I feel as if I was victualling my ship, with these damned books. But also, somewhere they are the crumpled wings of my soul. They get me free before I get myself free. I mean in my novel I get some sort of wings loose, before I get my feet out of Europe."[13]

Letters to Edward Garnett in 1913 offer the same contradictory endorsements, suggesting that this project blurred the boundaries between "pure" art and commercially viable or low art from its very inception.

"I think you will hate it," Lawrence concedes to Garnett, adding quickly that "it might find a good public amongst the Meredithy public" when rewritten. As he goes on to describe the project in more detail, however, the tone of his remarks shifts. The preliminary obeisance before Garnett's aesthetic standards gives way to a more positive characterization of both the novel and the readership Lawrence hopes to engage:

It is quite different in manner from my other stuff – far less visualised. It is what I *can* write just now, and write with pleasure, so write it I must, however you may grumble. And it is good too. I think, do you know, I have inside me a sort of answer to the *want* of today: to the real, deep want of the English people, not just what they fancy they want ... [T]his novel is perhaps not such good art, but it is what they want, need, more or less.[14]

Was *The Lost Girl* dashed off quickly to make a buck or is it "real" art? Obviously enough, both Lawrence's ambivalence about the "Meredithy public" and his defensiveness when writing to highbrow friends about his interest in this market for fiction is powered by a modernist notion of what Andreas Huyssen has so usefully termed the great divide between high art and the "culture industry."[15] Significantly, though, *The Lost Girl* slips from one category to the other, sometimes in the same letter. Rather than dismissing low culture out of hand, Lawrence both disparages it and defends it. He stands behind *The Lost Girl* both as a money-making project that "is good too" and one that speaks to the "real, deep want" of his readers.

Similarly mixed signals about low culture strongly mark the opening chapters of the novel as well. As I have argued in *New Women, New Novels: Feminism and Early Modernism*, New Woman fiction of the 1890s disrupted the high/low culture divide that was being organized, at least in part, in response to the New Woman novel's popularity. Because fiction about the New Woman resists classification as either popular or high art fiction, its commercial success was very threatening to the critical establishment at the turn of the century.[16] By alluding prominently to texts such as George Gissing's *The Odd Woman* in his opening chapter, Lawrence not only invites thematic comparisons between *The Lost Girl* and earlier New Woman fiction; he also refuses to honor a distinction in kind between popular and good art.

At the same time, however, even though James Houghton is mocked in Chapter 1 for not being able to satisfy his customers' tastes, the narrator characterizes the latter in entirely negative terms:

He thought he had not been clever enough, when he had been far, far too clever already. He always thought that Dame Fortune was a capricious and fastidious dame, a sort of Elizabeth of Austria or Alexandra, Princess of Wales, elegant beyond his grasp. Whereas Dame Fortune, even in London or Vienna, let alone in Woodhouse [the north-of-England mining town where this story takes place], was a vulgar woman of the middle- and lower middle-class, ready to put her heavy foot on anything that was not vulgar, machine-made, and appropriate to the herd. (5)[17]

"Like an author on his first night in the theatre" who watches "his work fall more than flat," Houghton's first business fails miserably, the narrator notes, because he "could never learn" to accept and cater to this vulgarity (5). The narrator's repetition of this analogy several times and his characterization of Houghton's yard goods shop as a "commercial poem" (3) encourage a comparison between Houghton's relationship to his prospective customers and Lawrence's to the readers of *The Lost Girl*. Critics rarely talk about James Houghton, choosing instead to focus on his daughter Alvina, whose story begins in Chapter 2.[18] But the focus in the opening pages on James should not be ignored. For through him Lawrence begins to address the concerns about the cultural hierarchy of discourses about art and the impact this has on the production of "literary" and popular fiction, as raised in his letters about *The Lost Girl*.

These issues are also addressed in Chapter 1 through the abrasive self-reflexiveness of the narration. Consider, for example, the opening paragraph, which asks readers to imagine a place and a character who inhabits it – and then abruptly tells us to forget him:

Take a mining townlet like Woodhouse, with a population of ten thousand people, and three generations behind it. This space of three generations argues a certain well-established society. The old 'County' has fled from the sight of so much disembowelled coal, to flourish on mineral rights in regions still idyllic. Remains one great and inaccessible magnate, the local coal owner: three generations old, and clambering on the bottom step of the 'County,' kicking off the mass below. Rule him out. (1)

This chapter has been read as a send-up of Arnold Bennett's fastidious detailing of social class distinctions.[19] But surely there is something more fundamental at stake in this opening gambit, in the first sentence even, than the relationship between Lawrence's and Bennett's work. The studied casualness of the initial directive – "Take a mining townlet like Woodhouse" – functions as a rhetorical challenge. Imagine a place; then imagine a person who inhabits this place, a "great and inaccessible magnate, the local coal owner." Now "rule him out." Forget him, in other words. In a nineteenth-century novel, an omnicient narrator's direct address to the reader typically functions as a means of engaging the reader in the verisimilitude of events being described.[20] By contrast, the direct addresses to the reader punctuating the first two pages of *The Lost Girl* both invite and dis-invite our realization of a scene.[21] Instead of asking a reader simply to accept its representationality, this narrative teases us with that possibility through its stops and starts, abrupt shifts of focus, and development by negation.

Readers might well ask: will this narrative satisfy the expectations of formal realism invoked by the sociological detailing of the opening paragraphs? That is, will Lawrence satisfy a 'Meredithy' public's appetite for readerly writing? Or will this book continue to proffer, then withdraw, its stories? Significantly, Lawrence does not sustain this level of playfully disruptive but also disorienting self-reflexivity past the first several chapters. Instead, the questions raised initially about an artist's relationship to his audience are taken up with regard to cinema and music hall theater in Chapters 6 through 9.

James Houghton's Pleasure Palace – a small-time nickelodeon vaudeville theater featuring both short films and music hall acts in an evening's program – is the last of his long line of spectacularly unsuccessful business ventures. Or rather, it is the last that readers of *The Lost Girl* see before his daughter Alvina runs off to southern Italy with one of the music hall performers. As will be discussed in further detail below, historians of cinema and vaudeville have argued that this particular vaudeville format played a crucial role in the establishment of cinema as the premier entertainment industry of the twentieth century. But, as Mr. May, the American manager, notes early on, the Pleasure Palace is "second-rate" from the start (114). The program of entertainment Houghton has chosen – three short films and two music hall turns – is as historically anachronistic in 1913 as the building itself, a renovated traveling theater show-house furnished with pews from an early nineteenth-century chapel. The Pleasure Palace's main competitor, the Empire Theatre in Woodhouse, charges higher prices for its middle-class decor and its exclusive showings of films, yet it never fails to pack a crowd. By contrast, Houghton's Pleasure Palace is doomed because the colliers come only if they cannot afford to travel farther or pay more for an evening's entertainment.

Contemporary readers are easily frustrated with Lawrence's very detailed and historically specific characterization of nickelodeon vaudeville cinema and traveling music hall theater in *The Lost Girl*. Moreover, film's current legitimacy as an art form makes it easy to dismiss the debates about cinema's effect on viewers that plagued this new medium at the turn of the twentieth century, the flavor of which is captured so beautifully in *The Lost Girl*. At the level of pure "story,"[22] what matters of course is that Alvina meets her future husband while working at the Pleasure Palace, not that her father has chosen an outdated format for his new theater, or that she herself objects to the voyeuristic passivity cinema imposes on its viewers. But these details figure crucially in Lawrence's characterization of aesthetic production in turn-of-the-century Britain. They establish the terms and the historical specificity of the comparisons he invites readers to make between early cinema and two other art forms: music hall the-ater, and the novel. Thus, it is worth dwelling on the historical specificity of Lawrence's representations of early cinema before proceeding.

In *Vaudeville and Film, 1895–1915: A Study in Media Interaction*, Robert Allen argues for the historical importance of the small-time vaudeville format that Lawrence's James Houghton has chosen for his Pleasure Palace. This format, rather than that of the large-scale review, was sig-nificant in the history of film because cinema was first introduced in this context. As "a visual novelty whose drawing power immediately eclipsed that of lanternry, shadowgraphy, pantomime, and moving pictures," film transformed music hall theater from the inside out, Allen argues. In other words, although Lawrence presents Houghton's Pleasure Palace and the Empire Theatre as contemporaries, in actuality small-time vaudeville theaters such as the Pleasure Palace paved the way for feature-film theaters such as the Empire. Vaudeville proved "itself to be a marketing outlet around which an entire film industry could be built – from the manufacture of equipment and the production of film subjects to the supplying of hundreds of vaudeville theaters with programs of film."[23]

James Cowan, Sam Selecki, and Linda Ruth Williams have analyzed Lawrence's treatment of early cinema in *The Lost Girl*.[24] They rightly note the similarity of his characters' and Lawrence's own views, as ex-pressed in poems such as "When I Went to the Film" and "Film Passion" (*Pansies*, 1929) as well as in essays such as "Sex versus Loveliness" (1928), "Pornography and Obscenity" (1929), and "Apropos *Lady Chatterley's Lover*" (1930). Their otherwise excellent discussions of this novel fail, however, to take full account of two things: Lawrence's focus on a very specific transition point in film's history through his characterization of the Pleasure Palace and the Empire; and the critique of music hall theater that is paired with that of early cinema. My own interest actually lies in Lawrence's presentation of the competition among *three* different forms of expressive culture at the turn of the twentieth century in *The Lost Girl*: cinema, music hall theater, and the novel. At least initially in this novel, this is a situation in which it is anything but clear that either the novel or "literature" more generally has priority in a rapidly changing scene of aesthetic production in which emergent media such as film are exerting pressure on older aesthetic forms such as music hall theater.

As Deborah Jacobs has reminded us, aesthetic production at the turn of the twentieth century was a varied, highly unstable, and contested field, and the literary field was only one among many newly specialized discourses struggling for legitimacy. Yet we tend to forget this because twentieth-century literary criticism's primary categories of analysis – categories such as 'the literary', 'the artist', and 'art' – were borrowed from modernism when both it and the discipline of English studies were institutionalized in the 1920s and 1930s.[25] As Lawrence Levine has also suggested, rather than trying to "understand the cultural classifications created around the turn of the century as products of that specific era which help to illuminate it, we have accepted them as truths and perpetuated them." And thus, by "confining something as variable and dynamic as culture into rigid hierarchical divisions, which are then projected back onto a past in which they did not yet exist," we have risked "misunderstanding not merely history but ourselves."[26]

Jacobs' and Levine's arguments can help us understand how the discussions of cinema and music hall theater in *The Lost Girl* expose the relative dis-organization of the literary field as Lawrence was working on this project. In the late 1910s new forms of mass media were gaining cultural centrality in Britain. In Lawrence's view, it was becoming less and less possible for an art form such as the novel "to enjoy simultaneously high cultural status and mass popularity" (Levine, 233). As noted earlier, Lawrence was still feeling the sting of *The Rainbow*'s scandalous withdrawal from circulation while working on *The Lost Girl*; it is also worth remembering that literary modernism more generally had not yet acquired its institutionally sanctioned status as a minority discourse in 1920. The great "masterworks" of high modernism, *Ulysses* and *The Waste Land*, had not yet been published in book form; nor had publishing venues such as the *Criterion* and *Scrutiny* begun providing respectably professionalized fora for the "sometimes suspicious contents" of avant-garde texts.[27] The hostility and hysterical contempt with which Lawrence's characters criticize film, together with the nostalgic defensiveness with which they mourn the impending "death" of music hall theater, suggest how threatened Lawrence must have been by high culture's relative disempowerment in the early postwar period.

Writing in 1920 about changes in the cultural hierarchy in Britain on the eve of World War I, questions such as the following would have been much on Lawrence's mind: what kind of an impact will America's increasing dominance in a newly international entertainment industry have on British cultural production? Can either the 'serious' novel *or* popular fiction compete with new, and primarily visual, forms of mass entertainment? Can something known, and cherished by British citizenry, as "the English novel" continue to wield the symbolic capital it had in the high Victorian period? These are questions to keep in mind in reviewing Lawrence's characterization of cinema and music hall theater in Chapters 6 through 9 of *The Lost Girl*. For they will help us appreciate how Lawrence arrives at a defense of 'the literary' through his criticisms of two popular, and primarily visual, art forms: film and music hall theater.

As has often been noted, Lawrence's chief criticism of film as a medium has to do with the way it isolates the visual from other modes of sensory experience.[28] According to Lawrence, the physical absence and visual presence of the film-viewer's objects of desire make film-viewing a modern, high-tech, and socially sanctioned form of voyeurism. As Alvina Houghton puts it, "film is only pictures, like pictures in the *Daily Mail*. And pictures . . . don't have any life except in the people who watch them. And that's why they like them. Because . . . they can spread themselves over a film, and they *can't* over a living performer. They're up against the performer himself. And they hate it" (116). Madame Rochard presents a similar case against cinema, and in defense of music hall theater, in Chapter 8. Anticipating arguments Lawrence makes elsewhere under his own name in poems such as "When I Went to the Circus," she values the sheer carnality of music hall theater, the physical spectacle of human beings transforming themselves into things and other people. In her view music hall theater is Bakhtinian carnival: a forum in which middle-class notions of bodily integrity and gender identity, as well as distinctions between human and animal life, animate and inanimate objects, are subverted, at least temporarily. Supplementing Alvina's critique of cinema, she argues that films "are cheap, and they are easy, and they cost the audience nothing, no feeling of the heart, no appreciation of the spirit . . . And so they like them, and they don't like us, because they must *feel* the things we do, from the heart, and appreciate them from the spirit" (148–9, emphasis in original). In ten years' time, she predicts mournfully, traveling music hall acts such as her own, which she acknowledges are already somewhat of an historical anachronism, will have disappeared entirely and cinema will reign supreme on the entertainment circuit.

Initially, music hall theater seems to be the preferred mode of expressive culture in these conversations in *The Lost Girl*. It is the art form endorsed by the characters whose opinions readers are encouraged most to respect in this novel. Ultimately, however, developments in the plot begin to suggest that it too falls short of the mark aesthetically, primarily because the integrity of a theatrical performance is so fragile. An actor can, for instance, speak out of character and disrupt a performance, as is the case when Ciccio almost ruins the Natcha-Kee-Tawara tribe's last show in Woodhouse by adlibbing a line in the dialogue. He tells the troupe afterwards that he was simply "tired of being dead" (162), that is, he was tired of playing a character whose role in the final scene is to lie flat on the stage while Madame delivers her last grand speech over his quiescent body. But this explanation does not satisfy the other members of the troupe, who recognize that the audience's engagement in the entire evening's performance was jeopardized by Ciccio's break through the so-called fourth wall. Notably, this is not avant-garde theater; this is what happens when, to borrow Alvina's phrasing, a theater audience is "up against the performer himself," a real body in real space and time who chooses to disrupt the dramatic integrity of the performance.

Lawrence's careful detailing of audience members' shifts in attitude *after* a theatrical performance also foregrounds the liabilities of this art form. In Chapter 7, for example, Miss Pinnegar's post-performance response to the Natcha-Kee-Tawara's staging of an Indian raid in Knarborough Road is described in great detail. During their performance, Miss Pinnegar is completely caught up in the spectacle: she screams when "Ciccio brushes her with his horse's tail and swings his spear so as to touch Alvina and James Houghton lightly with the butt of it" (141–2). Nonetheless, she dismisses the power of this performance once she is safely back in Manchester House serving tea. That kind of theater is "interesting in a way," she admits reluctantly, "just to show what savage Red Indians were like." But then she defends cinema by calling it ethnography for adults and dismisses music hall entertainment as ethnography for children:

[Music hall is] childish...I can't understand, myself, how people can go on liking shows...It's not like the cinema, where you see it all and take it all in at once; you *know* everything at a glance...I don't hold with idle show-people, parading round, I don't, myself. I like to go to the cinema once a week. It's instruction, you take it all in at a glance, all you need to know, and it lasts you for a week. You can get to know everything about people's actual lives from the cinema. I don't see why you want people dressing up and showing off. (142–3)

In light of Tom Gunning's recent work on early cinema as an "aesthetic of astonishment," Miss Pinnegar's characterization of film as ethnography for adults and music hall theater as ethnography for children can be read as a denial of cinema's fundamental spectacularity.[29] Miss Pinnegar values the ethnographic authenticity of film, its allegedly total replication of reality. Gunning's point is that early cinema never fulfilled the myth of total cinema: the experience of cinema's first audiences "was profoundly different from the classical spectator's absorption into an emphatetic narrative." Rather than being overwhelmed by, say, the real-ness of the train rushing headlong toward them on screen, early cinema audiences were both shocked by the illusion of danger and delighted by its pure illusion. "Placed within a historical context and tradition, the first spectators' experience reveals not a childlike belief [in the reality of the filmic image], but an undisguised awareness (and delight in) film's illusionistic capabilities" (Gunning, 129). Elsewhere in *The Lost Girl* theatricality is, as noted earlier, presented as something to be valued in the music hall tradition. But rather than recognizing similarities between the two modes of aesthetic production, Miss Pinnegar emphasizes their radical difference when she characterizes cinematic realism as an adult taste and dismisses as childlike an audience's pleasure in theatricality.

Given her characterization in earlier scenes, readers know better than to respect Miss Pinnegar's opinions. Nonetheless, her dismissive comments act like "a douche of cold water" on Alvina, destroying the "delicious excitement" she had continued to feel after the Natcha-Kee-Tawara's performance (143). Alvina is forced to concede Miss Pinnegar's point, and hates her for this:

They *were* unreal, Madame and Ciccio and the rest. Ciccio was just a fantasy blown in on the wind, to blow away again. The real, permanent thing was Woodhouse, the *semper idem* Knarborough Road, and the unchangeable grubby gloom of Manchester House . . . And Ciccio, splashing up on his bay horse and green cloth, he was a mountebank and an extraneous non-entity, a coloured old rag blown down the Knarborough Road into Limbo. (143)

The ritualistic renaming of Alvina as Allaye in Chapter 9 is an even more important reminder of theatrical illusion's fragility. It has been argued that this scene, in which the Natcha-Kee-Tawara initiate Alvina into their "tribe" in a lewd parody of a wedding ceremony, anticipates the grand enactments of primitive rituals in *The Plumed Serpent*.[30] This is certainly true insofar as the presentation of the ritual itself is concerned; yet the inefficacy of this ceremony is worthy noting. When Alvina rejoins the troupe for breakfast the next morning, after having sex with Ciccio for the first time, she is disoriented when Madame and the men greet her as Allaye. "It was all so solemn. Was it all mockery, play-acting?" she wonders. "She felt bitterly inclined to cry," and she is physically disoriented by the actors' continuation in real life of their stage roles: in fact, she "wonder[ed] where she was" (203). The re-naming ceremony in which she had participated so eagerly the night before has failed to transform her, and she leaves the troupe shortly thereafter.

Granted, there is more at issue in both of these scenes than the power of a theatrical performance. At least in part, the "delicious excitement" theatrical spectacle arouses in both of these women is the result of their sexual attraction to a particular player. Yet Lawrence struggles mightily in these scenes to make specific to one medium limitations faced by any art form. *Any* artistic performance, in *any* medium, is vulnerable to its audience's or its readers' refusal to suspend disbelief. Rather than acknowledging this, however, Lawrence emphasizes music hall theater's distinctive weakness in this regard in *The Lost Girl*. Having used music hall theater to point up the limitations of cinema, he now exposes the formal liabilities of this medium as well. Lawrence was not, of course, the only modernist to express hostility and hysterical contempt toward film as a medium during its rise to preeminence in the early part of the twentieth century; nor was he the only one to mourn the death of music hall theater. Indeed, he was in very good company in both regards, as recent work on T. S. Eliot, Virginia Woolf, and James Joyce suggests.[31] What is distinctive about *The Lost Girl*, however, is his emphasis on the historical relationship between these two media.

Robert Allen's characterization of early cinema's "grafting" onto vaudeville theatre is useful here. As Allen notes, by 1913 entertainment had become a big business, and a shift had been made from local to national and/or international marketing of music hall acts. Moreover, as the quality of film stock improved, it became possible to produce longer films; this in turn made it possible for progressively minded theater owners (like the owner of the Empire Theatre in Woodhouse) to feature cinema either centrally or exclusively in an evening's program. These changes in program content went hand in hand with the physical transformation of the theaters themselves to appeal to cross-class, mixed-gender audiences. Historians of music hall theater describe its political subversiveness in the mid-nineteenth century; they view it as a genuinely 'popular' expression of working-class culture in its early years. As all the changes described above might suggest, though, it is no longer appropriate to talk about music hall theater in the 1910s as "popular" culture in this same sense. Instead, by 1913, as Lawrence's characterization of Houghton's Pleasure Palace emphasizes, music hall theater was becoming a vehicle for a new kind of mass entertainment. As Allen notes, the latter would ultimately replace the very form of expressive culture which had originally nutured its growth.

Writing thus in 1920 about cinema's "grafting"[32] onto music hall theater, Lawrence knows already that Madame Rochard's predictions will come true: music hall theater will indeed be obsolete in ten years. For in 1913 not only the localness but also the 'Englishness' of English working-class culture was rapidly being lost as audiences indulged their preference for cinema's visual novelty and their appetite for American films.

The class politics informing Lawrence's discussion of aesthetic production in early twentieth-century Britain are worth noting too before considering Alvina's decision to leave Britain altogether at the end of *The Lost Girl*. Film historians quibble among themselves about whether cinema was ever marketed exclusively to a working-class urban population, but Lawrence leaves no room for argument on this point in *The Lost Girl*: he presents both cinema and music hall theater as working-class leisure-time activities. While the new Empire Theatre in Woodhouse caters to a more "respectable" mixed-class audience, Houghton's Pleasure Palace gets a rougher crowd: colliers who hoot and jeer at what they see on screen or on stage, "spoon" with their girlfriends, and generally refuse to treat art as an icon. Although Alvina and Mme. Rochard try hard to theorize cinema and music hall theater in formal terms, their arguments (most notably, Alvina's) keep collapsing back into characterizations of Woodhouse's lower-middle- and working-class citizenry.

Note is often made of the way Lawrence distanced himself from his working-class origins over the course of his career. Importantly, *The Lost Girl* articulates the connection between his self-imposed exile from working-class culture and his concern for its massification at the turn of the century through the development of a culture industry dominated by film – dominated, moreover, by American film. Unlike Walter Benjamin, for example, Lawrence is not bothered by cinema's potential use in aestheticizing politics. Instead, he seems to be suspicious of cinema's emergence as the working class's preferred leisure activity because it represents the potential loss of the opportunity to *escape* working-class culture and politics that 'literary' culture offered to Lawrence's generation of British working-class children, if not to many subsequent ones.

Both this backdrop of British educational and class politics and the historical specificities of an emergent film industry's evolving relationship to and impact on music hall theatre before and after World War I can help us understand the final sequence of Alvina Houghton's trajectory in *The Lost Girl*. When she travels to Italy with Ciccio Marasca, the dark-skinned Italian who embodies in real life the primitive masculinity of the Native American he plays in a music hall act, she leaves behind more than middle-class English sexual mores. She leaves behind modernity itself, as it is epitomized by her arguments with various characters about music hall theater's death and cinema's problematic rise to cultural centrality in the early 1910s. Critics have often noted how the narration in the final section of *The Lost Girl* differs from what precedes it; once Alvina reaches Italy, the satiric tone set in the novel's opening scenes is replaced by a more recognizably Laurentian voice honoring the stark beauty of the southern Italian landscape. Richard Aldington, for example, explains this shift in tone by suggesting that Lawrence himself, not his protagonist, "bend[s] in love" over the wild flowers that people this otherwise desolate place.[33] I would suggest instead that, in imagining this pre-modern world, Lawrence liberates himself from his concerns raised about the competition among cinema, music hall theater, and the novel for symbolic capital and audiences at the turn of the century. The narrative voice in these last few chapters is strikingly different not simply because of the autobiographical resonances of Alvina's situation but because writing in general and "literature" in particular are positioned differently in this pre-modern, pre-literate world.

In stark contrast to both the opening chapters and the conversations about cinema and music hall theater in Chapters 6 through 9, the final scenes of the novel resolve the debates about modernity, mass culture, and aesthetic production by simply taking us out of that world. The southern Italian landscape is rocky and harsh; but no "great divide" exists here between high and low culture, complicating the narrator's relationships with both his subject matter and his audience. Instead, the value of the narrator's verbalizations is simply taken for granted. Like the animals and flowers in Lawrence's poetry, these wild irises and gladioli *matter*, because their careful detailing manifests the observer's appreciation for what Lawrence describes elsewhere so often as the "quickness" of life:

The rose-coloured wild gladioli among the young green corn were a dream of beauty, the morning of the world. The lovely, pristine morning of the world, before our epoch began. Rose-red gladioli among corn, in among the rocks, and small irises, black-purple and yellow blotched with brown, like a wasp, standing low in little desert places, that would seem forlorn but for this weird, dark-lustrous magnificence. Then there were the tiny irises, only one finger tall, growing in dry places, frail as crocuses, and much tinier, and blue, blue as the eye of the morning heaven, which was a morning earlier, more pristine than ours. (335)

While the narration in Chapter 1 is abrasive, jarring, anxious, this is reassuringly mimetic. It leaves no room for questioning the verbal medium itself. Instead, as the narrator assumes the posture of the Romantic poet, we are invited to enjoy his loving visualization, in language, of a preindustrial landscape. Notably, this landscape elicits the poet's confidence in his ability to realize a world in words, not his anxieties about whether modern audiences prefer the easy, "pre-fab" visuality of cinema to the mental exertion required by reading.

In *Sex in the Head: Visions of Femininity and Film*, Linda Williams analyzes Lawrence's contradictory stance toward the visual. He claims to prefer "pre-linguistic, blind states of dark unknowing," she notes, and he condemns visual knowing as a destructive feminine activity.[34] Yet he takes great pleasure in the texture of words, and he spends a great deal of time and energy in all of his novels visualizing, in words, male bodies. Moreover, she shows how extensively Lawrence borrows from cinematic techniques of representation throughout his career in spite of his hostility toward that medium. I would highlight as well the usefulness of this contradiction to Lawrence in developing a defense of the literary field in *The Lost Girl*. Writing in 1920, Lawrence sees cinema emerging as the dominant aesthetic form of the twentieth century. That is, he sees an image-oriented form of literacy replacing alphabetic literacy; and he sees how cinema's dominance in a shifting hierarchy of aesthetic production makes it more difficult for a creative writer to function as what we would now term a public intellectual.

There is no overt debate among the characters about different modes of aesthetic production in the final chapters of *The Lost Girl*. Nonetheless, the confident readerliness of the nature descriptions in the closing scenes registers Lawrence's preference for the private visuality of the reading experience over the public spectacles of both cinematic and theatrical representation. Moreover, the poetic cadences of these passages – the incantatory rhythms, repetitious phrasings, and lush similes – speak to Lawrence's faith in the civilizing powers of aesthetic responsiveness to "Literature" (understood here as an analog of both "poetry" and "civilization").

Readings of modernism typically stress modernism's sexualization of the primitive. As in Forster's *A Room With a View*, for example, it could be argued that Italy represents non-Englishness, and specifically a non-English attitude toward sexuality, in *The Lost Girl*. The fact that the celebrated white cliffs of Dover look to Alvina like "a long, ash-grey coffin slowly submerging" (347) beneath the horizon on the first part of their voyage could thus represent the death of the traditional novelistic heroine: the virginal Clarissas and Emma Woodhouses of the "Great English Tradition" that are consciously invoked, and rejected, in *The Lost Girl*. Instead of withering up into spinsterhood like Miss Frost, her governess, Alvina's exposure to her Italian lover's "primitive" male sexuality will bring her to life, will transform Lawrence's version of Bennett's Anna Tellwright into a proto-Lady Chatterley. And yet, *The Lost Girl* does not play out this familiar modernist troping of the British subject's discovery of his/her sexuality on foreign soil entirely to pattern. Significantly, Alvina does not in fact go to Italy to discover herself sexually; her (re)birth through the discovery of her sexuality is achieved in a cheap north-of-England boarding house while she is on tour with a traveling music hall company. Moreover, she first encounters "authentic," "primitive" male sexuality through her Italian lover's performance of a native American Indian's role in a music hall production. That is, as will be discussed further below, Lawrence's twist on the familiar troping of "Italianness" as phallic sexuality emphasizes the performance of "authentic" sexuality and raced subjectivity, not its pre- or non-discursive innateness.

What is unique about *The Lost Girl* is, I think, Lawrence's association of a pre-modern world with "literary" culture. Alvina's trip to Italy is crucial to Lawrence's meditation on aesthetic production in *The Lost Girl* not because it enacts a familiar trope of sexual self-discovery in turn-of-the-century British novels but because Italy represents the Eden of a non-alienated, non-commercial realm of literary production. In other words, what is at stake in this travel narrative is not sexual self-discovery but cultural rebirth. In the pre-modern Italy of *The Lost Girl* print culture does not compete with image-oriented media for an audience. Instead, through his lush poetic descriptions of the southern Italian landscape Lawrence reclaims the Romantic artist's privilege to speak to and interpret the world for a nonliterate populace. He records both his nostalgia for and his attempt to restage an earlier era in Western history: an era when the value of alphabetic literacy could be taken for granted and in which the creative writer's role as legislator of the world could be plausibly argued. The latter are key issues in Lawrence's travel writing of the 1920s and his prose essays written in defense of a particular kind of high-art novel's cultural capital in a world increasingly dominated by visually oriented mass media. Think, for example, of the way his "ethnographic travesties"[35] of Aztec culture in *The Plumed Serpent* and "The Woman Who Rode Away" articulate his disenchantment with modernity. Think too of both his criticisms of popular fiction and his testimony to the cultural work of "real" novels in late essays such as "Why the Novel Matters," "Surgery for the Novel – or a Bomb," and "Pornography and Obscenity." I noted earlier how unstable the literary field was when Lawrence started working on this novel in December 1919. If he assumes its stability in subsequent work, perhaps it is because he has settled something in *The Lost Girl*. He has delimited the literary field and established its unique contribution to modern culture through his critique of cinema and music hall theater and his narrative of cross-cultural travel.

And yet my reading of *The Lost Girl* to this point fails to account for the scenes in the closing chapters that contradict the dominant characterization of Italy as a utopian alternative to modernity. Through the narration of Alvina's experience in and of Italy, Lawrence does indeed endorse alphabetic literacy and "the literary." At the same time, however, and in stark contrast to Alvina's valuation of this pre-modern world, conversations among Ciccio's Italian relatives and neighbors about their modeling work for Royal Academy artists in London at the end of the nineteenth century offer a very different view of art, modernity, and this pre-modern alternative.

Unlike Alvina, Ciccio's relatives are more interested in making a living than in appreciating the beauty of either the natural world or art. Rather than complaining about their commodification in the production of high art, they mourn the life they had in London – the easy money and interesting distractions they had in that urban environment. These conversations are an important counterpoint to Alvina's celebration of Italy's pre-modernity in two regards. They describe "contact zones"[36] between modern and pre-modern cultures; and they expose the system of labor undergirding the production of high art. Like Alvina, the Royal Academy artists for whom these models worked believe in art's autonomy and in the civilizing powers of aesthetic responsiveness. But what their models comment on is their economic exploitation and their performance, for hire, of "authentic," "primitive" sexuality. In other words, a scene such as the following, in which Alvina listens to Pancrazio's stories of Lord Leighton's treatment of his models, undermines the valorization of high culture that powers both Lawrence's critique of cinema and music hall theater and his rapturous characterization of the Italian landscape in *The Lost Girl*. Pancrazio notes:

Leighton, he was cruel to his model. He wouldn't let you rest. "Damn you, you've got to keep still till I've finished with you, you devil," so he said. Well, for this man on the cross, he couldn't get a model who would do it for him. [Other Italians] all tried it once, but they would not go again. So they said to him, he must try Califano, because Califano was the only man who would stand for it. At last then he sent for me. "I don't like your damned figure, Califano," he said to me, "but nobody will do this if you won't. Now will you do it?" "Yes," I said, "I will." so he tied me up on the cross. And he paid me well, so I stood it. (325)

Alvina listens silently to Pancrazio's stories, noting only how strange it is to look at the battered figure of Pancrazio, and think how much he had been crucified through the long years of London, for the sake of late Victorian art. It was strangest of all to see through his yellow, often dull, red-rimmed eyes these blithe and well-conditioned painters. Pancrazio looked on them admiringly and contemptuously, as an old, rakish tom-cat might look on such frivolous well-groomed gentlemen. (326)

In reading *The Lost Girl* as a self-reflexive commentary on aesthetic production in Britain at the turn of the twentieth century, I have tried to show how Lawrence establishes the distinctiveness of literary discourse by discrediting cinema as an emergent and Americanized low-culture art form as he mourns the disappearance of British working-class music hall theater and characterizes Italy as a pre-modern utopia. But Alvina's conversations with Italians who modeled for nineteenth-century British Academicians in the novel's last few chapters complicate matters substantially.

On the one hand, Lawrence's endorsement of "the literary" in *The Lost Girl* and his negative characterizations of cinema and music hall theater begin to explain his usefulness to a critic such as F. R. Leavis, for whom literary modernism would prove instrumental in the institutionalization of English studies. Even though Lawrence does not fit the Joyce–Pound–Eliot paradigm of modernism in so many other ways, his work, as *The Lost Girl* demonstrates so clearly, lends support to the argument that English literature is – to borrow Terry Eagleton's phrasing – "not only a subject worth studying, but *the* supremely civilizing pursuit, the spiritual essence of the social formation."[37] Although it may have been "desperately unclear" to the public at large "why English was worth studying at all" in the early 1920s (Eagleton, 31), it certainly wasn't to Lawrence. As someone who made his living as a teacher before devoting himself exclusively to his creative writing, Lawrence was acutely aware of the way English literature was beamed at populations deemed to be lacking (an appreciation of) culture. Even though he argues in *Fantasia of the Unconscious* that illiteracy will save the mass populace from those "tissues of leprosy," books and newspapers,[38] he also was extremely sensitive to the connection between access to literacy and access to the means of literary production and consumption. Moreover, he was deeply committed to what might be termed literary literacy, if not to newspaper and pulp fiction literacy. In this regard, and in spite of his notorious objections to mass education, his work would and could be easily co-opted by a Leavisite/New Critical paradigm of modernism that associates artistic autonomy with the articulation of a high/low culture divide and equates a great literary tradition with "civilization." This version of modernism has been an important component of mass university education in the U.S. (and more modestly in Britain) since the 1930s. As Antony Easthope has noted, for example, literary study was founded in the 1930s on the classic (if now contested) modernist characterization of an opposition between high and low culture. The modernist paradigm of close reading discriminates between "literary" texts and popular culture, and then demonstrates the former's thematic, structural, and aesthetic unity. This was standard pedagogy in English departments well beyond the point at which New Criticism began to be challenged by poststructuralist theory.[39]

On the other hand, scenes like the above in the final chapters of *The Lost Girl* expose Lawrence's ambivalence about his own modernist defense of the literary. He supports *and* challenges classic Romantic and modernist arguments about the civilizing powers of aesthetic responsiveness. He calls into question high art's claims to aesthetic autonomy even as he characterizes fine writing as a welcome alternative to the passivity and alienation of modern life, as exemplified by cinema's rise to dominance in the culture industry and the death of a "native" art form, music hall theatre. As David Chinitz has suggested, these kinds of contradiction entail a complete rethinking of modernism in general, not of a single work, or a single author's work. A "reappraisal of modernism as a whole" is thus necessary "if our understanding of the transformation of culture during the twentieth century is to continue to grow" (Chinitz, 246).

Having said this, though, the point to be made in concluding this section is that the process of monumentalizing modernism described so eloquently by Raymond Williams and Lyn Pykett entails the suppression of precisely these kinds of contradiction. Ian MacKillop's brilliant recent biography of F. R. Leavis certainly documents with painstaking (and painful) detail just how precarious Leavis's association with Cambridge was, how liminal he was for so many years to "Cambridge English."[40] Yet when Leavis reproduces Lawrence's own moves to distance himself from a (in Leavis's case) lower-middle-class background and begins declaiming the value of "serious" literature, Lawrence's place in an ideal order of literary tradition is secured. As the historical avant-garde "accede[d] to cultural legitimacy" in the early 1920s,[41] as it transformed itself and was transformed by its most influential interpreters into "modernism," a literary movement with an academic home in English studies, the contradictions that pepper *The Lost Girl* became unreadable – as in fact *The Lost Girl* itself became unreadable in a burgeoning mini-industry of Lawrence criticism.

"(C)LEANING UP A GREAT LOT OF RUBBISH": WYNDHAM LEWIS'S *TARR* AND THE MODERNIST CASE AGAINST LITERARY REALISM

Reviewing Wyndham Lewis's *Tarr* for the *Egoist* in 1918, T. S. Eliot describes it as "impressively deliberate [and] frigid."[42] Writing in 1922 for the *Dial*, he identifies two novels, Wyndham Lewis's *Tarr* and James Joyce's *Ulysses*, as *the* novels of the modern period, the only novels written to date that break effectively with what he terms "the narrative method" of nineteenth-century literary realism.[43] To a similar end but in characteristically more colorful and idiosyncratic terms, Ezra Pound describes *Tarr* in the *Little Review* as "the most vigorous and volcanic English novel of our time." Lewis and Joyce are "men who are once for all through with the particular inanities of Shavian-Bennett, and with the particular oleosities of the Wellsian genre."[44] "In so far as 'style' is generally taken to mean 'smoothness of finish', orderly arrangement of sentences, coherence to the Flaubertian method," Pound concedes that Lewis's writing is "faulty" by comparison with Joyce's in *Portrait of the Artist*. Nonetheless, he is quick to insist that Lewis's novel is of interest "not due to style . . . but due to the fact that we have a highly-energized mind performing a huge act of scavenging; cleaning up a great lot of rubbish, cultural, Bohemian, romantico-Tennysonish, arty, societish, gutterish" (428–9). The following is from Pound's 1920 essay:

What we are blessedly free from [in *Tarr*] is the red-plush Wellsian illusionism, and the click of Mr. Bennett's cash-register finish. [*Tarr*] does not skim over the surface. If it does not satisfy the mannequin demand for 'beauty' it at least refuses to accept margarine substitutes. It will not be praised by Katherine Tynan, nor by Mr. Chesterton and Mrs. Meynell. It will not receive the sanction of Dr. Sir Robertson Nicoll, nor of his despicable paper *The Bookman* . . . *Tarr* does not appeal to [the British reading public] nor to audiences which the [Public Libraries] have swaddled. (429)

Several things are of interest in these reviews of Lewis's first novel, which was originally serialized in the *Egoist* between April 1916 and November 1917 before being reprinted in book form twice in 1918 and then again in 1928.[45] Most importantly, both Eliot and Pound establish a binary opposition between realism and modernism, that is, between an aesthetic of mimetic representation ("Wellsian illusionism") and an aesthetic that refuses to organize itself around what Oscar Wilde termed in 1889 "the burden of the human spirit."[46] Literary modernism is figured in both of these reviews as a radical departure from, an absolute break with, not only the literary conventions but also the ethics of mimetic art. Thus, *Tarr* is praised because it does not document quotidian reality or "satisf[y] the mannequin demand for 'beauty'"; instead, it is "volcanic," "frigid." And because it does not observe or respect the formal and ideological conventions associated with realism, "we" – Eliot and Pound – like it. And "they" – the British reading public and conservative reviewers – don't. Modeled in these reviews are not only two different aesthetics but also at least two different audiences for literature and two different reading practices. As is also the case so powerfully in the work of other early "disciples"[47] of modernism's critical reviews, the contrast is neither innocent nor casual; rather, the defense of what "we" value is predicated on the dismissal of what "they" like. I argued in the first part of this chapter that Lawrence secured a defense of "literary" literacy through his critiques of cinema and music hall theater – and suggested how Leavis in turn secured his definition of the literary field through what Deborah Jacobs would term Lawrence's and other modernists' "distinction-making projects." I want to pursue further here the implications of the modernist avant-garde's investment in these kinds of cultural hierarchy through consideration of a scene in *Tarr* most critics have chosen, following Pound's lead, to pass over in silence: the rape scene in Part IV.

Chapter 9 of Part IV opens with Bertha Lunken realizing that she cannot construct a coherent narrative of the events that have just transpired. Estranged not only from her fiancé, Tarr Sorbert, but from her Parisian women friends as well, Bertha had met Otto Kreisler, a young German artist escaping his Italian creditors, at a party and agreed to

sit as a model for him one afternoon. Because "a separate framework
of time" exists for each of the images of her interaction with Kreisler
in his studio, she now looks back on the events of that afternoon as a
series of aesthetically and temporally discrete "roles" or tableaux.[48] After
the fact, "her hair hanging in wisps and strips...a heavy Susanna-like
breast heav[ing] uncontrollably," she is a "Salon picture" (191). Only "a
moment before," however, she had "improvised...with quick ostenta-
tious understanding... the most captivating moment of a lady's toilette,
the hair down, a comb in her hand – she had sat a humorous indulgence in her eye for her not very skilful colleague" (192). Galatea to his
Pygmalion, she had "repressed" her "sudden anxieties" about "his request to draw her 'shoulders' – her bare shoulders, arms and probably
breasts, she could not refuse her breasts" – by "jauntily" thinking of them
both, model and artist, as "priests of Beauty" (192). "She had come to sit
for him and her body of course was a beautiful thing, whereas the mere
idea that there was any danger was extremely repulsive where there was
any question of a beautiful thing" (192).

Significantly, Bertha cannot reconcile any of these tableaux with the
image of "an uncontrolled satyrlike figure" who attacks her "battling
Amazon" and leaves her "convulsed upon her back, her mouth smeared
with blood" (191). The following passage is crucial to my argument. Given
the frequency with which critics pass over this entire scene in silence, it
seems all the more important to reproduce its climax here.

"Your breasts are good!" he almost shouted, shooting up a hand to finger one –
she thrust his hand away with force and shouted back:

"Yes, they are good. But I don't wish you to touch me: you understand that?"

With the fury of a person violently awakened to some insult he flung himself
upon her: her tardy panting expostulation, defensive prowess, disappeared in
the whirlpool towards which they had both, with a strange deliberateness and
yet aimlessness, been steering.

An iron curtain rushed down upon that tragedy: he was standing there at
the window now as though wishing to pretend that nothing had passed to his
knowledge; she had been dreaming things, merely. The monotony and silence
of the posing had prepared her for the strangeness now: that other extreme
joined hands with this. She saw side by side and unconnected, the silent figure
engaged in drawing her bust and the other one full of blindness and violence.
Then there were two other figures, one getting up from the chair, yawning, and
the present lazy one at the window – four in all, that she could not for some
reason bring together, each in a complete compartment of time of its own. It
would be impossible to make the present idle figure at the window interest itself
in these others. The figure talked a little to fill an interval; it had drawn: it had

suddenly flung itself upon her and done something disgusting: and now it was standing idly by the window, becalmed, and completely cut off from its raging self of the recent occurrence. It could do all these things. It appeared to her in a series of precipitate states: in this it resembled a switchback, rising slowly, in a steady innocent way, to the top of an incline, and then plunging suddenly down the other side with a catastrophic rush. The fury of her animal hostility did not survive this phase for long. She had come there, got what she did not expect and must now go away again, it was simple enough: to Kreisler there was nothing more to be said. There never had been anything to say to him: he was a mad beast as everyone had always been right in remarking.

Now she had to take her departure as though nothing had happened. It was nothing actually, nothing in fact had happened: what did it matter what became of her? The body was of little importance: what was the good (seeing what she knew and everything) of storming against this person? (193–4)

It could be argued that this scene is less significant than many others in the novel. The early scene at the Bonnington Club in which Kreisler catapults around the dance floor with the woman he refers to as the "Merry Widow"; the late sequence leading up to Kreisler's duel with Soltyk; and the remarkable conversations between Anastasya and Tarr in Part VII of the novel: all are arguably more important than the rape scene, if for no other reason than that they receive a great deal more attention in the narrative itself as well as in critical commentary. In contrast, this scene surfaces momentarily and then is whirled away again in the novel's vortex (to borrow Lewis's own aesthetic vocabulary). I would like to suggest, however, that this "minor" scene – like other instances of liminality that this study has moved to center stage – is worth lingering over because it epitomizes the modernist avant-garde's establishment of its own cultural centrality through the articulation of formal, cultural, and historical hierarchies.

The cluster of stylistic practices that have been most commonly associated with literary modernism are: aesthetic self-reflexiveness; non-linear narrative organization; paradox, ambiguity, and uncertainty; and the fragmentation of subjectivity.[49] This scene is, I suggest, a powerful example of all four. Highly stylized, narrated so as not to re-present a sequence of events but to juxtapose contrasting perceptions of these events (and thus to undermine any sense of epistemological certainty about what has transpired), this scene also models the dis-unity of the human subject. As Tarr notes elsewhere, personalities are things that we take on and off like suits of clothing. There is no core to human identity; rather, the self is a "painted mummy-case" containing "innumerable other painted cases inside," like so many Chinese boxes (55).[50] Thus,

all of the figures of Kreisler that Bertha sees are Kreisler, and none of
them is the "real" Kreisler. Nothing happened, as Bertha notes, because
her perceptions of what transpired do not give her access to objective
reality. As in Lewis's Vorticist paintings such as *The Creditors* or *Timon of
Athens*, what Susan Stewart has termed the logic of representation is not
honored here.[51] Cause–effect sequence is not recognized as an appropriate or useful means of ordering experience; unity of character is not
something Bertha and Kreisler either presuppose or seek to achieve.

It could be argued that Bertha's fragmented perceptions and her difficulty remembering what has happened are accurate and sympathetic
representations of the psychic mechanism of denial triggered by Kreisler's
shocking attack.[52] Not unlike the patterns of affect and perception in
incest and rape survivors' stories, Bertha cannot construct a coherent
narrative about this traumatic sequence of events. To read the scene in
this manner would be to understand literary modernism as an updated
version of classic nineteenth-century realism. In this view, the Vorticist
narration in *Tarr* or the stream-of-consciousness technique in *Ulysses* or
"Mrs. Dalloway on Bond Street," for example, provide a more realistic
representation of "human character" than the nineteenth-century novelist could produce through what Olive Schreiner once termed "the stage
method" of narrative, whereby the novelist describes the setting and her
characters before letting the latter speak the parts she has written for
them.[53]

On the one hand, the argument that literary modernism is a new and
improved representational art finds support in, for example, Virginia
Woolf's "Modern Fiction," Ford Madox Ford's "On Impressionism,"
and D. H. Lawrence's "Surgery for the Novel – or a Bomb." But on the
other hand, I doubt whether such a reading of modernism and of this
particular scene in *Tarr* addresses the tension generated and sustained
by Lewis's presentation here. Making reference once again to Pound's
review of *Tarr* for the *Little Review* can help explain this point.

In spite of its "demonstrable faults," Pound writes, *Tarr* is "a *serious*
work" (425, emphasis added). The "'average' novel," he goes on to note,
"the average successful commercial proposition at 6*s.* per 300 to 600
pages is nothing of the sort; it is merely a third-rate mind's imitation of
a perfectly well-known type-novel; of let us say Dickens, or Balzac . . . or
some other and less laudable proto- or necro-type" (425). If Tarr tends
to be preachy, and if the reader suspects that Tarr is a rather obvious
mouthpiece for the author, Pound insists nonetheless that the talkiness
of this novel "differs from the general descriptiveness of cheap fiction

in that these general statements are often a very profound reach for the expression of verity" (426). Lest his readers miss his point he reiterates it again: "This sort of catalogue [of characters] is not well designed to interest the general reader. What matters is the handling, the vigour, even the violence of the handling" (428).

Notably, Pound is not referring to Otto Kreisler's violent handling of Bertha Lunken's body in this comment. As is also true of many other early as well as recent critical essays on this work, Pound never mentions the rape scene in his review.[54] Instead, he distinguishes *Tarr* from "cheap fiction" on the basis of the "violence" and the "vigour" with which it handles – shapes, controls, structures – its material. Form is paramount; or rather, the shock value of form is paramount. I suggested earlier that Eliot's and Pound's reviews of *Tarr* establish a distinction between two different aesthetics (modernism and realism), two different reading publics, and two different reading practices. In other words, these re-views position Lewis's novel in what Andreas Huyssen would term the dialectic between the avant-garde and mass culture, as the latter is represented here by "classic" nineteenth-century realism and a feminized British reading public that enjoys the "red-plush Wellsian illusionism" Pound mocks. These essays teach us, in fact, to value avant-garde culture; they show us how to read texts such as *Tarr*. And they do so by bracketing off or de-legitimizing any other response we might have to the actions represented here. The shock value of this "violent" and vigorous new formal presentation is predicated on the denial or erasure of the kind of ideological response to violent content (i.e., a rape) associated with a realist tradition of narration. If this is indeed the case, then it is not enough to say that the rape scene in *Tarr* epitomizes literary modernism's effort to break with the narrative method of Victorian realism. Rather, its stylistic innovativeness *depends upon*, is subtended by, its violations of literary realism's formal and ideological conventions. Scholars such as Lynne Hapgood and Nancy Paxton are encouraging us to understand "realism and modernism as terms which describe literary techniques rather than define conflictual literary movements," and to appreciate "how these two techniques interac[t], complemen[t] and coexis[t] with each other, often within the same text."[55] Realism and modernism, as literary techniques, do in fact coexist in *Tarr* – and for precisely this reason Lewis uses the one to discredit the other as he establishes what Michael North nicely terms the "cordon sanitaire" separating the work he values from that which he deems aesthetically retrograde.[56]

Pound's own characterization of this divide is, of course, less polite: recall his language regarding Lewis's "huge act of scavenging," his "cleaning up [of] a great lot of rubbish." Significantly, though, Lewis refrains from sensationalizing and eroticizing the violent interaction between Kreisler and Bertha, as D. H. Lawrence, for example, will argue is the case with all popular novels in "Surgery for the Novel – or a Bomb," his essay that, with Q. D. Leavis's influential work, finds the epitome of lowbrow culture in E. M. Hull's *The Sheik* (1922).[57] By contrast, Lewis's treatment of violent sex is deliberately classical: when Kreisler's attack leaves Bertha "convulsed upon her back, her mouth smeared with blood," she images this interaction, you will remember, as that of "an uncontrolled satyrlike figure" and a "battling Amazon" (*Tarr*, 191). Lewis also refrains from encouraging the reader to judge Kreisler's actions on moral or ethical grounds. As Bertha notes about her own objections to what has transpired, to read this scene as a representation of violence against a woman is as "inane" as Bertha's tears (191), because the morally centered, sequence-oriented reading strategies that work for classic realism (and that would fuel Bertha's interpretation of Kreisler's action as a violation of her personhood) simply do not obtain here. Still, these other ways of reading and responding to this material – both the titillation of the reader through the erotic sensationalism that the modernist avant-garde associated with lowbrow fiction and the bourgeois ideologies they associated with classic realism – are evoked in this scene; held in abeyance, as it were, but evoked nonetheless.

In this regard, the rape scene functions as a kind of litmus test: if Lewis is indeed training the reader to appreciate the violence and vigor of his handling of material in *Tarr*,[58] then this scene proves his success. For if the reader can read this scene and appreciate its formal innovativeness without either eroticizing or objecting on ethical grounds to its violent content, then she can join the company of Eliot and Pound. That is, she will no longer be one of the "general" readers whose opinions are swayed by the likes of Katherine Tynan, G. K. Chesterton, Alice Meynell, and the *Bookman*'s reviewers, all of whom Pound scorns in his *Little Review* essay on Lewis's work. Instead, as a reader who can take pleasure in the "impressively deliberate frigidity" of Lewis's formalism, she will be a member of what Peter Rabinowitz would term Lewis's authorial audience; she will be reading "as a modernist," having accepted "the author's invitation to read in a particularly socially constituted way."[59]

The larger issues at stake in this reading of *Tarr*, this attempt to denaturalize a modernist reading protocol, can be stated thus in the form of two questions. What kind of subject position is constructed for the reader in a modernist text like *Tarr*? And how is this subject position gendered?

One way to begin answering these questions is by situating this discussion of *Tarr* in relation to two important "traditions" of revisionary feminist scholarship on literary modernism, the first of which has viewed literary modernism as always or inherently misogynistic and the second of which, conversely, has assumed that a radical textual practice necessarily constitutes a radical politics. This reading of *Tarr* seeks, in fact, to navigate between what might be termed the Scylla and Charybdis of early feminist revisionary work on modernism: on the one hand, the facile indictment of modernism's misogyny, and on the other, the blanket endorsement of modernist experimentalism as an instance of *écriture féminine*. Both of these revisionary feminist approaches to modernism are problematic; the first, more obviously, because views expressed by literary characters are naively equated with those of their authors. The second approach must be questioned as well, however, because critics who employ poststructuralist theories of *écriture* to defend the radicalness of modernist experimentalism often ignore the fact that "radical textual poetics" can "mas[k] a deeply conservative politics."[60] Moreover, they typically assume "static oppositions between realism and modernism" that fail to account for "the changing social meanings of textual forms."[61]

Rather than contributing to either of these now well-established "traditions" of feminist scholarship on modernism, this reading of *Tarr* follows the lead instead of work by feminist narratologists such as Susan Lanser, who call for a narratology that explores the "rhetorical context of narrative": a narratology that moves beyond its own roots in structuralism to focus on the historically and culturally specific circumstances in which textual strategies of narration are deployed.[62] This reading is substantiated as well by the work of scholars of modernism such as Wayne Koestenbaum and Ina Verstl. In keeping with the insights of the feminist narratologists mentioned above, Koestenbaum, for example, in his reading of Pound's collaboration with Eliot in *The Waste Land*, encourages us to pay attention to the way in which texts such as *The Waste Land* (and *Tarr*) function within a "homosocial economy" requiring the collaboration of a male reader.[63] The "maleness" of literary modernism's implied reader is not determined by the possession of male genitalia; rather, as Verstl makes clear in her work on Lewis's theory of comedy, it is a function of the subject position the reader assumes, "his" participation in the "ambience of a 'men-only' space" designed for the exchange of "female" texts among "male" artists, critics, and readers.[64]

In this larger context, the present discussion of Wyndham Lewis's *Tarr* should not be understood as an attempt either to reject or reclaim this text for the "new modernist studies." I am interested neither in castigating Lewis for his sexism nor in praising his *écriture féminine*. Rather, my point has been to call attention to the reading practices whereby T. S. Eliot and Ezra Pound – two of the modernist avant-garde's most influential impresarios during its self-appointed and self-celebrated heyday, two of the most influential *readers* of early twentieth-century British literature – attempted to fit this particular text for canonization as a modernist masterwork by discrediting other ways of reading, other aesthetic practices that were flourishing in the early twentieth century. Insofar as the dialectic between avant-garde and mass culture is played out through reading practices, patterns of *response* to narrative strategies, as well as through discursive practices themselves, the rape scene in *Tarr* that performs its nonrepresentationality so "violent[ly]" and "vigor[ously]" epitomizes how a modernist aesthetic is powered by its opposition to classic literary realism. As this scene teaches us how to put the formal and ideological conventions of representational art under erasure, as it affronts the sensibility of a reader who is trained in the conventions of classic realism – and indeed might even identify with Bertha Lunken – it teaches us how to read "as a modernist," that is, as a reader who takes pleasure in the anti-humanist brilliance of Lewis's stylistic innovations, rather than either objecting to or being titillated by the sexual violence enacted upon the body of the female character from whose perspective we view this scene.

I grant the narratological innovativeness, the technical brilliance, of this particular scene in *Tarr*. As suggested above, it exemplifies modernist stylistics: aesthetic self-reflexiveness, non-linear narrative organization, ambiguity, the fragmentation of subjectivity. But I have also tried to call attention to what a modernist reading protocol would have us ignore: namely, the implications of presenting a rape as the site of *Tarr*'s most prototypically modernist stylistics. Precisely because Lewis (and, in reviewing his work, Eliot and Pound) associates representational art with the feminine – that is, with a feminized mass reading public, a public which, like Bertha Lunken, presumably cannot ever quite appreciate the genius of the modernist avant-garde – his own nonrepresentational narration of a rape emblematizes both his contempt for that "female" mass-market reading audience and his positing of a very different authorial audience for his work. Lewis's preferred readers are "male" not because they have male genitalia but because they assume a certain stance toward the actions he depicts. They notice certain things and ignore others in his text. They feminize what they devalue. And they dismiss the reading strategies associated with classic realism as an inappropriate, outdated, narratological paradigm through which to interpret something like the actions narrated in Part IV, Chapter 9 of *Tarr*.

On the one hand, Anglo-American feminist critics of modernism such as Sandra Gilbert and Susan Gubar might consider the rape scene in *Tarr* reason enough to view Lewis's work as yet another reactionary expression of male modernism's misogyny. On the other hand, feminist critics of modernism influenced by poststructuralist theories of textuality might chide Gilbert and Gubar for ignoring the performativity of a text such as *Tarr* and treating it as a direct expression of an author's own gender ideology, thereby failing to appreciate the revolutionary character of modernist textual poetics. What both sets of critics fail to address, I would suggest, is the tension generated and sustained in this scene by the juxtaposition of two different reading protocols. In the hands of Pound and Eliot, this tension is recast as an historical dynamic pitting "modern" against "old-fashioned" ("antiquated" was Terence Hewet's term in *The Voyage Out*) novelistic methods.

Scholars such as Vicky Mahaffey, Peter Nicholls, Michael North, and Marjorie Perloff have objected strongly to the characterization of literary modernism as a "monolithic ideological formation."[65] "Modernism," Mahaffey suggests, is a "misleadingly singular rubric" for a "diverse synchrony of movements" that have only subsequently been treated as aesthetically coherent.[66] Following the lead of critics such as Rita Felski, Susan Suleiman, Nancy Paxton, and Lyn Pykett, however, I would suggest instead that there is good reason, as Felski has argued especially persuasively in *The Gender of Modernity*, to retain the specificity of the term "modernism" as a "designation for... texts which display... formally self-conscious, experimental, [and] antimimetic features... while simultaneously questioning the assumption that such texts are necessarily the most important or representative works of the modern period."[67] Only by doing so can we recognize the will-to-be *the* aesthetic of modernity that powers so many influential modernist manifestos, early reviews, and literary works. Only by doing so can we register the full force of hostility toward bourgeois culture, toward representational art, and toward *women*, that is a constituent feature of the men of 1914's defense of their own cultural centrality.

The work on modernism that is re-energizing scholarship on the turn of the twentieth century typically pluralizes modernism: it find spaces within *modernisms* for women writers and other minorities; it charts the range and diversity of "popular modernisms";[68] and it rethinks received wisdom regarding modernism's relationship to modernity. As this chapter has sought to suggest, however, retaining a focus on the modernist avant-garde's exclusionary tactics is an important complement to such efforts to provide a more expansive definition of modernism. The new modernist studies' "return to the scene of the modern," as North puts it, should not simply ignore the modernist avant-garde's exclusionary moves and anxious territorialism. Or rather, we do so at the risk of reinscribing the modernist mapping of the literary field and of "modern" culture, a mapping that I have tried to show here is exactly that: *a* mapping, not *the* mapping, of either the literary field or "modern" culture.

NOTES

1. Raymond Williams, *The Politics of Modernism*, p. 35.
2. Lyn Pykett, *Engendering Fictions*, pp. 10–11. "Discipline of reading" is Richard Poirier's phrase, as used in *The Renewal of Literature* (London: Faber, 1988), p. 95; "the intellectual hegemony of Eliot, Leavis, Richards and the New Critics" is Edward Said's phrasing, in "Critism," *Boundary 2*, 8 (1979), 17.
3. Kelly, *Our Joyce*.
4. Pykett, *Engendering Fictions*, p. 11; Williams, *The Politics of Modernism*, pp. 32, 33.
5. Obviously, this is much less the case with *Tarr* than with *The Lost Girl*, given the recent flurry of interest in Lewis; nonetheless, it can still be said that both texts have remained outside the curriculum if not the research program in modernist studies.
6. Eagleton, "The Rise of English Studies," p. 44.
7. John Worthen, "Introduction," *The Lost Girl* (Cambridge University Press, 1981), p. li.
8. See Worthen's introduction to the Cambridge edition for a detailed explanation of *The Lost Girl*'s genesis: it began as a story entitled 'Elsa Culverwell', which Lawrence worked on after finishing *Sons and Lovers* in 1912, then quickly abandoned in favor of a novel provisionally titled 'The Insurrection of Miss Houghton.' The latter in turn was abandoned in favor of 'The Sisters', which eventually became *The Rainbow* and *Women in Love*. Lawrence left 'The Insurrection' in Bavaria when he and Frieda stayed there in 1913; after several unsuccessful attempts to recover it during the war, he finally had it in hand again in December of 1919 when he sat down to write to Secker about this novel whose high sales would support Secker's investment

in *Women in Love* if he were to publish both. Interestingly enough, even though *The Lost Girl* is the least well-known of Lawrence's texts today (it has generated even less commentary than *The White Peacock* and *The Trespasser*), it won the James Tate Black prize in 1921.

9. Worthen, "Introduction," *The Lost Girl*, p. xxvi.

10. D. H. Lawrence, *The Collected Letters of D. H. Lawrence*, ed. Harry T. Moore (New York: Viking Press, 1962), vol. I, p. 602.

11. As quoted by Worthen, "Introduction," *The Lost Girl*, p. xxvii.

12. *Ibid.*, p. xxxiii.

13. *Ibid.*, p. xxxi.

14. Lawrence, *Letters I*, p. 183, emphasis in original. See also letters to Garnett dated 11 March 1913 and 15 March 1916, and Worthen's discussion of these, "Introduction," *The Lost Girl*, pp. xxiii–iv.

15. The "culture industry" is the Frankfurt School theorists' dismissive term for popular culture. See in particular, Theodor Adorno and Max Horkheimer, *The Dialectic of Enlightenment* [1944] (New York: Continuum, 1993) and the essays by Adorno reprinted in *The Culture Industry* (London and New York: Routledge, 1991).

16. Ardis, *New Women, New Novels*, p. 4.

17. D. H. Lawrence, *'The Lost Girl,'* ed. John Worthen (Cambridge University Press, 1981), p. 5. All subsequent references to this edition will be cited parenthetically in the text.

18. As Worthen notes, James Houghton is Lawrence's recreation of George Henry Cullen (1845–1915), an Eastwood merchant who "was secretary of the Congregational Sunday School, started an unsuccessful shirt factory . . ., took the lead in the creation of the Eastwood Brick and Pottery Works, made more than one effort to work the Hill Top Colliery in Eastwood, and opened a cinema" (*The Lost Girl*, p. 362, n. 2: 20). I feel obliged to note here that my own reading of *The Lost Girl* is going to neglect Alvina Houghton. There is much to be said about her coming-of-age story, but my concern here is with a different story: the story Lawrence tells about the culture that produces, and the novel that will house, such women.

19. See David Norton, "Lawrence, Wells, and Bennett: Influence and Tradition," *Journal of the Australasian Universities Language and Literature Association* 54 (1980), 171–90.

20. See Robyn Warhol, *Gendered Interventions: Narrative Discourse in the Victorian Novel* (New Brunswick: Rutgers University Press, 1989).

21. For an interesting discussion of a similar strategy in *Mr. Noon*, which Lawrence started writing immediately after finishing *The Lost Girl*, see Linda Williams, *Sex in the Head: Visions of Femininity and Film in D. H. Lawrence* (Detroit: Wayne State University, 1993), pp. 61–2.

22. I am borrowing here Seymour Chatman's useful distinction between story ("the what of narrative") and discourse ("the way of narrative"); see *Story and Discourse: Narrative Structure in Fiction and Film* (Ithaca and London: Cornell University Press, 1978).

23. Robert Allen, *Vaudeville and Film, 1895–1915: A Study in Media Interaction* (New York: Arno Press, 1977), p. 115.

24. James C. Cowan, "Lawrence and the Movies: *The Lost Girl* and After," *D. H. Lawrence and the Trembling Balance* (University Park and London: Pennsylvania State University Press, 1990), pp. 95–114; Sam Selecki, "D. H. Lawrence's View of Film," *Literature/Film Quarterly* 1,1 (Winter 1973), 12–16; Williams, *Sex in the Head*.

25. Jacobs, "Feminist Studies/Cultural Studies/Modernist Texts," p. 277.

26. Lawrence Levine, *Highbrow/Lowbrow: The Emergence of Cultural Hierarchy in America* (Cambridge, M.A.: Harvard University Press, 1984), pp. 241, 242. Subsequent references to this work will be cited parenthetically in the text.

27. Levenson, *A Genealogy of Modernism*, p. 213.

28. For detailed discussion of this critique, see Cowan, *D. H. Lawrence and the Trembling Balance*, pp. 95–114; Selecki, "D. H. Lawrence's View of Film," pp. 12–16; and Linda Williams, *Sex in the Head*, especially, pp. 1–39.

29. Tom Gunning, "An Aesthetic of Astonishment: Early Film and the (In)Credulous Spectator," in Linda Williams (ed.), *Viewing Positions: Ways of Seeing Film* (New Brunswick: Rutgers University Press, 1994), pp. 114–33. Subsequent references to this essay will be made parenthetically in the text.

30. Daniel Albright, *Personality and Impersonality: Lawrence, Woolf, and Mann* (University of Chicago Press, 1978), pp. 63, 65.

31. Work on modernists' attitudes toward early cinema is proliferating, but see in particular Leslie Hankins, "'Across the Screen of my Brain': Virginia Woolf's 'Cinema' and Film Forums of the Twenties," in Diane F. Gillespie (ed.), *The Multiple Muses of Virginia Woolf* (Columbia: University of Missouri Press, 1993), pp. 149–79; Cheryl Herr, "Blue Notes: From Joyce to Jarman," in John B. Brannigan, Geoff Ward, and Julian Wolfreyes (eds.), *Re Joyce: Text, Culture and Politics* (New York: St. Martin's Press, 1998), pp. 221–3; Lisa Hotchkiss, "Writing the Jump Cut: *Mrs. Dalloway* in the Context of the Cinema," in Beth Rigel-Daugherty and Eileen Barrett (eds.), *Virginia Woolf: Texts and Contexts: Selected Papers from the Fifth Annual Conference on Virginia Woolf* (New York: Pace University Press, 1996), pp. 134–9; and Paul Tiessen, "Literary Modernism and Cinema," in Patrick McCarthy and Paul Tiessen (eds.), *Joyce/Lowry: Critical Perspectives* (Lexington: University of Kentucky Press, 1997), pp. 159–76. The similarity between Lawrence's views of cinema's relationship to music hall theater and T. S. Eliot's is particularly strong. In his famous elegy for Marie Lioyd, whose death in 1923 he describes as "a significant moment in English history," Eliot describes both media in almost exactly the same terms that Lawrence uses. Lawrence would not tolerate Eliot's patronizing glorification of the innate "dignity" of the working classes (see T. S. Eliot, "Marie Lloyd," *Selected Essays* [New York: Harcourt, Brace and World, 1964], p. 407).

32. Grafting is Robert Allen's term for the relationship between cinema and vaudeville theater. See also Peter Bailey, *Leisure and Class in Victorian England* (London: Routledge, 1978); Bailey (ed.), *Music Hall: The Business of Pleasure*

(London: Open University Books, 1986); Erik Barnoux, *The Magician and the Cinema* (Oxford University Press, 1981); J. S. Bratton, *Music-Hall: Performance and Style* (London: Open University Books, 1986); Bratton, Richard Allen Cave, Breandan Gregory, Heidi J. Holder, and Michael Pickering (eds.), *Acts of Supremacy: The British Empire and the Stage* (Manchester University Press, 1991); David F. Cheshire, *Music Hall in Britain* (Rutherford: Fairleigh Dickinson University Press, 1974); John M. MacKenzie (ed.), *Imperialism and Popular Culture* (Manchester University Press, 1986); Eileen and Stephen Yeo, *Popular Culture and Class Conflict 1590–1914: Explorations in the History of Labour and Leisure* (Atlantic Highlands: Humanities Press, 1981). As all the changes described above might suggest, though, it is no longer appropriate to talk about music hall theater in the 1910s as "popular" culture in this same sense. Instead, by 1913, as Lawrence's characterization of Houghton's Pleasure Palace emphasizes, music hall theater was becoming a vehicle for a new kind of mass entertainment. As Allen notes, the latter would ultimately replace the very form of expressive culture which had originally nurtured its growth.

33. Richard Aldington, "Introduction," *The Lost Girl* (Harmondsworth and New York: Penguin Books, 1977 [1920]), p. 10.
34. Linda Williams, *Sex in the Head*, p. 75.
35. Emily Apter, "Ethnographic Travesties: Colonial Realism, French Feminism, and the Case of Elissa Rhais," in Gyan Prakash (ed.), *After Colonialism: Imperial Histories and Post-colonial Displacements* (Princeton University Press, 1995), 299–325.
36. Mary Louise Pratt's term for sites of cross-cultural exchange, as developed in *Imperial Eyes: Travel-Writing and Transculturalism* (London and New York: Routledge, 1992).
37. Terry Eagleton, "The Rise of English Studies," p. 31. Subsequent references to this essay will be made parenthetically in the text.
38. D. H. Lawrence, *Fantasia of the Unconscious* (New York: T. Seltzer, 1922), p. 116.
39. Antony Easthope, *Literary into Cultural Studies*, pp. 12–21.
40. Ian MacKillop, *F. R. Leavis: A Life in Criticism* (London and New York: Penguin Press, 1995).
41. Levenson, *A Genealogy of Modernism*, p. 213.
42. T. S. Eliot, "*Tarr*," *Egoist*, 5 (1918), 105.
43. Eliot, "*Ulysses*, Order, and Myth," *Dial*, 5 (1923), 480.
44. Pound, "*Tarr*, by Wyndham Lewis," as reprinted in T. S. Eliot (ed.), *Literary Essays of Ezra Pound* (New York: New Directions, 1935), p. 425. Subsequent references to this essay will be cited parenthetically in the text.
45. For information on the publication of *Tarr*, see B. Morrow and B. Lafourcade, *A Bibliography of the Writings of Wyndham Lewis* (Santa Barbara: Black Sparrow Press, 1982), pp. 28–37.
46. Oscar Wilde, "The Decay of Lying," as reprinted in Karl Beckson (ed.), *Aesthetes and Decadents of the 1890s* (Chicago: Academy Press, 1981), p. 192.

47. "Disciples" is Michael North's term for critics such as Clement Green-
    berg, F. R. and Q. D. Leavis, and I. A. Richards, who took their lead from
    T. S. Eliot (even more so than from Pound) in establishing a "cordon sani-
    taire around the great works of aesthetic modernism" (North, *Reading 1922:
    A Return to the Scene of the Modern* [Oxford University Press, 1999], p. 141.)

48. Wyndham Lewis, *Tarr* (London: Chatto and Windus, 1928), p. 192. Subse-
    quent references to the novel will be cited parenthetically in the text. I have
    chosen to use the 1928 edition because this scene was extensively revised
    and expanded in the later edition.

49. Eugene Lunn, *Marxism and Modernism: A Historical Study of Lukàcs, Brecht,
    Benjamin, and Adorno* (London: Verso, 1985), p. 34. Michael North points
    out the risks associated with attempting to formulate a unified formalist
    definition of modernism (*Reading 1922*, p. 208). Yet, of course, formalist
    definitions of "modern" art are precisely what Eliot and Pound wield in
    their influential early reviews.

50. For further discussion of Lewis's treatment of personality in *Tarr*, see Michael
    Levenson, "Form's Body: Wyndham Lewis' *Tarr*," *Modern Language Quarterly*
    45, 3 (1984), 252; and Roger Henckle, "The Advertised Self: Wyndham
    Lewis's Satire," *Novel* 13 (1979), 95–108.

51. Susan Stewart, *Crimes of Writing: Problems in the Containment of Writing* (New
    York: Oxford University Press, 1991).

52. For groundbreaking work on trauma and narrative, see Cathy Caruth (ed.),
    Trauma: Explorations in Memory (Baltimore: Johns Hopkins University Press,
    1995); Caruth, *Unclaimed Experience: Trauma, Narrative, and History* (Baltimore:
    Johns Hopkins University Press, 1996).

53. Olive Schreiner, "Preface," *Story of an African Farm* [1883] (New York:
    Penguin, 1982), p. 27.

54. Hugh Kenner, for example, chooses to overlook this scene entirely in devel-
    oping an otherwise close reading of the novel in *Wyndham Lewis* (Norfolk:
    New Directions, 1954). By implication, such silence suggests either that
    the scene is too insignificant or too disturbing to merit attention. In other
    words, silence signifies either benign neglect or an effort to "save the text"
    by repressing offensive ideological features that distract us from the work's
    admirable formal innovations, as Barbara Herrnstein Smith might sug-
    gest ("Contingencies of Value," *Critical Inquiry* 10 [1983], 28.) Critics who
    do mention this scene often contrast Kreisler with Tarr, thereby distanc-
    ing Tarr, Lewis, and themselves as readers from Kreisler's violence. See,
    for example, Robert Chapman, *Wyndham Lewis: Fictions and Satires* (London:
    Vision Press, 1973), p. 70; Fredric Jameson, *Fables of Aggression: Wyndham
    Lewis, the Modernist as Fascist* (Berkeley: University of California Press, 1979);
    Thomas Kush, *Wyndham Lewis' Pictorial Integer* (Ann Arbor: UMI Research
    Press, 1981), p. 68; Timothy Materer, *Wyndham Lewis the Novelist* (Detroit:
    Wayne State University Press, 1976), p. 57; Valerie Parker, "Enemies of
    the Absolute: Lewis, Art, and Women," in Jeffrey Meyers (ed.), *Wyndham
    Lewis: A Revaluation* (Montreal: McGill-Queen's University Press, 1980),

pp. 217–24. Of these readings, Fredric Jameson's is by far the cleverest. Characterizing Tarr and Kreisler not as characters in the traditional sense but as "transindividual" psychic forces, Jameson dismisses all possible objections to the act of rape by reading this scene's actions as violence against the idea of the unified subject. Kreisler's assault, according to Jameson, signals the "eclipse of the subject or ego" as a new "energy model" "explodes... older psychic typologies" (p. 103). While I agree with Jameson's argument about the way this scene dismantles the notion of the unified subject, his reading ignores the tension generated in this scene as Lewis tests his readers' response to controversial subject matter. For a view of the gendered "pleasures" of reading *Tarr* that complements the present discussion, see Ina Verstl, *Tarr: A Joke Too Deep for Laughter? The Comic, the Body, and Gender," Enemy News: Journal of the Wyndham Lewis Society* 24 (1987), 4–9.

55. Lynne Hapgood and Nancy L. Paxton (eds), *Outside Modernism: In Pursuit of the English Novel, 1900–1930* (London and New York: Macmillan/St. Martin's Press, 2000), p. vii.

56. North, *Reading 1922*, p. 141.

57. Note, though, that Lawrence's and Leavis's characterization of lowbrow sensationalism is thoroughly reductive; for a very different reading of Hull's treatment of female sexuality in *The Sheik*, see my "E. M. Hull, Mass Market Romance and the New Woman Novel in the Early Twentieth Century," *Women's Writing* 3, 3 (Autumn 1996), 287–96.

58. When he first sent Pound a section of the manuscript in 1915, Lewis advised him to read it "in an incredulous and argumentative voice, full of [much] harsh emphasis" (Lewis, *Pound/Lewis*, p. 17).

59. Peter Rabinowitz, *Before Reading: Narrative Conventions and the Politics of Interpretation* (Ithaca: Cornell University Press, 1987), p. 22.

60. Schenck, "Exiled by Genre," p. 231. See also Felski, *The Gender of Modernity*; Susan Suleiman, *Subversive Intent: Gender, Politics, and the Avantgarde* (Cambridge, M.A.: Harvard University Press, 1990); Janet Wolff, "Feminism and Modernism," *Feminine Sentences: Essays on Women and Culture* (Berkeley: University of California Press, 1990), pp. 51–66.

61. Felski, *Beyond Feminist Aesthetics: Feminist Literature and Social Change* (Cambridge, M.A.: Harvard University Press, 1989), p. 161.

62. Susan Lanser, "Towards a Feminist Narratology," *Style* 20 (1986), 358.

63. Wayne Koestenbaum, *Double Talk: The Erotics of Male Literary Collaboration* (New York: Routledge, 1989), p. 136.

64. Verstl, "*Tarr*: A Joke Too Deep for Laughter?," p. 7.

65. Peter Nicholls, *Modernisms: A Literary Guide* (London: Macmillan, 1995), p. vii.

66. Vicky Mahaffey, "Heirs of Yeats: Eire as Female Poets Reinscribe Her," p. 100. See also Marjorie Perloff, *Radical Artifice: Writing in the Age of Media* (University of Chicago Press, 1991), p. 202.

67. Felski, *The Gender of Modernity*, p. 25.

68. North, *Reading 1922*, p. 141.

CHAPTER 4

Mapping the middlebrow in Edwardian England

We are sick to death of the assorted panaceas, of the general acqui-
escence of artists, of their agreement to have perfect manners, and
to mention absolutely nothing unpleasant.
    Realism in literature has had its run . . .
    The artist has been at peace with his oppressors for long enough.
He has dabbled in democracy and he is now done with that
folly . . . The aristocracy of commerce is decaying,
the aristocracy of the arts is ready again for its service
                                        . . .
    And the public will do well to resent these "new" kinds of art.
                                Ezra Pound, "The New Sculpture"[1]

Ezra Pound's essay for the *Egoist* on "The New Sculpture" in 1914 provides a useful point of departure for this chapter's consideration of an
arena of literary production that the Joyce–Eliot–Pound nexus of modernism obscures entirely from history: the sphere of the middlebrow in
Edwardian England. The work of Netta Syrett (1865–1943), a middlebrow writer of feminist women's fiction who published prolifically between 1895 and 1940, will provide the occasion in this chapter to register
depth and subtle contrast in a terrain that her avant-garde contemporaries viewed only as a vast, flat wasteland. Before introducing her or
looking closely at her work, however, it is helpful to unpack Pound's
contribution to the controversy raging in 1914 over Jacob Epstein's
sculpture.

Viewing this controversy in the visual arts as an opportunity to establish aesthetic policy in the realm of the verbal arts, Pound accomplishes
several things with his usual truculence in "The New Sculpture." First,
as is also the case in manifestos by D. H. Lawrence and Virginia Woolf
such as "Surgery for the Novel – Or a Bomb" and "Mr Bennett and
Mrs Brown," Pound collapses all distinctions among a plethora of non-
modernist contemporary writers in order to distinguish "new" art from

Edwardian realism, thereby identifying the writers with whom the history of art will go forward. In this classic modernist mapping of early twentieth-century culture, the history of the literary and visual arts is relentlessly teleological, and literary realism is jettisoned like so much portage in a sinking ship in order to allow truly "new" art to float more securely and distinctively above the flotsam and jetsam of contemporary popular culture.

Second, Pound's essay shares with other modernist manifestos certain assumptions about the politics of textual form. Asserting that particular forms – in this case, literary realism and avant-garde poetics – are automatically and necessarily freighted ideologically in a particular way, Pound creates a static opposition between realism and literary modernism. Realists, according to Pound, acquiesce to bourgeois social norms, "have perfect manners," and agree "to mention absolutely nothing unpleasant"; modernists, by contrast, shall proudly earn the public's resentment for their refusal to conform.

On this basis Pound then justifies dismissing literary realism because it is democratic – because it is accessible to what he mocks in this essay as the "half-educated simpening general" (221), the newly literate populace in Britain produced after the 1870 Education Act and the establishment of board schools, workingmen's institutes, and women's colleges. As his characterization of the "aristocracy of the arts" indicates, Pound prefers to limit rather than to broaden the general public's access to the realm of high culture. Quite clearly, he does not want to be another Charles Dickens, or to have the audience Dickens had. Thus, he assumes here the pugilistic stance that typifies so many of the modernist avant-garde's public pronouncements toward mass culture – and he writes this essay for the *Egoist*, a journal that in its heyday under his editorship had a circulation of two hundred.

We've seen this attitude before – not only in Pound's slash-and-burn characterization of *Tarr*'s "blesse[d]" freedom from "red-plush Wellsian illusionism . . . and the click of Mr. Bennett's cash-register finish" but also in Terence Hewet's exaggeration of the contrast between the literary writing he himself values and problem plays and 1890s novels he sees in Rachel Vinrace's room in *The Voyage Out*. These spokesmen for literary modernism as *the* aesthetic of modernity claim its centrality and high status in the cultural landscape by putting competing aesthetic paradigms and narrative strategies "behind" them. The long-term impact of this on our conceptualization of Edwardian middlebrow fiction is the focus of this chapter's discussion.

As noted in the previous chapter, scholars such as Lynne Hapgood and Nancy Paxton are shaking literary realism free of modernism's reductive association of it with the nineteenth century as they and the contributors to their anthology, *Outside Modernism*, move "outside" modernism in tracing the development of the English novel between 1900 and 1930. "[B]y understanding realism and modernism as . . . literary techniques rather than . . . conflictual literary movements, and by demonstrating how these two techniques interac[t], complemen[t] and coexis[t] with each other, often within the same text," Hapgood and Paxton argue that Edwardian writers "repositioned the English tradition" and "transformed realism by making it a flexible, fluent tool for describing modernity." "Literary realism and literary modernism," they suggest, "meet on this common ground."[2] Yet, as we also saw in the previous chapter, literary modernists themselves don't necessarily acknowledge this "common ground"; instead, they promote a characterization of realism and modernism as "conflictual literary movements" – movements in historical succession, moreover, not contemporaneous competitors. Their failure to recognize the middlebrow as a distinctive in-between space is an offshoot of these practices.

As Janice Radway has noted, although the terms "highbrow" and "lowbrow" were in common usage early in the twentieth century, "middlebrow" is a post-World War I invention. The *Oxford English Dictionary* attributes its first use to a 1925 article in *Punch* to describe people "who are hoping that someday they will get used to the stuff they ought to like"; it does not "mov[e] into common parlance" until the mid-1930s, when Margaret Widdemer uses it in the *Saturday Review of Literature* and "Virginia Woolf used it extensively in a letter (which she never sent) to the *New Statesman* protesting a recent review of one of her books."[3] The etymology of this third term should not lead us to conclude, though, that the phenomenon did not exist prior to its naming as such. I would like to suggest that literary modernism's simplification of the "scene" of British literary production in the early twentieth century resulted in not only the classic modernist exaggeration of a "great divide" between high and low culture but also the belated identification of the middlebrow. "Talking back" is bell hooks's term to describe the ways in which the allegedly passive consumers of a hegemonic popular culture respond to, challenge, and re-purpose its meanings and messages.[4] I will argue here that a middlebrow writer such as Syrett "talks back" to the "aristocracy of the arts" that Pound and other modernists were intent on promoting.

Her work thus can help us re-map an arena of literary production in early twentieth-century Britain that the Joyce–Eliot–Pound nexus of modernism obscured entirely from history's view through its characterization of a high/low cultural dichotomy.

* * * * * * * * *

Netta Syrett began her literary career in the early 1890s publishing short stories in *Longman's*, *Macmillan's*, *Temple Bar*, and the *Yellow Book*; her first two novels were published in 1896 and 1897 as part of John Lane's prestigious "Keynotes Series." After the premiere performance of her play, *The Finding of Nancy*, was reviewed disastrously in 1902,[5] she lost a teaching position and supported herself almost exclusively for ten years by writing plays for children and short stories for journals such as *Harper's*, *Everybody's Magazine*, *The Acorn*, and *Venture*. In the late 1910s – as T. E. Hulme, Ford Madox Ford, Ezra Pound and others were beginning to write lectures and manifestos celebrating a radical break with all things Victorian – Syrett's literary production shifted again somewhat. Although she continued to publish children's fiction and histories throughout the rest of her career, she turned her hand increasingly once more to fiction for adults. In her short story collection, *Women and Circumstance* (1906), and novels such as *The Child of Promise* (1907), *Anne Page* (1908), *Olivia Carew* (1910), *Drender's Daughter* (1911), *Three Women* (1912), *The Victorians* (1915), *Rose Cottingham Married* (1916), and *Troublers of the Peace* (1917), she writes about young middle-class women who struggle with their own as well as their culture's deep conflicts about women's entrance into the public labor force at the turn of the century. Altogether, and under the imprimature of twenty different presses, she published thirty-eight books, seventeen short stories, four plays, an autobiography, and twenty children's books between 1896 and 1940.[6]

At the end of her autobiography, *A Sheltering Tree* (1939), Syrett herself concedes that she is not someone whose writing has been granted trans-historical value. She is not, according to Michel Foucault's definition, an "author"; nor does she conceive of herself as an "artist" – the kind of alienated genius figure literary modernists both celebrate and mock in their fiction. "In a few years, or even less," she notes, "everything I have written will be as dead as a dodo. Already my novels are being swamped by those of the beginners in the art of fiction." "But what does it matter?," she goes on to ask. "The interest and excitement of writing, with any luck, will sustain these newcomers for their lifetime, and no sensible person should ask of our transitory existence more than this" (259).

Writing an autobiography in and of itself might seem to constitute an act of individualization, and therefore a claim to the authority and privilege of authorship. Syrett's self-deprecation thus could perhaps be read as the expression of false modesty that often precedes a grand expression of ego. Other evidence suggests overwhelmingly, though, a different reading of Syrett's gesture of self-effacement. Even though Syrett's background is solidly middle-class,[7] her autobiography conforms to the conventions of what Regenia Gagnier has termed working-class "memories," autobiographies written to preserve local history for members of a community.[8] Not only does Syrett repeat tag-lines like the above about her ordinary-ness throughout the autobiography, but she also introduces the whole volume by suggesting that it was inspired by a new generation of writers' misrepresentations of the Victorian era. She claims to be writing, in other words, as a witness to the local history of late Victorian and Edwardian England that was lost when later writers represented the pre-war world as the Dark Ages. As her title suggests, Syrett wants to preserve a sense of that culture as a "sheltering tree" harboring any number of life forms alien to itself.[9]

Syrett never identifies by name these later writers who demonize the Victorian period. Given her representation of the modernist avant-garde in novels such as *Anne Page* (1908), *Troublers of the Peace* (1917), and *Strange Marriage* (1930), it is nonetheless appropriate, I would suggest, to associate her critique of anti-Victorianism with the modernist avant-garde's "make it new" rhetoric – and to view Syrett's career as an attempt to sustain and carry forward a turn-of-the-century middlebrow feminist fictional tradition that the latter overdetermines as a form of cultural conservatism. At a point in time when the men of 1914 were proselytizing the modernist avant-garde by promoting the production of what Roland Barthes would later term "writerly" texts, Syrett was making a living publishing "readerly" fiction.[10] Writing novels when the modernist avant-garde privileged poetry; writing realistically when their privileged mode was experimental, formally complex, and "difficult"; writing for a middlebrow audience when their preferred stance was anti-bourgeois and anti-sentimental, she produced roughly a book a year for over forty years. Looking carefully at some of the best fiction she produced during the first half of her career can help us map the larger cultural scene in which the modernist avant-garde first promoted its hegemonic views on literary value and "modern" culture. Before turning to her work, though, it will be useful to contextualize it with a brief material history of middlebrow Edwardian literary production.

MAPPING THE EDWARDIAN MIDDLEBROW

Following upon the changes in the British publishing industry discussed in Chapter 2 – e.g., the circulating libraries' loss of dominance in the literary marketplace, the establishment of new venues of publication (both publishing companies and periodicals), changes in international copyright law, the increasing effectiveness of literary agents in brokering contracts, the Society of Authors' attempts to professionalize and unionize writers, and publishers' increased use of advertising – the market for fiction exploded in the early twentieth century. As the editors of *Edwardian Fiction: An Oxford Companion* note, "Between the decline of the three-volume novel in 1895 and the outbreak of the First World War lay twenty years in which fiction was the most important section of the leisure industry."[11]

A less well-charted but equally significant new development in the publishing industry during this period is the extensive expansion by accretion accomplished by a number of firms. We tend to think of corporate buy-out as a phenomenon unique to our own turn of the century. To read the official histories of British and American publishing firms of the early twentieth century, however, is to see an industry transformed through consolidation. Many of the grand old Victorian publishing firms continued to wield considerable power in the early twentieth century – though not necessarily as conservative forces in the literary marketplace, for they often, as we shall see, took significant risks on unknown writers and contemporary social controversies even as they were reaching out to an increasingly literate populace, seeking to capitalize on its anxiousness to be taught what to read.[12] Companies were also, however, changing hands right and left: small speciality firms were being absorbed by larger, more diversified operations, American and British companies were buying each other's British and American offshoots, and reputations were being made and remade in the process.

It is also worth noting that the women's suffrage campaign generated an extensive female-centered network of institutionalized as well as informal publishing outlets for pro-suffrage writings during this period.[13] Although Syrett's decided ambivalence about women's educational institutions and suffrage organizations (as will be discussed further below) kept her from taking advantage of these resources, it is nonetheless important to remember that this very female-centered world existed in counterpoint to the "official" world of British publishing, which continued to operate much like a Victorian men's club in many regards.

Archival materials documenting Syrett's life and her negotiations with her publishers are sparse. A handful of extant letters and play scripts are scattered in research libraries at Eton School Library, the National Library of Scotland, the Bodleian, the Merton College Libraries at Oxford, and the Toronto Public Library.[14] Not surprisingly, they are more typically archived in the collections of her correspondents – Max Beerbohm, Thomas Hardy, Evelyn Sharp, May Sinclair – than under her own name. Searching for her history in the history of her publishers, it is disappointing to find that she consistently falls through the cracks in the "official" historical records of the publishing industry as well. In several instances, entire archives of publishing houses were destroyed and no records remain of any kind. In most cases, though, the men appointed to write official histories of the most prominent among the twenty firms with whom she published – Hutchinson, John Lane, Chatto and Windus, Roberts Brothers, Duckworth, Frederick Stokes, T. Fisher Unwin, Methuen, Samuel French, Dodd, Mead – simply do not seem to consider her worthy of mention, even though she published multiple titles with a number of these firms.[15]

What can be documented, however, is the reputation of the publishing houses that carried her work and the names and reputations of other authors being published by them. When Roberts Brothers acquired Syrett's *Nobody's Fault* (1896) and *The Tree of Life* (1897) along with the other titles in John Lane's Keynotes Series, the Boston-based firm had a strong reputation for publishing British imports (including Christina Rosetti, William Morris, Swinburne, Olive Schreiner, George Meredith, and W. B. Yeats) and had been ranked on par with the major New York publishing houses since the early 1880s. The Keynotes Series itself had been praised as by far the most elegant fiction series of the nineteenth century – and featured, as noted above, not one but two titles by Syrett. Chatto and Windus, which also published Arnold Bennett between 1902 and 1907, was still known as an experimental publisher when Syrett published *Anne Page*, *Olivia Carew*, and *Three Women* in 1908, 1910, and 1912, respectively. Duckworth, which published Syrett's *Castle of Four Towers* in 1909, would publish D. H. Lawrence's *The Trespasser* in 1912 and Virginia Woolf's *Night and Day* in 1917. When Syrett was publishing with T. Fisher Unwin in the mid-1910s, the firm had a reputation for taking risks with unknown writers – and losing them once they'd achieved some success, because Thomas Fisher refused to offer any additional compensation. In addition to publishing Olive Schreiner's *Trooper Peter Halket of Mashonaland* and H. G. Wells's *Ann Veronica*, Unwin published Ethel Dell, Vernon Lee,

Mark Rutherford, Somerset Maugham, and John Galsworthy during this period. Methuen, which published *The Jam Queen* (1914), had almost 170 authors on its list by 1910, and was attracting more and more well-known writers through its growing success. One of the relative upstarts in the British publishing industry at the turn of the century (having opened in 1889, just before the demise of the circulating libraries), Methuen had acquired Arnold Bennett's *Hilda Lessways* in 1911; other authors published under its imprimature between 1900 and 1915 include Hillaire Belloc, Henry James (*The Golden Bowl*, 1905), Oscar Wilde (*De Profundis*, 1905), H.G. Wells, George Gissing, A. E. Milne, Marie Corelli, Arthur Conan Doyle, Jack London, John Masefield, Frances Thompson, and Kenneth Graham. T. S. Eliot would debut here with *The Sacred Wood* in 1920. Although Syrett also published with some smaller and more short-lived firms such as Rich & Cowan, Lawrence & Bullen, and Thornton Butterworth, certainly those mentioned above are among the most prosperous and innovative in the Anglo-American publishing industry in the early twentieth century. That Syrett was able to place multiple titles with many of them is no minor accomplishment.

Harder to trace, but no doubt equally significant in trying to understand the arc of her career, are two things: first, the impact that various acquisitions and mergers and the business practices of particular firms in the literary publishing industry might have had on her; and second, the fact that she worked simultaneously in several distinct fields – children's literature, adult middlebrow fiction, and drama. Over the course of her life, Syrett worked with twenty different British and American firms. Except for John Lane, Hutchinson, and G. Bles, none of these houses handled more than four titles. Thus, until Syrett established herself first with Hutchinson, which published five of her novels between 1923 and 1931, and then Geoffrey Bles, which published eleven novels and her autobiography between 1928 and 1940, she would have been negotiating with a new publisher almost every two years. Although she notes in *The Sheltering Tree* that "a novel became for me a sure thing" (126), and that it was no hardship to focus her energies on fiction-writing after the scandal surrounding her play, *The Finding of Nancy*, the brevity of her association with most of these firms suggests otherwise.[16]

I would suggest that Syrett's erasure from the official histories of these early twentieth-century publishing firms is related to her work in the burgeoning field of children's literature. My primary interest in her in this context is as a writer of adult middlebrow fiction. It is worth noting, however, that her theater work and her success in writing history and fiction for children adds to the scattershot feel of her publishing career – and the complexity of her negotiations in the literary marketplace. While she was publishing adult fiction with Chatto and Windus, T. Fisher Unwin, G. P. Putnam, John Lane, Duckworth, Methuen, and others throughout the 1910s, Syrett was also working with Lane, Lawrence & Bullen, Mowbray, and the Clarendon Press to publish children's plays and histories such as, respectively, *The Story of St. Catherine of Sienna* (1910), *Old Miracle Plays* (1911), *Stories from Medieval Romance* (1913), *Robin Goodfellow and Other Fairy Plays* (1918). During the 1920s and early 1930s, the period of her most secure alliances with Hutchinson and G. Bles, Samuel French, the largest supplier of plays for amateur and stock theatre companies in the U.S. and Great Britain, published *Two Domestics* (1924); Frederick Stokes, known for its distinguished line of children's literature (and for Stokes's opposition to book clubs and the use of bestseller lists), published *Toby and the Odd Beasts* (1922), *Cupid and Mr. Pepys* (1923), and *Rachel and the Seven Wonders* (1923); John Lane published *Tinkelly Winkle* (1923); Thornton Butterworth published *Magic London* (1922); and John Murray published *Sketches of European History* (1931).

Clearly, Syrett was working multiple markets with considerable success throughout her career. But her success as a writer of children's fiction and histories in particular might be a key source of posterity's amnesia regarding this prolific writer. In this regard, the argument Suzanne Clark makes about Edna St. Vincent Millay can be adapted to pertain to Syrett as well: as Clark argues in *Sentimental Modernism*, when women writers in the early twentieth century chose to write for an audience that included 'the ladies' – and, in Syrett's case, children – they opened themselves up "to the most terrible critical scorn" of the literary modernists. "The more successfully they wrote, both to appeal to a feminized community of readers and to help readers feel part of the literary community," the less they could be considered "serious" artists. "The more clearly they appealed to the shared feelings of a popular community, the more they risked being labeled 'sentimental' or merely popular."[17] In Syrett's case, as she notes in her autobiography, this meant being "cursorily read" by the likes of Edward Garnett, Duckworth's reader during this period, even though servicemen at the front during World War I sent her fan letters about the novels she wrote when she failed to find any other kind of work that would allow her to participate in the war effort (*Sheltering Tree*, 257, 233).

Garnett alone cannot be held responsible for Syrett's current obscurity, of course – or that of the Edwardian middlebrow more generally.

For that we also need to recognize the impact of Syrett's failure to be interested in what she terms "self-advertisement" (*Sheltering Tree*, 10) and the lack of fit between her work and dominant critical paradigms of literary value. Because Syrett was not interested in promoting her own work by producing critical documents to ensure its correct reception among readers, she did not "blast and bombadier" her way into modern memory, as did Ezra Pound, Wyndham Lewis, T. S. Eliot, and company. Nor is she an Edwardian whose work benefited by association with modernism once the latter gained steam in institutionalizing itself as a privileged subject of academic literary study. The career of her friend, May Sinclair, whose early fiction such as *The Creators* bears a significant resemblance to Syrett's fiction in theme and content, differs strikingly from Syrett's in this regard, as recent scholarship on her is beginning to suggest.[18] As Syrett notes in *The Sheltering Tree*, she would have been better off financially if she had done more to promote her work. Instead, "even as a novelist reached that dull eminence known as 'established,'" she "receive[d] very little attention of any kind from modern reviewers" (*Sheltering Tree*, 258).

The fact that her work does not fit the critical paradigms reigning in academic literary circles either in her own time or today is yet another reason Edwardian middlebrow writers such as Syrett have disappeared into the backwaters of history. Her realist novels are not prime specimens of the "experimental writing" valued so highly by both literary historians of the 1920s, 30s, and 40s, and late-twentieth-century feminist critics and historians of the modernist avant-garde. Thus, alongside other Edwardian realists such as Alice Meynell, Anna Wickham, Charlotte Mew, and Eleanor Wylie, she was ignored entirely by her avant-garde contemporaries, treated to brief dictionary-style mention in influential academic literary histories of the 1920s such as Harold Williams's *Modern English Writers, 1890–1914* (1925) – and "exiled by genre" from the first generation of feminist revisionary work on modernism in the 1980s and early 1990s.

Work by scholars such as Rita Felski, Celeste Schenck, and Talia Schaffer provides the critical leverage required for effectively challenging the academy's over-investment in modernist experimental writing and concomitant neglect of non-modernist (and even anti-modernist) writings. In *Beyond Feminist Aesthetics*, for example, Felski argues that "feminist theories of 'textual politics' grounded in a modernist aesthetics" are open to criticism because "they continue to draw upon static oppositions between realism and modernism without taking into account the changing social meanings of textual forms." Objecting in particular to French feminists' overestimation of the radical effects of linguistic indeterminacy, Felski suggests that "the supposedly revolutionary function of experimental techniques is increasingly questionable in late capitalist society, while the 'conservative' status of realism as a closed form which reflects ruling ideologies has been challenged by its reappropriation in new social contexts" by oppositional movements such as feminism.[19] Felski thus defends contemporary women writers' production of realist fiction for the following reasons: "while it is no longer possible to believe... that a text can transmit an unmediated representation of the real, this does not negate [realism's] strategic importance... as a medium of self-exploration and social criticism." Therefore,

given that all discursive positions are constructed, and that there is no privileged space beyond ideology, the question which confronts women is that of the relative value of particular discursive and textual forms in relation to their changing needs and interests. The use of realist forms in feminist fiction in this context denotes a concentration upon the semantic function of writing rather than its formal and self-reflexive component. (79)

Felski's phrasing – "it is no longer possible... to believe that a text can transmit an unmediated representation of the real" – is curious, I think, and speaks to her strong sense of embattlement in the late 1980s as she responded to poststructuralist critics' charge that realists believe naively in their unmediated representations of the real. (One only has to remember the famous chapter in *Adam Bede* "In Which the Story Pauses a Little" and George Eliot interjects a short metanarrative about her art to doubt whether realists *ever* claimed access to an unmediated reality.) That particular characterization of realism's naivete powers postmodernism's view of itself as the more sophisticated (and therefore) superior aesthetic.

More immediately to the point: while Felski's primary concern in *Beyond Feminist Aesthetics* is with women writers' production of realist fiction in the 1970s, feminist historians of modernism such as Schenck and Schaffer have interrogated the same set of assumptions about the textual and political radicalism of experimental writing as they focus on Edwardian women writers who have been left out of the most recent revisionary histories of modernism. In "Exiled by Genre: Modernism, Canonicity, and the Politics of Exclusion," Schenck asks: "Shouldn't the canonization of Stein and H.D.... give us pause, if it is accomplished at the expense of striking poets like [Anna] Wickham and [Charlotte]

Mew, [Eleanor] Wylie and [Alice] Meynell, from the modernist register?"
And she continues: "if... the radical poetics of Modernism often masks a
deeply conservative politics, might it also possibly be true that the seemingly genteel, conservative poetics of women poets whose obscurity even
feminists have overlooked might pitch a more radical politics than we
had considered possible?"[20]

Schaffer has taken this line of argument still further in her recent work
on Alice Meynell, noting not only Meynell's pioneering work in feminist
literary historiography but also Virginia Woolf's deliberate suppression
of both Meynell herself and Woolf's extensive borrowings from Meynell
in her construction of a female literary tradition. "What Woolf's modernist imperative condemned as ladylike indecisiveness or outmoded
gentility can be read as an interestingly complex mode of meditating
among competing female identities at the turn of the century," Schaffer
writes, glossing Meynell's struggle to reconcile her responsibility, as a
professional writer, to "publish tidbits that fed her readers' hunger for
autobiographical information" with the duty of a Victorian lady "to keep
her personal life sacrosanct."[21] Building on the work of Gillian Beer and
Barbara Green, Schaffer concludes by suggesting that Woolf's relationship with Meynell, her "complicated appropriation and subversion of the
past – along with a corresponding attempt to erase that relationship –
was fundamental to modernist self-fashioning" (16).

In tandem with the work of critics such as these, I have argued elsewhere that the realist fiction Netta Syrett produced during the heyday of
the modernist avant-garde does indeed "pitch a more radical politics"
than might otherwise be considered possible, given our continued valorization of experimental writing; that is, given the familiar assumption
that realism is conservative and that an avant-garde poetics constitutes
a radical politics.[22] I am not, perhaps I need to emphasize, mounting
a Lukàcsian attack on modernism that doubles as a defense of realism
on both formal and ideological grounds. Nor am I arguing that realism
constitutes some sort of "privileged space beyond ideology," to borrow
Felski's phrasing. Rather, I am interested in what continues to be left
out of revisionary histories of modernism, and why. Expanding these
histories to include consideration of writers who have been "exiled by
genre" allows us to interrogate not only "'the presumed chasm between
experimental and realist writing'"[23] but also the critical paradigms that
continue to sustain such oppositions. Even more fundamentally, investigating what is entailed in this kind of exile invites us to review the way
we conceptualize the ideology of form. It is one thing to reconfigure

the traditional opposition between form and content by arguing that form *is* content; form is always already ideological. (This is, of course, the highest high-modernist doctrine, as expressed by Samuel Beckett in writing about James Joyce's "Work in Progress" in his essay, "Dante . . . Bruno. Vico . . Joyce," for example.[24]) But it is quite different to then assert that a particular form is necessarily freighted ideologically in a particular way. That second critical move formalizes ideology, ignoring entirely certain kinds of question about both literary production and reception. Which is why, by contrast, I find Felski's concern for the "changing social meanings of textual forms" so appealing. And why I think Syrett's middlebrow manipulation of "traditional" modes of representation during the modernist avant-garde's heyday is worthy of our attention.

Through close readings of *Anne Page* and *Three Women*, I have shown, too, how Syrett undermines the bourgeois ideologies commonly associated with literary realism even as she employs its strategies of narration. In spite of the fact that her writing was "unwarranted" (as Suzanne Clark would say) by the modernist avant-garde, she subjects bourgeois political, social, sexual, and aesthetic conventions to critique in her middlebrow Edwardian novels of manners. I have also shown how, in both *Anne Page* and *Strange Marriage (1930)*, she extends this critique to include the counterdiscourse of *fin-de-siècle* aestheticism as well, challenging its antagonistic self-differentiation from bourgeois culture and its bipolar figurations of femininity while at the same time savoring and extending its aestheticization of everyday life. Importantly, though, the vehicle for such critique is realism, not "experimental writing." Expanding on those arguments here, I want now to explore the ways in which Syrett's middlebrow fiction offers a counterdiscourse to literary modernism, which she views as both perpetuating aestheticism's misogynistic representations of women and functioning hegemonically through its manifestos on literary value.

WRITING IN THE SHADOW OF SOCIALIST, FEMINIST, AND MODERNIST COLLECTIVISM

Syrett gained her entrée into the "Yellow Book" crowd with a pair of novels, *Nobody's Fault* (1896) and *Tree of Life* (1897) that, like so many other New Woman novels, take issue with the colonization of young middle-class women by Victorian culture's domestic agenda. Interestingly enough, however, and as is true of her later fiction as well, her earliest novels are distinctive among New Woman novels by their refusal to blame or demonize the Victorian angel in the house. Not unlike Virginia Woolf's characterization of Lily Briscoe's difficult, but not unaffectionate, relationship with Mrs. Ramsay in *To The Lighthouse*, Syrett's New Women do not sever their ties with Victorian patriarchy; instead, they find ways to avoid co-optation by Victorian domestic ideology while at the same time maintaining powerful emotional ties with family members (especially mothers) who cannot even begin to grasp their non-domestic ambitions let alone endorse their refusal to contain the expression of sexuality within the confines of a lifelong heterosexual partnership.

Early twentieth-century "lowbrow" mass-market novelists such as E. M. Hull played an important role in carrying forward the late nineteenth-century New Woman writers' popularization of "advanced" views of sexuality.[25] While most women's suffrage campaigners steered clear of sexuality in order to secure the respectability of their political campaigns, early twentieth-century mass-market romance writers were continuing the work of *fin-de-siècle* New Woman writers – writing about sexuality, reworking the romance plot to incorporate women's non-domestic ambitions, and renegotiating women's access to the public sphere in the process. Although Syrett never sensationalizes female sexuality, and though she never treats sexual desire as the exclusive, or even the primary, focus of female ambition, her work, like Hull's, does indeed carry forward this particular legacy of *fin-de-siècle* New Woman fiction. Equally importantly, however, it carries forward a second legacy of *fin-de-siècle* New Woman fiction: a legacy of political critique that is powerfully articulated in the novels I want to consider in some detail now, *Drender's Daughter* (1911), *The Jam Queen* (1914), *The Victorians* (1915), and *Rose Cottingham Married* (1916), before turning to the novels focused specifically on avant-garde aesthetics and politics, *Troublers of the Peace* (1917), *Strange Marriage* (1930), *Three Women*, and *Anne Page*.

Although Syrett says nothing in her autobiography about her own exposure to turn-of-the-century utopian and reformist socialism, the references to both are extensive in her fiction – as is her critique of their highly conservative gender politics. *Drender's Daughter*, for example, takes issue with socialist eugenics by exposing the misguidedness of a country gentleman-turned-Tolstoyan's scheme to raise his bailiff's daughter as the perfect wife. Not only does Nancy Drender turn out to be the illegitimate daughter of an aesthete roué (so much for her pure working-class background); she grows up deeply resentful of her guardian/husband's interest in disciplining her into perfect submission to his will. Leonard Chetwynd's utopian reform scheme for the village near his estate may make him a middle-class radical. But his gender politics are a throwback to high Victorian gender ideology.

The Victorians and *Rose Cottingham Married*, the pair of novels Syrett wrote in the mid-1910s about a young middle-class girl who marries a working-class socialist, extend Syrett's critique of socialist gender politics to "gradualist" socialism as well. Her heroine, Rose Cottingham, makes an entrée into an only slightly fictionalized version of London's *Yellow Book* "set" as a writer, is quickly disillusioned by its "sort of mania for trying to shock people, and for turning things upside down," "converts" to socialism, and falls in love with John Derring, a socialist working toward the establishment of a labour party.[26] Against the advice of her middle-class 'Yellow Book' friends – "you are an artist, not a social reformer," a friend notes (109) – Rose first becomes active in a working-class women's club organization and then marries Derring. She quickly finds herself in a more rigidly gendered and gender-segregated world than any she has inhabited to date. Not only does her new husband believe that "the Woman Question should and can wait till more pressing matters are settled" (260); political debate of any kind at all is considered off-limits to the wives of her husband's political cohorts.

In the first four months of her marriage, Rose quickly comes "to be aware that in the class she had entered, women were negligible quantities whenever serious discussions were on foot, and her early attempts to join in the conversation met with such speedy discouragement that she had long ago desisted" (265). John Derring is clearly "not anxious to share with her the serious side of his life." Moreover, he is contemptuous of her modest fame as a novelist; or rather, he is contemptuous of fiction-writing itself, viewing novels as "only the playthings of the rich" (266). At least in part, as Rose surreptitiously observes, this attitude stems from "jealousy and fear of his wife's superior education" (281). But when Derring hires a "boorish product of the new educational system for women" (281) to work at Rose's desk in their home on the question of proper working-class housing, she finally challenges him openly: "I didn't understand then [i.e., when she married him] that your socialism implied drudgery for the women, while the men [and middle-class bluestockings] did all the intellectual work. I married you to work with you, not to live in the kitchen" (283).

John Derring's working-class background makes him a fairly unusual character in Syrett's fiction. More often than not, the socialists she writes about are men and women of the middle- or upper-middle-classes who have taken on the cause of the working classes. Whether she is writing about an organic intellectual or about middle-class radicals such as

Leonard Chetwynd in *Drender's Daughter*, though, Syrett is consistently
critical of social reformers who presume to know better than the working class itself what the latter needs or wants. Rejecting, as noted above,
"progressive" eugenics, she rejects as well both radical and reformist
socialist educationalism.

The Jam Queen, for example, revolves around the conflict between
Frederick Benn, an Oxford-educated young gentleman who proclaims
that "capitalism [is] the unforgiveable sin" and proposes to "devote his life
to the cause of Socialism," and his aunt, the eponymous Jam Queen, an
ex-Houndsditch match factory worker who married into money and then
made a fortune making that staple of British consumerism: jam.[27] Mrs.
Quilter is willing to support him (at the handsome rate of two thousand
pounds a year) while he and his fiancée make themselves "instruments
for help in this evil world of greed and capitalism, and money-grubbing"
(89). Yet she refuses to support his Institute, a barely fictionalized Toynbee
Hall that is to serve as a "lighthouse," a "beacon of light, to lighten mental darkness," to factory workers such as her own, he argues. Frederick
dismisses a friend's objections to his characterization of his aunt's "blind
prejudices... [and] her lack of faith" in his utopian scheming (153).[28] He
is brought up short only after he is caught in a scheme to swindle her into
supporting the Institute, and his aunt offers the following reminiscences
as she bails him out. What first "saved" her from her marginal existence
as a match factory child worker, she concedes, was a pub owner's kind-
ness to her in teaching her to read. After meeting her future husband
in an entertainment gallery, she set herself still higher educational goals.
Although Frederick has accused her of refusing to support any kind of
"big coordinated scheme in which the individual perishes after working
for the good of the race," her success as an entrepreneur should in fact
be proof of her "brains for a big scheme" (234). Yet she chides him for his
naively optimistic faith in "big coordinated [reform] schemes" and the
orchestration of social change through education by noting the following
about the children with whom she worked as a child.

In that Houndsditch match factory there were fifty girls and boys whose opportunities, or lack of them, were equal to mine. I have been at pains to trace their
careers. Their grandchildren are now in Board Schools, and not one of them,
in three generations, has ever risen above the rank of a domestic servant, or an
operator of some description. (265)

"I know," she warns him, "that the needs of nine-tenths of [the people] and, for
that matter, of nine-tenths of the world, are simple, material needs... I wanted
just as much learning as would make it not impossible to be rich, so that I should

never be cold and hungry again" (265–6). She will continue to make charitable contributions, she observes. But "I will not trouble about the educational faddist," she concludes before cutting him out of her will (267).

If Syrett is critical of socialist educational "faddism," she is even more critical of emergent alternatives to these attempts to continue a nineteenth-century tradition of working-class auto-didacticism. Specifically, she views socialists' increasingly exclusive focus on parliamentary politics and their willingness to promote a narrowly economic theory of culture as dangerously limiting and inappropriately dismissive of visual and literary art's cultural work. The fact that Leonard Chetwynd, in *Drender's Daughter*, and John Derring, in *Rose Cottingham Married*, are both absolutely lacking in aesthetic sensibility is a strong indication of their limitations of character. John Derring's defensive disdain for book-learning – even toward an education in classic Marxist theory – and his naive belief that "what I've learnt by personal experience" will provide him with a sufficient basis of argument in political debate make his effectiveness as a political leader still more suspect (294). Rather than simply renouncing parliamentary socialism and endorsing a different form of socialist instead, though, *Rose Cottingham Married* traces Rose's gradual disenchantment with all forms of organized politics. Acknowledging to herself that "humanity, writ large, no longer appealed to her, and that she "cared more for books, for pictures, for music, for amusing, stimulating talk with her equals than for any socialistic theories in the world," she withdraws, albeit somewhat ambivalently, from her husband's circle of political influence and absorbs herself again in fiction-writing.

Reclaiming her life as an artist need not be viewed, however, as an entirely conservative or reactionary move to separate art from politics and claim some sort of ground "above" politics for art. Instead, as Rose's successful enlargement of John Derring's world view through his exposure to *her* circle of artist friends in the last third of *Rose Cottingham Married* would suggest, and as her comments in *The Sheltering Tree* about her own fiction-writing as a kind of war work also reinforces, Syrett views art as a means of engagement with the world, not an escape from it. Notably, though, it is a means of individualized engagement with the world, not a function of collective activism.

This is, importantly, where Syrett's critique of socialism dovetails with her critique of both feminist collectivism and the modernist avant-garde as well. Syrett was never an activist for women's suffrage. In fact, the references to organized feminism in her fiction are as negative as those to socialist organizations in her fiction, suggesting that she was suspicious of any and all political movements because of her concern for the way individuals are co-opted into dissenting orthodoxies – which can still be orthodoxies, even if they position themselves in opposition to institutionalized centers of power. Victorian bluestockings and Victorian educational reforms are presented very critically, for example, in *The Victorians*. Nor does suffrage activism capture the imagination of Syrett's heroines. In *Drender's Daughter* Rose Derring is skeptical of her friend Helen Ambrose's renunciation of the suffrage movement once "a mad, hysterical, unbalanced element" creeps in and suffragists resort to "undignified" behavior; she associates this decision with Helen's abandonment of Rose as a child when the latter behaved, according to Helen, outrageously.[29] Although she sustains a certain amount of guilt regarding her political quietism, Rose Cottingham refuses to throw herself into either the suffrage movement or her husband's Labour Party campaign. Instead, she insists upon John's and Helen's recognition of her deliberate self-positioning as "a non-combatant" (445).

In one sense, this term aptly describes as well Syrett's heroines' characteristic relationship with the modernist avant-garde, as the latter is figured in novels such as *Anne Page, Troublers of the Peace, The Jam Queen*, and *Three Women*. Cubism, Fauvism, and other avant-garde "isms" make frequent – but typically very marginalized – appearances in Syrett's work; most often they are something that *other* people are involved in, not her heroines. Rosamund Steele, for example, the third of the three female characters in *Three Women*, is a Fauvist whose artwork is never observed by either Phillida Thorold or Katharine Verney, the art connoisseurs and business partners featured in the novel's main plot line. Anne Page, the eponymous heroine of Syrett's novel about a woman who hosted a salon in Paris during the 1860s before retiring to a tiny, and terribly hidebound, English village, notes with relative equanimity and mild amusement a younger generation of artists' contempt for her seemingly conventional life and their failure to appreciate her artful gardens and domestic landscapes in the novel's final scene. Joan Wickham in *Troublers of the Peace* is unusual among Syrett's heroines in being immersed, for a time, in Futurism; but, as shall be discussed further below, she quickly withdraws from this circle, choosing to opt out of the sexual as well as the artistic experimentation being conducted by her avant-garde friends.

In another sense, however, Syrett is anything but a "non-combatant" *vis-à-vis* the modernist avant-garde. If her characters typically observe the avant-garde's grand assault on bourgeois social and aesthetic values from the sidelines – and typically, as well, from the vantage point of a slightly older generation – they are not without criticisms of its tactics. If Syrett objects to socialist and feminist collectivism for their cooptation of the individual, she is equally suspicious of avant-garde aesthetic orthodoxy, particularly as practiced hypocritically by artists who claim to be de-institutionalizing art. As Anne Page notes, there is something curiously "business-like" about all the "new doctrines." There is "no fire" about any of them; "they are all eminently cool, calculating, and dull," in spite of the self-presentation as the antithesis of bourgeois commercialism.[30] *Three Women* pursues a similar line of critique when a minor character notes how the self-styled radicalism of a young couple is nothing more than conformity to one of two possible "schools" of "modern" thought:

> Not a symptom of anything escapes them. They behave inscrutably, and I watch with unholy curiosity. Is it a platonic attachment, I ask myself, and hope for the worst. Are they reading Tolstoy, and soaring into unimpassioned realms of philosophy? Or, on the other hand – and here I hope for the best – are they trampling underfoot all the "man-made," vulgar, stifling conventions, and "living" their little lives, and all that sort of thing? Is it, in fact, Shaw and Carpenter they're reading, or is it Tolstoy? (51).

A related feature of Syrett's characterization of the modernist avant-garde is her concern for the disassociation of avant-garde style from radical politics. At the opening of Frederick Benn's Institute in *The Jam Queen*, for example, porters "in Futurist livery," charwomen "in cubist attire," bath officials, and gymnasium instructors in black silk tights mill about among the factory workers who have been gathered for the occa-sion (201). The latter, as Frederick's fiancée Betty notes, neither "knew [nor] cared for what purpose this great building had arisen in their midst" (157). "'Those people outside the institute,' she keeps wondering. 'Were they typical? If so, what was the use? *Was* there any use?,'" she asks herself, though she also "tries to stifle her doubts" (157). Betty's en-dorsement of Frederick's Utopian socialist scheming in *Drender's Daughter* ultimately results not in the success of the Institute but in their retire-ment to the Malvern Hills to lead a "Simple Life." As is also the case in Syrett's presentation of Rosamund Steele as a Fauvist whose studio allows her to entertain a series of lovers privately in the afternoons and to live "mid-way between Bohemia and the set vaguely labeled 'Society,'" avant-garde style serves as a convenient disguise for nothing more radical or revolutionary than bohemian sexual behavior (64). Scholars such as Susan Rubin Suleiman and John Lucas have urged us to recognize when the allegedly radical poetics of modernism mask a deeply conservative politics.³¹ In Syrett's fiction, the deeply conservative *sexual* politics of the "moderns" is never simply a matter of women's victimization. Rather, the political or aesthetic stylishness of women such as Rosamund (*Three Women*) and Betty (*Drender's Daughter*) can be a convenient disguise for a very old-fashioned Victorian sort of sexual entrepreneurialism – à la Thackeray's Becky Sharp – that enables them to channel all their ambitions through their sexual control of men and keep the latter, as Betty notes of her fiancé at the end of *Drender's Daughter*, "completely in tow" (267). The truly "modern" women in Syrett's fiction are those, like Phillida Thorold and Katharine Verney in *Three Women*, who mock "the theory of love as 'a woman's whole existence'" and work to achieve artistic and economic autonomy (29).

If the masking of conservative politics by avant-garde style is an issue of concern in many of Syrett's novels, her characters also question the modernist avant-garde's theoretical inconsistencies. After her friend Winifred visits to explain why she is "dropping out" of Bernard Coulson's "set" in *Troublers of the Peace*, Joan Wickham is left to reflect on her own ambivalence about the "clever and brilliant" men and women with whom she has been associating, alienating herself from her mother while also neglecting her studies in the process:

Joan understood ... and sympathized with Winifred's distress about the 'muddle' in which she found herself as the result of conflicting arguments and constantly varying 'convictions.' She, too, often found herself in a whirl. What did they really want, all these champions of advanced thought amongst whom she perforce classed herself? Towards what goal, if any, were they, and she among them, moving? She had heard, and taken part in, conversations upholding by turns standards of mutually exclusive moral and unmoral conduct and outlook upon life. What did it all mean? Did it mean anything except a welter of crude undigested ideas with nothing so definite as an opinion among them? (98–99)

Joan listens silently to Bernard Coulson's grand pronouncements about the avant-garde's war on "all the sickly rot that passes for art and morality" among her mother's generation of artists and Society friends (39). She chooses not to respond in particular to his accusations that women are responsible for the stifling "herd" mentality that continues to deaden the world:

"You women will never do anything that matters, because in your hearts you're afraid of violence ... [O]f course you're going to tell me that you've broken windows, and that sort of footle ... That's mere childishness. I'm talking about real 'frightfulness' in the German sense of the word ... It's violence we want ...

Revolt. Destruction. A clean sweep of old-fashioned lumber . . . There would be elbow-room then, for real creative genius and for the men and women with free spirits. But there's not enough courage. You women, especially, are afraid. You funk it. You'd continue to let the herd rule the world!" (38–9)

Although it will take her most of the rest of the novel to extricate herself successfully from his influence, she has enough independence of mind even at this point in the novel to wonder momentarily "what kind of world Bernard looked fit to rule" (39). He rants about supermen, and "she knew he was very clever – but he was so small. So undersized! His ugliness repelled her" (39). Moreover, while what he says "[is] always desperately interesting," she can't ignore the inconsistencies among his many pronouncements (40).

Novels such as *Anne Page*, *Strange Marriage*, and *Three Women* are highly critical as well of the modernist avant-garde's refusal to find value in "traditional" aesthetic and social conventions – both Victorian and Edwardian traditions in particular and anything pre-twentieth century more generally. Literary modernism's anxiety of influence has been a subject of much discussion among scholars, as has its denigration of its most immediate rivals, the Edwardians. As noted earlier, modernists never simply make evaluative distinctions between the work of earlier artists and their own. They invent literary history as a theory of plate tectonics, describing their own emergence out of the total destruction of "outworn conventions," as Bernard Coulson puts it in *Troublers of the Peace* (40). To a female protégé's question, "What would you have us destroy," he responds with a classic avant-garde rhetoric against the institutionalization of art that shocks Joan Wickham: "Most of the things in London. The Albert Memorial. The British Museum. The National Gallery. St. Paul's . . . One could go on indefinitely . . . [T]hey're all lumber. Symbols of outworn conventions. Impediments to progress. Destruction is the first step to power" (40). Joan is actually quite unique among Syrett's protagonists insofar as she is willing – for a time – to endorse this kind of oppositionality, this exaggeration of difference from both the past and from the contemporary status quo. This particular scene, for example, becomes "one of the test cases" for her, pitting social propriety, familial obligation, and allegiance to an "old" aesthetic against her newfound social and aesthetic allegiances to Coulson and his friends (41). When the discussion turns to making arrangements to attend "Marinetti's lecture next week," Joan is tormented privately by her internal conflict: should she keep a promise to her mother to attend the latter's dinner party, or should she join her friends for supper at the Café Royal and the lecture? Notably, this conflict is pitched in terms of aesthetic as well as social choices: "Was she to stay at home and listen to Mr. Franklin talking about Whistler when she might be learning really important things from Marinetti" (41). "She would rather have refused," the narrator notes. "It seemed mean to break her promise to her mother," and "it would be difficult to get out of the engagement." But her conviction that she will be learning "really important things from Marinetti" overrides her sense of familial obligations. She can't enjoy the irony here: that Whistler is being cast as a late Victorian fuddy-duddy along with the other "dull old men and women" her mother accuses "you young people" of despising (21).

An interest in responding to modernist mis-characterizations of Edwardian and Victorian traditionalism powers the plotting of *Anne Page* as well, which takes a stock Victorian character – the aging virgin spinster – and fleshes her out with a complexity and an unconventionality modernists never associate with the Victorian period. When the reader is first introduced to Anne Page, twenty years have passed since her affair with a French artist, and she is hosting a dinner party at her country estate in Dymfield, at which she introduces one of her ex-lover's Parisian artist friends, now a famous artist himself, to some of her neighbors, the rector of her parish church, the village doctor, and their wives. The women are very surprised to learn that this elegant Parisian is an old friend of Anne's, surprised, too, to realize that she is a "brilliant conversationalist," capable of holding her own in "the sort of conversation [about literature and art] to which Dymfield was unaccustomed" (13). As the doctor's wife notes, it is difficult to reconcile this "new view of her hostess" with the "Miss Page who would spend hours in discussing the organization of a mothers' meeting, of a local flower show, of a Church bazaar" (14). As the doctor notes on a separate occasion, she is a "curious anomaly": she is capable of both maintaining friendly relations with Carfax, the archtypally closed-minded village rector, and making reference to Huysmans's *À Rebours* when characterizing a color scheme in her gorgeous garden. "Huysmans, a country practice, and Carfax – and you! It's an amazing world. I hope some intelligent Being doesn't miss the exquisite humour of many human juxtapositions" (81–2).

Anne changes the subject abruptly rather than respond to the doctor's comment, and the narrator does not interject to confirm or deny his observations. But Syrett's point is made nonetheless: at fifty-seven, Anne Page is a worldly aesthete who lives comfortably among the stolid, unworldly gentry of Dymfield. She is capable of speaking intelligently about both avant-garde French art and mundane village affairs. She has a past that would be scandalous if it were known, yet she leads the life of a Victorian Lady Bountiful, beloved of everyone in Dymfield, sought after to solve every personal and social problem that arises. Rather than defiantly differentiating herself from bourgeois values – by flaunting either her past or present ties to a cosmopolitan world of art and culture far from her tiny English village – she seems to live in accordance with the village's precepts. Her garden may remind her of "an elaborately arranged 'sensation' scheme, planned by that madman in *À Rebours*." But she reserves this observation for the one man in her immediate circle who can appreciate it, Dr. Dakin. And she explains the significance of this garden's having been planted in "homely natural flower[s]," English cottage garden flowers, that Huysmans's Des Esseintes "would have despised," to no one (81).

Elsewhere I have discussed this novel as a prime example of Syrett's inversion of *fin-de-siècle* aestheticism's characteristic figurations of art's autonomy from nature and women's degenerate fleshliness.[32] In novels such as *Strange Marriage* and *Three Women* as well as *Anne Page*, Syrett's female aesthetes refute what Linda Hughes has termed "dominant masculine aestheticism's" standard pattern of associations.[33] As in *Anne Page*, art is figured as a collaboration with nature, not an alternative to it: Anne's art *is* her garden, her house, and her elegantly aging self. And she cherishes the prosaic bourgeois realities of life in Dymfield every bit as much as she cherishes the fine paintings and furniture she has collected and her memories of other places and another life. She lives simultaneously in the mundane world of church bazaars and village socials and in a world of ideas and artistic genius. That no one in her immediate social circle guesses the real value of the art hanging on her walls does not keep her from enjoying it. Moreover, far from being like the Cumaean sybil, the prophetess who was granted eternal life but failed to ask for eternal youth invoked in T. S. Eliot's epigraph to *The Waste Land*, Anne ages not simply gracefully but beautifully, appearing more and more radiantly self-possessed to her old friend Fontenelle each time he visits her. In her dress of "grey-green and purple" that "might have been suggested by the lavender borders" of her Shakespearean garden in the novel's opening scene, she commands our attention as an "artist in life" (4). Having made "a perfect memory for herself" (231) of her three-year affair with René Dampierre, she now lives in perfect visual and emotional harmony in a quaint country village that is as narrow-minded morally and aesthetically as its thatched roofs and cottage gardens are stereotypically English.

The point to be emphasized here is that Syrett's attempt to counter the counterdiscourse of *fin-de-siècle* aestheticism incorporates a response to high modernism's caricatures of Victorian and Edwardian conventionality as well. Unlike her more influential avant-garde contemporaries, Syrett associates genuine artistic sensibility *with* bourgeois culture rather than setting it entirely apart from dominant culture or insisting upon its inevitable opposition to bourgeois norms. In Syrett's view, artistic sensibility is not entirely compatible with bourgeois culture: Anne Page lives in the country, but she does not bury herself among the narrow-minded *petite bourgeoisie* of her aptly named village, Dymfield. Similarly, Jenny Ferris, the protagonist of *Strange Marriage*, falls in love with a handsome but ordinary young country gentleman and bears his child – yet realizes she would be painfully lonely married to him, given his inability to share her intellectual and artistic passions. Phillida Thorold and Katharine Verney do business with the American soap magnate intent on purchasing all the trappings of nobility, but their own connoisseurship is carefully distinguished from his crass, *nouveau-riche* conspicuous consumptionism, while their extra-marital sexual affairs are never discovered by their Society friends.

Notably, even if these female aesthetes do not live their lives entirely in accordance with *petit bourgeois* standards of morality, they are not outspokenly critical of bourgeois culture either. Anne Page, for example, does not share the vicar's closed-mindedness; but she never challenges him directly – and her influence over him is all the more powerful for its invisibility to him. Although Jenny Ferris conceives a child out of wedlock, she finds a way to shelter him within a traditional legal marriage, while discovering her own as well as her husband's sexual and artistic creativity in the process. And Phillida and Katharine's unconventionality, as suggested above, goes entirely unnoticed by their peers. In Syrett's novels, in other words, scandal is avoided by her heroines – not because her female aesthetes do not behave scandalously but because they do so without flaunting their defiance of bourgeois social and sexual norms, without engaging in the oppositional politics practiced by both late Victorian male aesthetes and the modernist avant-garde. These thoroughly "modern" (if not modernist) women see the value of radical aesthetics, they live their radical gender politics, yet they still want to have a decent house with a nice garden and a life free of violence.

In *Anne Page* if not in the other novels discussed above, the quietness of these female aesthetes' rebellions from not only Victorian and Edwardian but also from avant-garde convention is a tribute to

Shakespeare's "sweet Anne Page." Without any of the bold fancifulness of Shakespeare's play (and without any help from an older generation of women, for Syrett's Anne Page plays the roles of both Mrs. Page *and* her daughter in this novel), Syrett's soft-spoken heroine manages to debunk the Falstaffs of her world, whether they are village vicars or famous French artists. To borrow Shakespeare's language, she "pinch[es]" away at the art world's considerable misogyny – but she is never oppositional.[34] This stance needs to be understood finally, I would like to suggest, not as a tribute to Shakespeare (whom Syrett incorporates into a feminized tradition of landscape gardening, by the way, rather than celebrating as any kind of transhistorical and universal figure of "genius") but as an Edwardian woman writer's survival strategy. Given what happened to Syrett's promising career as a playwright in 1902, we need be neither surprised nor overly critical of her refusal to play oppositional politics. We should instead appreciate the subtlety with which her middlebrow Edwardian novels "talk back" to a hegemonic high-culture discourse of aesthetics.

Syrett was never a major player in the London literary scene, either in the 1890s or subsequently. She never enjoyed, or suffered, the kind of meteoric success and notoriety that other women writers who debuted in the 1890s experienced. Moreover, as noted earlier, unlike her friend May Sinclair, she is not an Edwardian whose work benefited from association with literary modernism mid-career. Nor was her work "ghosted" by a major modernist, as was the case, as Schaffer has argued, with Virginia Woolf's extensive unacknowledged borrowings from Alice Meynell. Nonetheless, I would suggest, Syrett's long if not "distinguished" career can help us understand the Edwardian middle-brow publishing world in which women such as these worked, a world occluded entirely by modernist histories of the period. Recent attempts to rethink "the great divide" between high and low culture have both enhanced and greatly altered our mappings of turn-of-the-twentieth-century literary and cultural history. But there is a great deal of work still to be done on this other cultural space, a space that complicates familiar, easy, oppositions of modernist high and low culture, a space inhabited by writers and a reading public with a more sophisticated appreciation of aesthetics – and a more critical view of the modernist avant-garde – than the latter's contemptuous characterizations of both the Edwardian era and the vast publishing world lying outside the modernist "submarket" would suggest.[35]

NOTES

1. Ezra Pound, "The New Sculpture," *The Egoist* 1, 4 (16 February 1914), 68; as reprinted in Baechler, Litz, and Longenbach (eds.), *Ezra Pound's Poetry and Prose: Contributions to Periodicals, Volume One: 1902–1914*, p. 222.
2. Hapgood and Paxton (eds.), *Outside Modernism*, pp. vii, viii.
3. Janice Radway, *A Feeling for Books: The Book-of-the-Month Club, Literary Taste, and Middle-Class Desire* (Chapel Hill: University of North Carolina Press, 1997), p. 219.
4. bell hooks, *Talking Back: Thinking Feminist, Thinking Black* (Boston, M.A.: South End Press, 1989).
5. Syrett notes in her autobiography that Clement Scott, a reviewer for the *Daily Telegraph*, objected to her female protagonist's decision to have an affair with a married man; Scott also ruined Syrett's own sexual reputation by insinuating that the play was autobiographical. Thus, even though Max Beerbohm wrote enthusiastically about Syrett's play in the *Morning Post*, the St. James Theatre decided to cancel its run, rather than "sully the purity" of the theatre (*The Sheltering Tree* [London: G. Bles, 1939], p. 125). Syrett was subsequently asked to resign her teaching job after a student's mother read Scott's review. Subsequent references to *The Sheltering Tree* will be cited parenthetically in the text.
6. For a complete bibliography of Syrett's work see Jill Owen, "Netta Syrett: A Chronological, Annotated Bibliography of Her Works, 1890–1940," *Bulletin of Bibliography* 45, 1 (1988), 8–14.
7. Bonnie J. Robinson notes that Syrett's father was a silk mercer; at the age of 11 she left a "financially privileged home in Landsgate, Kent, to attend England's first high school for girls, the famous London North Collegiate. After four years there, she went on to the Cambridge Higher Local, where she prepared for a teaching career." (Robinson, "Netta Syrett," in William B. Thesing [ed.] *Dictionary of Literary Biography 153, British Short-Fiction Writers, 1880–1914: The Realist Tradition*, [Detroit: Gale Research, 1994], p. 357.)
8. See Regenia Gagnier, *Subjectivities: A History of Self-Representation in Britain, 1832–1920* (Oxford University Press, 1991), p. 168.
9. "Sheltering tree" is a phrase Syrett borrows from Coleridge's 1823 poem, "Youth and Age"; a line from this poem, "friendship is a sheltering tree," appears as the epigraph to the autobiography.
10. Roland Barthes, *S/Z* (New York: Hill and Wang, 1974), pp. 4–6.
11. Sandra Kemp, Charlotte Mitchell, and David Trotter (eds.), *Edwardian Fiction: An Oxford Companion* (Oxford University Press, 1997), p. xv. See also Anthea Trodd, *Women's Writing in English: Britain 1900–1945* (London and New York: Longman, 1998), especially ch. 2, "The Conditions of Women's Writing"; Joseph McAleer, *Popular Reading and Publishing in Britain 1914–50* (Oxford: Clarendon Press, 1992); Michael Joseph, *The Commercial Side of Literature* (London: Hutchinson, 1925); Claude Cockburn, *Bestseller: The Books that Everyone Read 1900–1939* (London: Sidgwick and Jackson, 1972).

12. See Ian Norrie, *Mumby: Publishing and Bookselling in the Twentieth Century*, 6th edn (London: Bell and Hyman, 1982), especially "Fathers and Sons," pp. 28–39. Anthea Trodd also notes that "in the Edwardian period and thereafter publishers were torn between two particular models for their relations with their writers. One was that of the traditional paternalist, who nurtured his stable of talent, exemplified by John Murray's hopes for Rose Macaulay . . . The other model was that of the risk-taker backing a hunch on an unknown writer, as Fisher Unwin did when they gambled on the often rejected manuscript of Ethel M. Dell's *The Way of an Eagle* (1912)" (*Women's Writing in English*, p. 33).

13. See Barbara Green, *Spectacular Confessions: Autobiography, Performative Activism, and the Sites of Suffrage 1905–1938* (New York: St. Martin's Press, 1997); Wendy Mulford, "Socialist-Feminist Criticism: A Case Study, Women's Suffrage and Literature 1906–14," in Peter Widdowson (ed.), *Re-Reading English* (London and New York: Methuen, 1982), pp. 179–92; Janet Lyon, *Manifestos: Provocations of the Modern* (Ithaca and London: Cornell University Press, 1999), pp. 92–123; and Lisa Tickner, *The Spectacle of Women: Imagery of the Suffrage Campaign, 1907–1914* (University of Chicago Press, 1988).

14. Robinson, "Netta Syrett," p. 361. Margaret Stetz and Mark Samuels Lasner have also located un-catalogued play scripts in the Toronto Public Library.

15. See Edward H. Dodd, Jr., *The First Hundred Years. A History of the House of Dodd, Mead 1839–1939* (New York: Dodd, Mead & Co.,1939); Maureen Duffy, *A Thousand Capricious Chances. A History of the Methuen List 1889–1989* (London: Methuen, 1989); Raymond L. Kilgour, *Messrs. Roberts Brothers Publishers* (Ann Arbor: University of Michigan Press, 1952); Robert Lusty, *Bound to be Read* (Garden City: Doubleday & Co., 1976); George Haven Putnam, *Memories of a Publisher 1865–1915* (New York and London: G. P. Putnam's Sons, 1915); Frank Swinnerton, *Authors and the Book Trade* (London: G. Howe, 1932); Swinnerton, *The Reviewing and Criticism of Books* (London: J. M. Dent and Sons, 1939); Philip Unwin, *The Publishing Unwins* (London: Heinemann, 1972); Oliver Warner, *Chatto and Windus: A Brief Account of the Firm's Origin, History and Development* (London: Chatto and Windus, 1973). See also Katherine Lyon Mix, *A Study in Yellow: The Yellow Book and Its Contributors* (Lawrence: University of Kansas Press, 1960); Margaret D. Stetz and Mark Samuels Lasner, *England in the 1890s: Literary Publishing at the Bodley Head* (Washington, D.C.: Georgetown University Press, 1990); and Stetz and Lasner, *The Yellow Book: A Centenary Exhibition* (Cambridge, M.A.: Houghton Library, 1994).

16. Unfortunately, few of the documents that might make it possible to learn more about Syrett's relationships with her publishers have been archived. To know something about the complex mergers and acquisitions in the industry during this period, however, is to wonder whether and how Syrett either benefited from or lost out in these transitions. Hutchinson, for example, which was known in the industry for its huge output and its rejection of manuscripts that were "too highbrow," had purchased Skeffington, a small

house specializing in religious works, in either 1919 or the early 1920s. Did Hutchinson acquire Syrett, who had published both *The God of Chance* (1920) and *The Wife of a Hero* (1918) with Skeffington, in that process? The answer to that question will remain unknown because Hutchinson's records were destroyed in a famous Paternoster Row fire in 1940. Did Dodd, Mead "discover" Syrett through its purchase of the American branch of John Lane in 1922, subsequently publishing four of her titles, *Fairy Doll* (1922), *Moon out of the Sky* (1932), *Portrait of a Rebel* (1931), and *Strange Marriage* (1931) in fairly quick succession, the latter being Syrett's retrospective tribute to the Yellow Book "scene" of the 1890s? This too can't be known, because *The First Hundred Years: A History of the House of Dodd, Mead 1839–1939* fails even to list Syrett as one of its authors.

17. Suzanne Clark, "The Unwarranted Discourse: Sentimental Community, Modernist Women, and the Case of Millay," *Genre* 20 (1987), 139, 133. This essay was subsequently incorporated into Clark's book-length study, *Sentimental Modernism*.

18. See Lyn Pykett, "Writing Around Modernism: May Sinclair and Rebecca West," *Outside Modernism*, pp. 103–22; and Suzanne Raitt, *May Sinclair: A Modern Victorian* (Oxford: Clarendon Press, 2000).

19. Felski, *Beyond Feminist Aesthetics*, p. 161.

20. Schenck, "Exiled by Genre," pp. 230–1.

21. Talia Schaffer, "Writing a Public Self: Alice Meynell's 'Unstable Equilibrium,'" in Ann Ardis and Leslie Lewis (eds.), *Women's 'Experience' of Modernity* (forthcoming, Baltimore: Johns Hopkins University Press), pp. 18, 2.

22. Ann Ardis, Toward a Redefinition of 'Experimental Writing': Netta Syrett's Realism, 1908–1912," in Alison Booth (ed.), *Famous Last Words: Changes in Gender and Narrative Closure* (Charlottesville and London: University Press of Virginia, 1993), pp. 259–79; Ardis, "Netta Syrett's Aestheticization of Everyday Life: Countering the Counterdiscourse of Aestheticism," in Talia Schaffer and Kathy Alexis Psomiades (eds.), *Women and British Aestheticism*, pp. 233–50.

23. Susan Stanford Friedman, "Forbidden Fruits of Lesbian Experimentation," unpublished essay (as quoted by Schenck, "Exiled by Genre," p. 245).

24. Beckett writes of Joyce's "Work in Progress": "Here form *is* content, content *is* form. You complain that this stuff is not written in English. It is not written at all. It is not to be read – or rather it is not only to be read. It is to be looked at and listened to. His writing is not *about* something; *it is that something itself*" (*Disjecta* [New York: Grove, 1984], p. 27).

25. For further discussion of Hull in this context, see my "E. M. Hull, Mass Market Romance and the New Woman Novel in the Early Twentieth Century," *Women's Writing* 3, 3 (Autumn 1996), 287–96.

26. Syrett, *The Victorians* (London: Unwin, 1915); republished as *Rose Cottingham* (Chicago: Academy Press, 1978), p. 101. Subsequent references will be made parenthetically in the text.

27. Syrett, *The Jam Queen* (London: Methuen, 1914), pp. 82, 83. Subsequent references will be made parenthetically in the text.
28. His friend notes: "Here is a woman who from the smallest beginnings has built up one of the largest and certainly the best-conducted businesses of the time in England. She concerns herself with the health of her work-people. The factories are models of all that such places should be, and often are not, in the way of light, and ventilation, and general sanitation. The employees are well paid" (p. 126).
29. Syrett, *Drender's Daughter* (New York: John Lane, 1911; London: Chatto and Windus, 1911), p. 445. Subsequent references will be made parenthetically in the text.
30. Syrett, *Anne Page* (London: Chatto and Windus, 1908), p. 315.
31. Suleiman, *Subversive Intent*; John Lucas, "From Realism to Radicalism: Sylvia Townsend Warner, Patrick Hamilton and Henry Green in the 1920s," Hapgood and Paxton (eds.), *Outside Modernism*, pp. 203–24.
32. Ardis, "Netta Syrett's Aestheticization of Everyday Life."
33. Linda Hughes, "A *Fin-de-Siècle* Beauty and the Beast: Configuring the Body in Works by 'Graham R. Tomson' (Rosamund Marriott Watson)," *Tulsa Studies in Women's Literature* 14, 1 (1995), 101.
34. The passage from *The Merry Wives of Windsor* to which I'm alluding here reads in full: "Fie on sinful fantasy!/Fie on lust and luxury!/Lust is but a bloody fire,/Kindled by unchaste desire,/Fed in heart, whose flames aspire,/As thoughts do blow them, higher and higher./Pinch him, fairies, mutually;/Pinch him for his villainy;/Pinch him, and burn him, and turn him about/Till candles and starlight and moonshine be out" (William Shakespeare, *The Merry Wives of Windsor*, ed. Giorgio Melchiori [Walton-on-Thames: T. Nelson, 2000], 5.5.90–102 [pp. 282–3]). See my "Netta Syrett's Aestheticization of Everyday Life" for discussion of Syrett's very deliberate de-Hellenization of Shakespeare and her characterization of a homegrown, country-based, "old-fashioned" *English* aestheticism that "talks back" to "decadent" European aestheticism.
35. Joyce Piell Wexler's term, as used in *Who Paid for Modernism? Art, Money, and the Fiction of Conrad, Joyce, and Lawrence* (Fayetteville: University of Arkansas Press, 1997).

CHAPTER 5

"Life is not composed of watertight compartments": the New Age's *critique of modernist literary specialization*

BLAST GRAMMAR,   BLESS CLICHE,
BLAST SPELLING,   BLESS BIG PRINT,
BLAST REASON,   BLESS BLOOD,
BLAST SENSE, SO   BLESS SELF, SO
BLAST THE NEW AGE.   BLESS WYNDY LEWIS.

C. H. Bechhöfer, "More Contemporaries," *New Age*, July 30, 1914[1]

Twinkle, twinkle, Ezra Pound,
Like a candle underground.
Cubes, potatoes, prunes and prisms
Summarise your witticisms...
Twinkle, twinkle, my NEW AGE;
Star shells burst on every page,
By whose light you boldly tilt
At the mills of England's guilt.

L'Hibou, *New Age*, July 15, 1915[2]

The advertising flyer for Brown University's "Modernist Journals Project" introduces this exciting, and massive, new digital research initiative by noting its commitment to "providing on-line editions of English-language journals that were important in shaping those modes of literature and art that came to be called modernist." "At the MJP site," the flyer continues,

readers will find keyword-searchable texts of modernist journals, as well as essays on general topics related to modernism, and discussions of particular publications and their historical and cultural background. Our first project is an edition of *The New Age: A Weekly Review of Politics, Literature and Art*, edited in London by A. R. Orage from 1907 to 1922. *The New Age* offered its readers an in-depth view of the political, social, and cultural landscape of England at the time. During the 15 years when A. R. Orage presided over the paper, it published many of England's best writers and became one of the chief organs for cultivating public opinion about modern art and literature.

On the one hand, by making a previously all-but-inaccessible archive available to many on-line researchers, digitalization of the *New Age* promises to facilitate the kind of "ric[h], thic[k]" historical contextualization that scholars such as Michael Levenson have described as one of the unique contributions of "the new modernist studies."[3] The *New Age* was indeed one of the most interesting political and literary journals of Edwardian Britain; moreover, it is an excellent source of information about the entire British newspaper industry in the early twentieth century because its range of references to dailies, weeklies, and monthly periodicals across the political and literary spectrum – from large-circulation dominant culture newspapers and periodicals such as the London *Times*, the *Spectator*, and the *Daily Mail*, to mid-range as well as small-circulation regional and special-interest literary and political weeklies and monthlies such as the *New Statesman*, the *Christian World*, the *Liverpool Courier*, the Bristol *Venture*, the *English Review*, and the *Clarion* – is truly extraordinary. Because of its commitment to reporting on "politics, literature and the arts" and its refusal to separate the aesthetic from the political sphere, its coverage is unusually synthetic as well.

On the other hand, the fundamental assumptions about the *New Age* as a *modernist* journal that saturate the MJP's promotional materials should give pause to anyone who has worked extensively in the *New Age* archives. Certainly it is easy to see how this characterization of the *New Age* has been perpetuated, given all the famous modernist manifestos redacted from its pages and published subsequently elsewhere under separate, and more prestigious, cover – in Sam Hynes's edition of T. E. Hulme's essays, *Further Speculations*, for example; in T. S. Eliot's *Literary Essays of Ezra Pound* as well as in the more recent and inclusive edition of his writings for periodicals, *Ezra Pound's Poetry and Prose: Contributions to Periodicals*.[4] To read the journal cover to cover, issue by issue, year after year, however, can leave a very different impression. For every article or letter to the editor or sample of modernist writing or art that is featured in its pages is counterbalanced by a parody or critique or countermanifesto. We are used to seeing modernist avant-gardists dismiss rival aesthetic traditions in intemperate and idiosyncratically colorful terms. But over and over again in the pages of the *New Age*, modernists themselves are critiqued with gusto, in feature articles, regular columns, letters to the editor, and the dialogue essays with which the periodical so often pursues its case about the need for "brilliant common sense."[5] If Netta Syrett "talks back" to the modernist avant-garde in her Edwardian middlebrow fiction, she does so quietly, and with a great deal of self-deprecation. By contrast, the *New Age* shouts its "quarrels" (as Orage himself describes them) with modernism.

Studies to date of the *New Age* have, alternately, either emphasized Orage's "catholic editorshop"[6] or described its evolution from Socialism to modernism in terms very similar to those frequently used to characterize the *Freewoman*'s transformation into the *Egoist*.[7] In his fascinating study of Orage's early involvement in the Leeds Art Club, Tom Steele, for example, describes the *New Age* as a vehicle for "such divergent emergent currents that it was almost impossible to label politically." Taking the opposite tack, Wallace Martin (one of the consulting editors for the Brown Modernist Journals Project), concentrates exclusively upon "those aspects of the magazine that are of enduring interest in relation to cultural history" – and assumes *a priori* that these are limited to, in turn, its promotion and subsequent rejection of (socialist) realism in drama and fiction (1908–1910) and its presentation of modernist movements in art (1911–1914).[8] I would like to suggest in this chapter that the *New Age*, as Orage himself insists, is anything but eclectic in its literary and social views. It was, indeed, determined to provide "some neutral ground where intelligences may meet on equal terms" in a public debate about politics, literature, and the arts, and it voices strongly its objections to monologic special-interest literary and political periodicals alike whenever possible because of their failure to do just that.[9] It was equally committed, though, to promoting Guild Socialism's unique theory of economic reorganization and to radicalizing turn-of-the-century Arts and Crafts and Clarion movement socialisms, which Guild Socialists perceived as, respectively, too complacent about art's association with luxury in a capitalist commodity culture and too willing to harness the lures of mass-market advertising in support of an allegedly revolutionary socialist cause. In other words, to call the *New Age* a modernist journal is to ignore its very unique political and aesthetic commitments to Guild Socialism, a radical fringe socialist movement in the early twentieth century in Britain that sought "the mould of a new civilization" in the creation of national labor guilds.[10] As this chapter will show, these commitments color the journal's presentation of modernist visual and literary art quite strikingly – and often quite negatively.

Insofar as one of the real strengths of literary modernism lies in its ability to incorporate its opposites, it could be argued that the *New Age*'s presentation of nonmodernist and even antimodernist material alongside modernist art and literature is precisely what makes this a quintessentially modernist journal. I would insist, however, on recognition of a crucial distinction between the journal's modernist *style* of presentation and its socialist politics, which are insistently and consistently differentiated from modernism's by the editors. Granted, the journal dedicates considerable real estate to the promotion of modernist art and literature. Nonetheless, the *New Age*'s willingness to feature work by critics and artists such as Pound, Lewis, and T. E. Hulme should not be confused with an unqualified endorsement. This is not to suggest that modernists weren't capable of mocking themselves, contradicting themselves, and changing their stances on any given topic. Rather, it is to emphasize that the *New Age* is a journal whose agenda is not contained by modernism's own anti-modernist impulses. As a proponent of Guild Socialism, Orage harbored the modernist avant-gardist for quite some time within the pages of the *New Age* – but he never unequivocally approved what he in fact terms its "fads," "absurd theories," and "charlatanism."[11]

"Good God, I have almost made them significant," he notes sarcastically in 1914 at the end of a review in which he ridicules fawning references to Pound and Imagism in a recent issue of the *Little Review*.[12] When the first issue of *Blast* had appeared several months earlier, he had written:

I can see now, from the appearance of "Blast" and from the number and quality of its probable victims, that THE NEW AGE must be more definite than ever in the future. To tell the truth, the work is at present incredibly difficult. Even to think straight in these days requires an effort; as the alienist often finds it hard to preserve his sanity among his patients.[13]

In reviewing the second issue of *Blast* almost exactly a year later, he details his specific disagreements with Wyndham Lewis, then throws down the gauntlet:

J'accuse Mr. Lewis of being, to the best of his ability, disloyal to Nature. We agree that Nature should not be imitated. The second commandment must be obeyed in art as well as in ethics. But we are hopelessly at variance when the next step is to be taken. Mr. Lewis is for creating a "Nature" of his own imagination. I am for perfecting the Nature that already exists in strenuous imperfection. He is for Vorticism; I am for the idealization of the actual. *It is worth quarrelling about.* (emphasis added)[14]

Orage's "quarrels" with modern avant-gardists are both reiterated and supplemented by the witty but nonetheless pointed criticisms offered by other contributors to the *New Age* – as exemplified by the poems featured as epigraphs to this chapter. The *New Age* can be canalized into the history of modernism, I would thus like to suggest, only by ignoring these very prominently displayed debates with and ribaldry at the expense of the modernist avant-garde. Undoubtedly, the *New Age* under Orage's editorship was an important venue of publication for these modernist critics and artists. What this chapter will demonstrate, though, is that the journal's commitment to the kind of "revival of the arts" Guild Socialists viewed as a "necessary factor in social salvation" (read, a socialist revolution) was never satisfied by modernist experimentalism.[15] The historical record this early twentieth-century socialist journal leaves us, of open, spirited, and acrimonious debate about art and art's role in culture, allows us to gain a much better sense of the competition among emergent aesthetic and political traditions animating British cultural life at the turn of the century than we will ever find in modernism's own histories of the period. The new modernist studies' historical recontextualizations of modernism must include awareness of such competition – if, that is, we're not to be accused of preserving modernism "in intellectual amber," to borrow Michael North's phrasing, retrospectively accomplishing "by critical consensus" modernism's "insulation from the cultural world into which it was introduced."[16]

"LET DERISION BE OUR WELCOME"

So be it. For I know that the dark comes before the light and that, like the gods, new movements usually come to birth hindparts foremost. I see, moreover, in imagism what perhaps the imagists themselves would be shocked to discern – the prefiguration of a more brilliant common sense than we have known before: common sense in the sphere of the aesthetic emotions. But until this side appears it is wise to laugh at the side now presented to us. *Let derision be our welcome.*
    "R. H. C.," "Readers and Writers", November 19, 1914
(emphasis added)[17]

Several examples of the *New Age*'s characteristic humor at the expense of the modernist avant-garde were featured as this chapter's epigraphs. But consider the following as well. Having published several of F. T. Marinetti's Futurist manifestos in 1913, the journal offers "A Post-Impressionist Parable" lampooning Futurism and Cubism on January 1, 1914, which traces, in the form of a parable, the "progress" of modern aesthetic ideologies from Impressionism through Cubism and Futurism and ends with the following dismissive remarks:

In course of time these two groups fell into controversy. But in order to win the public ear each wrote in the public language. So busy were they in mutual destruction that they had neither time nor energy for their peculiar practices. Thus they cancelled one another out, and mankind was restored to sanity.[18]

Publishing this broadside does not, however, preclude the publication of more of Marinetti's work. A translation of "Geometric and Mechanical Splendour in Words at Liberty" will be featured five months later, on May 7, 1914, without any kind of editorial over-voicing, positive or negative.[19] As is so often the case, though, the *New Age*'s presentation of avant-garde work is then counterposed again in the next week's issue, May 14, 1914, by a brilliant parody exposing the gender politics of this experimental writing:

FUTURISTICS A LA MARINETTI
AT THE RESTAURANT
Sinuosity and woman. Wine and barren passion. Waiters
    and the lusts of the flesh. Stagnation.
Cease, breath; and let me whirl in geometric splendour
    amongst the whizzing spheres.
A comma crawls upon the menu card. My sluggish heart
    faints at a full stop.
Joy! Geometric and mechanical joy! A half-brick –
    dear cube – sweet architectural slab – shatters the wide
    window, and in irrestible [*sic*] impetuosity hisses by me.
What triangles of space appear in yonder glass!
What parellely fissures! – opening parellelier fissures in
    my swelling heart!
A flying trapezoid of clear-cut glass severs my fair com-
    panion's jugular with a dispatch that defies Time
    and Space, while Lightning hides its head.
The scintillating perfection of the speedy act carries away
    my spirit like a feather in a hurricane.
A waiter clears up the bloody mess and removes
    the inanimate female.[20]

Four weeks later, on June 18, 1914, the journal offers yet another devastating, and hilarious, send-up of Futurism in "Futile-ism. Or, All Cackle and No Osses," one of a series of dialogue essays Charles Brookfarmer wrote that takes issue, on other occasions, with Fabian Socialism, the suffrage movement, Bernard Shaw's *Pygmalion*, and mysticism ("Mrs. Tism"). Reporting on Marinetti's and C. R. W. Nevinson's lectures about "Vital English Art" at the Doré Galleries six days earlier, Brookfarmer begins his essay by mocking the audience in attendance: "The hot room is full for the most part of elderly (passées?) ladies, including such half-forgotten crimes as Messrs. Cunninghame-Graham and Nevinson père." Then he savages the keynote speakers, mainly through very roughly edited quotations, parenthetical commentary, and descriptions of the audience's response. Both the ellipses and the parenthetical exclamations in the following are Brookfarmer's phrasings:

Mr. NEV.:...Also important from a commercial point of view...barbarians of the West End (some giggles)...putting a pony on Durbar Two...backwoods of Chelsea (more giggles) the modern artist must advertise...Selfridge's...materials are extremely expensive...Nobody listens to the singing of a corpse or the histrionics of a dead actor (more giggles)...virile, original, and, above all, English...(He reads the manifesto, in which occurs, "Immortality in art is a disgrace"!! As he cries, "Forward! hurrah for motors! hurrah for speed! hurrah for draughts! hurrah for lightning!" an assistant fires a small piece of magnesium wire. Tremendous Futurartistic effect. Then, "We call upon the English public to support, defend, and glorify the genius of the great Futurist painters or pioneers and advance-forces of vital English art: Atkinson, Bomberg, Epstein, Etchells, Hamilton, Nevinson [!!!], Roberts, Wadsworth, Wyndham Lewis." Mr. NEV. sits down amid laughter and shouting of names. MARINETTI rises and commences to wander on and on and on with much emphasis and gesture and mopping of sweaty brow.) (Exclamation marks in brackets in the original)[21]

By no means is Italian Futurism the only avant-garde movement singled out for this kind of treatment in the *New Age*. Cubism comes under fire, for example, not only in the "Post-Impressionist Parable" mentioned earlier but also each time T. E. Hulme weighs in to educate the *New Age* readers on the pleasures of contemporary art. Critics such as Wallace Martin have viewed Hulme's critiques of Walter Sickert and the representational artists he was promoting throughout the spring of 1914 as proof of the *New Age*'s commitment to modernist aesthetics. This ignores, however, the simple fact that Hulme himself is quite moderate in his initial presentation of "Contemporary Drawings." Readers familiar with the swagger and bluster of "Romanticism and Classicism" or "The Kind of Rubbish We Oppose" might be surprised by the patient and teacherly manner with which Hulme explains innovations in style and technique to *New Age* readers in this particular essay – without demanding their agreement with his own assessment. The jury is still out on contemporary artists' work, he insists. "You have before you a movement about which there is no crystallised opinion." And thus readers of the *New Age* will have "the fun of making your own judgments" about contemporary art.[22] The journal itself demands this kind of "fun," this level of independent judgment, from its readers because of its simultaneous publication of critics and artists on both sides of the current debate about representational versus abstract art. When, however, the *New Age* features Hulme's and Walter Sickert's and Anthony Ludovici's art criticism side by side in issue after issue; when it publishes in quick succession "Tom Titt"'s caricatures of Anthony Ludovici and Roger Fry, Will Dyson's cartoon, "Progress," and a host of verbal equivalents of these artists' visual mockery of modernism, the strong aftertaste of critique in its presentation of modernism is hard to miss.[23]

Given the journal's current reputation as a vehicle for modernism, the frequency with which proponents of modernism are challenged in letters to and from the editors as well as in leaders and columns might also seem surprising. Yet they are a very telling index of the skepticism with which readers and editors of the *New Age* greeted all of the feature articles propagandizing on behalf of the modernist avant-garde. Letters to the editor written in response to T. E. Hulme's essay, "Mr. Epstein and the Critics," sound a characteristic tone in this regard.[24] On January 8, 1914, Arthur E. Hight writes:

Sir – Could you not persuade Mr. T. E. Hulme to explain to us, in an Essay not "clumsy, hurriedly-written, and unrevised," "Why it is the duty of every honest man at the present moment to clean the world of these sloppy dregs of the Renaissance"? and especially why we shall benefit by substituting God Epstein for God Michelangelo. Some of us also would like to know with what credentials Mr. Hulme sets himself up as an Apostle, and rides his silly hobbyhorse into your classical columns, shouting his war-cry, "Modern feeling be damned!" when he ought, were he consistent, to be squatting naked in Easter Island surrounded by the pre-historic Art he admires, and dieting himself on roots and toadstools after the manner of savages.[25]

Douglas Fox Pitt chimes in next in the lineup of letters to the editor, taking issue with Hulme's *ad hominem* remarks about Ludovici's inability to appreciate Jacob Epstein's work:

Sir,–Although I admire Mr. Epstein's work, I do not admire the methods whereby he expects to inculcate appreciation of his work amongst the public. Mr. Epstein must know that he only makes himself ridiculous in threatening to blacken the eyes of an individual who dares to write adversely of his work. Mr. Hulme as the champion of Mr. Epstein was equally unfortunate in his choice of language toward Mr. Ludovici, who had ventured to refer to the sculptor as a "minor non-value-creating ego." Liberty to express oneself freely in marble implies equal liberty to criticise in writing.[26]

Two weeks later, two additional readers weigh in not so much in Ludovici's defense but to object to Hulme's rhetorical pugilism. "If I were Mr. Ludovici, I would run away," J.A.M.A. writes. "After due consideration, it seems clear to me that Mr. Hulme's remarks on 'plastic criticism' (see his 'hasty notes,' NEW AGE, December 25) resolves itself into a desire to re-mould the curvature of Mr. Ludovici's spine. Why? Because Mr. Ludovici talks sense, I suppose."[27]

Arthur Rose literalizes the metaphoric violence of the conflict over Jacob Epstein's work between the two art critics and develops the conceit still more elaborately when he offers the following suggestion:

If Mr. Hulme will state his weight, I will undertake to match him with a pugilist of equal weight. The said pugilist shall sincerely hold and state similar opinions of Mr. Epstein's art to those stated by Mr. Ludovici . . . And I will lend my garden for the contest. It is a very large and secluded garden, capable of accommodating as many of THE NEW AGE readers as would care to witness so interesting an encounter.

When the pugilist has punched Mr. Hulme's right eye into Mr. Hulme's left ear, and Mr. Hulme's remains have been carried to a surgery on a shutter (I have several shutters in the garden) . . . I mean when the contest is over, those present will have leave to foregather to see whether the result aids them to a better understanding and appreciation of art in general, and Mr. Epstein's art in particular.[28]

Wyndham Lewis makes his first appearance as an author in the *New Age* in letters to the editor on this conflict by describing Ludovici's work as the "grimest pig-wash vouchsafed at present to a public fed on husks."[29] When he begins providing feature articles for the journal, he too earns the ire of readers and editors alike. While C. H. Bechhöfer's "More Contemporaries," an excerpt of which is the first epigraph to this chapter, mocks not only *Blast I* but also Lewis's play, *Enemy of the Stars*, and his involvement in the Omega Workshop, the editors' column, "Readers and Writers," finds fault with *Blast*'s philosophical and spiritual limitations in the following manner:

Mr. Wyndham Lewis' new quarterly magazine, "Blast" (Lane 2s 6d.), has been announced as the successor of the "Yellow Book." But that, I imagine, is no great credit to it, for who, looking back to that period, can admit that there was any philosophy in it? Aubrey Beardsley was something of a genius, but his mind was never equal to his talents; in other words, he was a decadent genius; and who else was there of the smallest importance on the "Yellow Book"? "Blast" has the relative disadvantage of being launched without even a decadent genius to give it a symptomatic importance. It is, I find, not unintelligible . . . – but not worth the understanding. Blake, it is certain, has gone into the making of it – but Blake without vision, Blake without spiritual certitude. More, no doubt, will be said of it in these columns, for in the absence of any movement of ideas, *any* movement must be discussed. All the same, its significance will have to be put into it; for of its own self it contains none.[30]

The following week, "Readers and Writers" opens with an admission that the editors hadn't read *Enemy of the Stars* before writing the previous week's column, and concedes that "it deserves to be called an extraordinary piece of work" – in sharp contrast to Rebecca West's short story, "Indissoluble Matrimony," which has "all the vices of the 'Blast' school, excessive and barbaric ornamentation, violent obscurity, degraded imagery; but unmixed with any idea."[31] Undoubtedly, "Readers and Writers" then admits, *Blast*:

will provide in the end fresh material for reason to elucidate. But for the moment the movement [Vorticism] appears to me to be the very devil. Brilliant common sense, which we of THE NEW AGE have taken as our watchword, is obviously in peril from the neo-mysticism; so, too, I fear, is reason itself. I'm afraid, however, that the plunge into the dark is going to be seductive of the young. It sounds romantic, it makes a great clatter both in the mind and in the world, it stirs the solar plexus, and it produces the illusion of life. All the same, it is past racial history; and the time-spirit will be revenged on such as stir its bones. I will return to the subject if nobody else deals with it. (253)

If Hulme and Lewis take some hard knocks in the *New Age*, Ezra Pound's treatment at the hands of its readers and editors is still more strikingly and wittily hostile – and hence exemplary of the journal's less-than-laudatory stance toward the modernist avant-garde. Pound published extensively in the *New Age*. As noted earlier, many of these articles found their way eventually into Eliot's *Literary Essays of Ezra Pound*; the rest surfaced again much more recently in *Ezra Pound's Poetry and Poetry: Contributions to Periodicals*, Volume I (1991). While Eliot's edition of Pound's writings redacts Pound's wide-ranging cultural writings into more narrowly "literary" fare, as Michael Coyle has noted, both Eliot and Pound's more recent editors isolate his writings from the controversies they inspired in the *New Age*, thereby creating a kind of authority for these essays that they certainly did not have in their original context.

Interestingly enough, Pound himself goes on record publicly as being very appreciative of the *New Age*'s interest in operating as a forum of open debate about the arts and politics, not an in-house modernist publication, so to speak. The second installment of his series, "Affirmations," for example, opens with the following endorsement of the *New Age*'s editorial policy:

THE NEW AGE permits one to express beliefs which are in direct opposition to those held by the editing staff. In this, THE NEW AGE sets a most commendable example to certain other periodicals which not only demand that all writers in their columns shall turn themselves into a weak and puling copy of the editorial board, but even try to damage one's income if one ventures to express contrary beliefs in the columns of other papers.[32]

This comment is undoubtedly a tribute to the *New Age*'s commitment to providing its writers and readers with an independent arena for public debate about politics, literature, and the arts. Still, the sheer number as well as the intensity and the range of negative responses Pound's work elicited from *New Age* readers and columnists are striking reminders that its presentation of modernist movements is not, *per se*, an endorsement.

Pound's reaction, for example, to a typographic error in the January 28, 1914 *New Age* printing of "Affirmations IV. As for Imagisme" certainly suggests his awareness of *New Age* readers' less than sympathetic response to his work. He writes – entirely without bluster, perhaps surprisingly – that "Your printer has put 'primary figment' instead of primary pigment' in the last paragraph of my last article (January 28). The phrase as it stands will doubtless give pleasure to many of your readers, but it does not convey my original meaning."[33] Yet even this concession doesn't prepare contemporary readers who think of the *New Age* as a modernist journal for the level of animosity (and hilarity) at his expense in the letters to the editor spawned in response to his work.

Writing under the pseudonym "Alice Morning," Beatrice Hastings, the *New Age*'s Paris correspondent and a "virtual co-editor" of the journal for a number of years while she was living with Orage and Katherine Mansfield in London,[34] leads the assault on Pound in a series of counter-manifestos in 1915. "I almost was about to believe," she writes,

while reading his article, "Affirmations," that Mr. Ezra Pound was about to wake up. But he sank quietly deeper on the pillow in his final paragraph, which is only an affirmation that he is a hopeless cultist. Bless my heart, Vortices and Quattrocentro! Why drag in physics? "Is it," asks Mr. Pound, "that nature can, in fact, only produce a certain number of vortices? That the Quattrocento shines out because the vortices of power coincided with the vortices of creative energy?" It is all fiddling with terms; and creative energy *is* power. Were there no vortices in nature before the Quattrocento? Yes; and whirlpools, and surges, and Charybdis, and the wheel of Ixion, whereon was bound the poor diable who embraced a cloud thinking it was Juno. I knew a woman once who had decided that everything went in spirals: and, by the way, she played little tricks on you with magic candles and perfumes that arose out of nowhere. The state of things in Art which Mr. Pound deplores is somewhat due to just such florid, pedantic, obscurantist critics as himself – Ixions whom not even an introduction to the almighty gods can clear of pretension.[35]

A slew of letters to the editor in the weeks that follow reiterate Hastings's objection to Pound's pedantic allusiveness. John Riddle complains of "the muddle" Pound has given us; Herman Scheffauer writes that "Mr. Ezra Pound might as well mask himself with the name of Ezra Ounce," and John Duncan writes: "It would be a delight to follow Mr. Pound into his magic wood of ribble-rows to stalk pattern-units and plunge the quivering spear into curlicubists, but bread and philosophy are very scarce nowadays, and we are not all fairy knights." "Be clear, Mr. Pound. Never say exiguous for narrow; nor talk of the intellectually-inventive-creative spirit when you mean what Englishmen once called wit, quick-parts and fancy."[36] And D. Lawrence concludes this series of exchanges with the following:

Your contributor, Miss Alice Morning, is right as usual when she describes Mr. Ben Ezra Pound as muddled. He is so busy borrowing ideas from all sources that he has no time to examine their meanings. He tells us that the present search is for intensity; but intensity by itself is of very little value. It must be intensity efficiently applied. Some verse-makers have intensity without efficiency; some have efficiency without intensity; only poets have both. Mr. Pound has no intensity and but little efficiency. If Mr. Pound wants to be efficient he must economise his means and stop running to waste like a British Museum on the loose.[37]

Other readers and editors of the *New Age* will take issue with other aspects of Pound's work even as the journal continues to allow him prime space in its pages. "Current Cant," for example, a regular column that cameos very brief excerpts from other periodicals, ridicules Pound's scientific rhetoric in "The Serious Artist,"[38] while Beatrice Hastings, writing as "T. K. L.," mocks Pound's seven-part "Approach to Paris" series quite uproariously in a counterpoint set of essays that occupies readers throughout the fall of 1913. The following excerpt from "All Except Anything," the penultimate piece in her series, epitomizes her deliciously wicked mockery, which is inspired primarily by Pound's championing of French poetry at the expense of English traditions.

Reader, when I began these articles I had no notion that there were so many Frenchmen! I thought they were doing these things better in France. But, alas, France is swarming: and every second individual is a poet exactly as over here in these chilly, but prolific islands. Exactly, too, as over here every one of these poets is unique, incomparable, defiant of computation; every one make his poems his very own; every one challenges in his especial person all the old poets and poetical trappings; every one sings of the commonplace, the ordinary you and the ordinary me; every one talks "normally" instead of posing as a Bard; every one prints his Bare Statement of Things in metrical lines. It begins to beat me to know one from another in spite of the fact that they are all unique.[39]

Although Pound isn't exactly handled with kid gloves in these pieces by both regular contributors and *New Age* readers, his toughest critic, and the one who offers the most sustained critique of his work, is the editor's column of the *New Age*, "Readers and Writers," which was written not only by Orage himself but also by Beatrice Hastings and other regular contributors to the journal under the pseudonym "R. H. C."[40] In September 1914, "Readers and Writers" calls attention to Pound's recent essay in the *Fortnightly Review* on Vorticism – and dismisses both Pound's promotion of the movement and his characterization of the relationship between Imagism and Vorticism in the following manner:

Whether or not [Mr. Ezra Pound] knows it, Vorticism is dead. It was, at best, only a big name for a little thing, that in the simmering of the pre-war period suddenly became a bubble, and is now burst. Of the magazine "Blast," which was devoted to the propaganda of Vorticism, I doubt whether another issue will appear. Compared with the war it is incomparably feeble. Mr. Pound, however, tries to establish some connection between "Vorticism" in painting and design and "Imagism" in verse. As usual, he is very obscure and the more so for the pains he takes to disguise the real relations. Mr. Pound happened to like Mr. Wyndham Lewis, and there you are! That this is a thousand times more probable than Mr. Pound's explanation appears from this: that while he defines Imagism, his own contribution to the common stockpot, quite clearly, he nowhere in the article has a clear word to say on the subject of Vorticism.[41]

Lest readers assume this is an endorsement of Imagism if not of Vorticism, the column concludes by challenging the formal innovativeness of Pound's most famous Imagistic poem, "In a Station of the Metro." After reprinting the poem, the column continues:

The image here, you are to understand, is Mr. Pound's imaginative equivalent for the scene of which he was a sensitive witness; and we ought further to conclude that it is the perfect image. But is it? On the contrary, I could invent a score of other images of quite equal equivalence. So could anybody. Meredith was perpetually doing such things: his "dainty rogue in porcelain" is the most familiar instance. Shelley was prolific in them. The Japanese have made their only literary art of such bon-bons. What of these, for instance, as other images of the same scene: white wheeling gulls upon a muddy weedstrewn beach; war medals on a ragged waistcoat; patches of blue in a sky of smoke-coloured clouds; oases in a sand-storm; flaming orchids growing upon a gooseberry bush; mistletoe on bare trees snow-clad; iridescence upon corpses; a robin's song on a dark autumn day. Had enough? I could go on ad infinitum. But I should not set up as an Imagist, but only as a journalist, on the strength of them! (449)

Reminding readers that the *New Age* "had the honour of first publishing" Pound's translation of "The Sea-Farer," which is "without doubt one of the finest literary works of art produced in England during the last ten years," but offering qualified praise for *Cathay* and characterizing Pound's poetic contributions to *Blast I* as "a hybrid . . . between the commonplace and the incomprehensible," "Readers and Writers" disparages Pound's aesthetic theorizing in an August 5, 1915 column. "However often we may have mentioned Pound's name, it is at least certain that we have never countenanced his theories," the *New Age* insists. "But then," the column goes on to note,

> Mr. Pound is so much better than his theories that to dispose of them is by no means to dispose of him. What, in fact, he does in the company his theories keep, it is hard to say; for they do not distinguish him, but link him with inferior schools; they do not influence his work, except when he is wilful [*sic*] like an American child; and they afford him no help. I would part Mr. Pound from his theories as often as I found him clinging to one, for they will in the end be his ruin.[42]

Condemning artists who "worship" Pound, and taking significant umbrage with the suggestion that Pound was "invented" by the *New Age*,[43] the *New Age* points up over and over again, in column after column, its differences with Pound – and its right to publish Pound nonetheless.

A 1913 "Readers and Writers" nicely summarizes this policy of both featuring and quarreling with Pound, and through him the modernist avant-garde more generally. Responding to readers' challenges regarding the appropriateness of publishing "T. K. L.'"s parodies of Pound while the latter's series of essays on French poetry, "Approach to Paris," was still being published, "Readers and Writers" defends this decision by making an analogy with the *New Age*'s presentation of Hillaire Belloc's critiques of Guild Socialism:

> Nobody, I suppose, thinks it odd that Mr. Belloc should write in THE NEW AGE in criticism of the National Guilds System; and nobody will think it odd if the editorial exponents of that system reply either currently or at the conclusion of the series. Why, then, should it be thought strange to publish Mr. Pound's articles and to subject them to criticism while they were still before our readers? But Mr. Pound, it will be said, was not attacking THE NEW AGE, he was only defending certain tendencies in French poetry. This view assumes too readily the eclecticism of THE NEW AGE which is much more apparent than real. We have, as discerning readers know, as serious and well-considered a "propaganda" in literature as in economics or politics. Why should it be supposed that the economic writers are jealous to maintain their views and to discredit their perversions or antitheses; and the critics of literature be indifferent? It will be found, if we all live long enough, that every part of THE NEW AGE hangs together; and that the literature we despise is associated with the economics we

hate as the literature we love is associated with the form of society we would assist in creating. *Mr. Pound – I say it with all respect – is the enemy of THE NEW AGE.* (emphasis added)[44]

The *New Age*'s respectful hostility – but hostility nonetheless – toward Pound in particular and the modernist avant-garde more generally cannot simply be ignored. Once the *New Age* is on-line it won't be buried in the archive either. If the above material from a multiplicity of articles, editorials, reviews, letters to the editors, and weekly columns suggests the inappropriateness of labeling the *New Age* a "modernist" journal, some background information on Guild Socialism and its equally tension-filled relationships with other British socialist movements of the period can help us understand the political commitments powering this critique of the modernist avant-garde, which the editors allude to in the above passage through reference to the *New Age*'s "serious and well-considered" "propaganda" in literature *and* economics/politics.

"THE TRAGEDY OF THE LAST THIRTY YEARS": REFORMIST V. REVOLUTIONARY SOCIALISM

British Guild Socialists were opposed to the political gradualism and the narrowly class-based politics of both Fabian Socialism and the Independent Labour Party. Although half of the funding for the *New Age* was provided by Bernard Shaw when Orage and Holbrook Jackson first took over the journal in 1907, the journal quickly outgrew its Fabian Art League support, and Shaw was featured along with Beatrice and Sidney Webb and H. G. Wells in political caricatures that provide visual reinforcement of the verbal critiques offered in the journal's regular columns.[45] Taking issue in particular with the Webbs, who believed in the gradual transformation of a capitalist economy through the nationalization of industry and development of the heavily centralized bureaucratic infrastructures of a modern welfare state – and were all too willing, in the view of Guild Socialists, to work with any government that would accept their advice – Guild Socialists wanted to "free workers from the unrelieved tedium of mass production and restore a sense of craftsmanship which would make labour satisfying and its products beautiful."[46] Unlike French Syndicalists, British Guild Socialists did not envisage the disappearance of the State; instead, as Wallace Martin notes, they proposed that citizens would elect a state government to regulate the guilds, enact a national legislation, and conduct international affairs. Borrowing heavily from John Ruskin and William Morris, but also challenging the latter's complacency regarding the association of art with luxury, A. J. Penty and Orage sought, in studies such as *The Restoration of the Guild System* (1906) and a multitude of editorials, feature articles, and letters in the *New Age*, to assist in creating a form of society that would be a genuine alternative to either capitalist commodity culture or Fabian Socialism. In such a society workers would no longer regard their labor as a market commodity. In such a society the words of the Apocrypha, which served as the motto of the movement, would come true: "They shall maintain the fabric of the world, and in the handiwork of their craft is their prayer."[47]

"Press Cuttings" is a regular column in the *New Age* in which the editors reprint a passage (usually a substantial paragraph) from another news source as a means of endorsing the latter's view without adding any additional commentary. A "Press Cuttings" from the Bristol socialist paper, the *Venture*, demonstrates the legacy to Guild Socialism of both Arts and Crafts and Clarion movement socialisms, while also hinting at the critique of science that places Guild Socialism in relation to Fabian Socialism as well.

Of the 'movements' which aspire to modify the social order, that which aims at instituting National Guilds is the most inclusively human, and appeals most completely to the whole gamut of Nature's finest faculties. It is scientific, but it always subordinates science – whether it be economics or sociology – to art, to the great art of living. We need to realise that economics alone, and that even science in general, is quite unequal to the task of controlling the destinies of man. To live, or rather, to live well, is an art. This is as true of human society as of the individual. The government of man is more than science; it is an art, based not on economics but on philosophy, and the building of an ideal, well-ordered society, such as Socialists dream of, is emphatically a work of art . . . The new order of society, if it is to be attained at all, calls for imagination, courage, devotion, and high-spirited allegiance to its great ideals. It is in that spirit that some of us see in National Guilds the mould of a new civilisation. The mark of that new fraternal civilisation will not be a false and impossible equality, but fair play and freedom in the fellowship of the Guilds. The Guilds will raise and expand the standard of life for the whole of their members. Leisure and plenty, culture and fine character will no longer be buried out of bounds for the many, as at present. To work for the coming of the Guilds is to work for the re-establishment of fellowship in the world of Labour. It is to work not merely for a new economic system, but for the humanising influences that would be liberated thereby.[48]

Guild Socialism's attempt to redirect, and thereby radicalize, not only the Arts and Crafts movement's commitment to the humanization of labor but also the Clarion movement's faith in human "fellowship" is fairly obvious in the *New Age*'s silent endorsement of the *Venture*'s views. On the one hand, Guild Socialists such as Ivor Brown follow William Morris's lead in suggesting that the two central human desires "neglected by socialists" and "crushed, mocked and perverted by the capitalists" are "the will to do good work" and the "craving for some freedom in personal choice and expression."[49] But on the other hand, Guild Socialists such as Penty and Ramiro de Maetzu criticize the Arts and Crafts movement for not having "a social theory which accords with its artistic philosophy."[50] Art needs to take "in hand the work of social reconstruction," rather than allowing itself to be "thrust out of society by the ever-increasing pressure of commercial conditions of existence," Penty writes.[51] Taking this same critique still further, de Maetzu stresses over and over again in his many articles for the *New Age* that Ruskin, Morris, and Oscar Wilde (presumably in "The Soul of Man Under Socialism") went wrong when they dreamed of turning society into a "corporation of artists who... discover their joy in the production of beautiful things."[52] "You cannot make workmen happy by utilising their energies in the production of beautiful things," he insists, arguing that the production of beautiful things, in a capitalist commodity culture, is harnessed inevitably "to the service of luxury, vice, and decoration."[53] Failing to distinguish between, for example, Kelmscott Press fine art editions and copies of the *Yellow Book*, which sold cheaply and were available at railway stations as well as in other venues, de Maetzu associates the Arts and Crafts movement with bourgeois luxury and seeks a more radical collectivism in a national guild system.[54]

As noted in Chapter 2, the modernist avant-garde's relationship with *fin-de-siècle* aestheticism is deeply complex and contradictory. Guild Socialism's is equally so. On the one hand, *New Age* Guild Socialists view aestheticism's alleged characterization of art's autonomy from the political sphere as counter-progressive;[55] on this basis they collapse any distinction between aestheticism and decadence. "The association of art with luxury, of beauty with disease, of aesthetic emotion with strange and sought sensations, is the unholy union of god and ape that we have set ourselves to annul," "Readers and Writers" announces definitively.[56] If *Blast* describes itself as a successor to the *Yellow Book*, this is a mark against it rather than in its favor. Indeed, this is "another sign of the spiritual anarchism of modern society," confirmation that the "spiritual character of our intellectuals has been declining. "There is no life in decadence...nowadays; its future is past...Only those writers belong to the new age and have a future before them who can write sense," the

New Age declaims. And the *New Age* "must be more definite" if it is going to succeed in battling the intellectual decadence of the age.[57]

On the other hand, the *New Age*'s borrowings from Wilde are more pervasive than it was willing to acknowledge. As noted in Chapter 2 was also the case with T. S. Eliot, there are "skeletons of influence" (to borrow Richard Shusterman's phrasing) in Guild Socialists' critical closet that could not be brought into the light of day, in this case not only because of Wilde's status as a "social pariah," an "isolated figure removed from 'the main current' of tradition," but also because of Guild Socialism's participation in what Christopher Hitchens has characterized as contemporary scholars' willful erasure of "The Soul of Man Under Socialism" from the record of turn-of-the-century British socialist debate.[58]

This last point moves the discussion too far afield from my main argument, however, which is to explain what the *New Age* means by "writing sense" versus succumbing to the intellectual decadence of the age. *New Age* Guild Socialism's insistence upon the value of logical, rational argument needs to be understood in the context of its strong antagonism to turn-of-the-twentieth-century idealizations of science and scientific method by both Fabian Socialists and modern avant-gardists alike. Although the *New Age*, as noted earlier, began its life under Orage's editorship with Fabian Art League support, it severed its association with Fabianism fairly quickly and Fabians are critiqued alongside Futurists and Vorticists for their "decadent" fascination with efficiency, machinery, and scientific objectivity. Recall the Bristol *Venture*'s claim: "[E]conomics alone, and . . . science in general, is quite unequal to the task of controlling the destinies of men. To live, or rather, to live well, is an art." As Guild Socialists use the term, "decadence" refers to both short-sighted scientific materialism and spiritual anarchism. Examples of decadent scientism include both the Fabians' neglect of "the spiritual and pyschological qualities" of the proletariat and the Vorticists' "cantings about Life-Force."[59] Examples of "decadent" spiritual anarchism include not only the writing in *Blast I* but also the poetry of Rabindranath Tagore. The fact that W. B. Yeats and Pound are promoting Japanese Noh drama and that Tagore's "mysticism is just now so much the rage of a large following" is, from a British Guild Socialist's perspective, as sure a sign of the failures of modern society as *Blast*'s "savage" views on "God as Energy, Action, and Dynamic Philosophy" and its "affection for gore."[60]

Rejecting all such efforts to map the "progress" of modern British society either through the achievements of science or through a false (false because it's non-English) spiritualism, Guild Socialists instead hold out hope for a "real revolution," a socialist revolution: "The tragedy of the last thirty years," Orage writes in his 1913 essay, "Journals Insurgent," a crucial statement of his editorial principles and commitments, "is now known to be this: a propaganda [i.e., socialism] assumed to be revolutionary was not revolutionary, but merely reformative." "[T]he real revolution is to be found in the destruction of wagery and not in political action; . . . the real revolution is the transformation of the wage-system into a labour monopoly,"which "can only be effective in the form of a guild – an organisation, that is to say, that can produce wealth more efficiently and distribute it more equitably than under present conditions."[61]

A second passage from "Journals Insurgent" can help us understand the *New Age*'s commitment to the presentation of literature and the arts as a key component of any truly revolutionary socialist platform for cultural change. "Not the least of the revolutionary journal's troubles," Orage writes, "is the difficulty to drive into the minds of its readers that life is not composed of water-tight compartments." "Although [i]t is quite usual for many so-called revolutionary journals to assume that the economic struggle can be maintained without affecting the canons that govern the writing of books, the painting of pictures, the preaching of sermons, and even the fabric and texture of religion," "[w]e are under no such delusions" (51). Thus, unlike the *New Statesman*, the official journal of Fabian Socialism, the *New Age* perceives itself as having literary and artistic as well as political work to do. Not only does it feature regular "literary" columns such as its theater review series; still more importantly, it conceptualizes its participation in debates about literature and art as part and parcel of its political work. Specifically, Orage argues that:

the literary work of the revolutionary journal, whether creative or critical, must cut across all modern canons of conduct, or literature, or of art. It is our experience that reviews and critiques so inspired hurt far more than our analysis of the wage-system, our attacks on the political parties or our advocacy of labour monopoly. But we know in fact as well as in reason that the economic emancipation of the workers is a dream until its conception has entered into and coloured and changed the minds and hearts of all who minister to our reason and imagination. (51)

Note how much further Orage goes here than in the "Readers and Writers" discussed above. Rather than simply claiming that "every part of THE NEW AGE hangs together," that the editorial stance taken on economic matters is related to that taken on literary and artistic concerns,

Orage insists that the "revolutionary journal's" literary and artistic reviews and critiques are even more effective politically than political commentary *per se*. They "hurt far more" than rational analysis of the wage
system, because literature and art "chang[e] the minds and hearts" of
readers by "minister[ing]" to reason *and* imagination.

This commitment to a view of the aesthetic realm as an integral component of the political and economic order, not a separate (and subor-
dinate) sphere fuels many of the *New Age*'s harshest criticisms of other
periodicals. If anything is "eclectic" about the *New Age* under Orage it
is the editorial staff's reading habits, not its political and literary commitments. As noted earlier, its range of reference to other periodicals in
regular columns such as "Current Cant" and "Press Cuttings," as well
as the editor's column, "Readers and Writers," is truly extraordinary.
And yet, precisely because of its political and literary commitments, the
New Age's line of argument about the periodical literature of its day is un-
mistakably partisan. Anxious to combat the fragmentation of the public
sphere exacerbated at the turn of the century by the proliferation of periodical publications; anxious, too, to reach and radicalize a newly literate
working-class populace, which it worries is increasingly drawn to the
spectacular attractions of commodity culture, it criticizes quite sharply
any and all periodicals that fail to live up to its own high standards
of integrative and politically progressive debate about politics and the
arts.

Its hostility to the narrowness of special-interest literary and political periodicals is particularly telling in this regard. Robert Blatchford's
Clarion, for example, one of its chief socialist competitors, is taken to
task regularly not only for its patent medicine advertisements but for
its failure to provide coverage of the full range of developments within
British socialism at the turn of the century. Similarly, the *Labour Leader*
is described as never having "risen higher than a parish magazine; it is
spiteful, narrow, and ignorant." And *Justice* is noted as having "lost in intellectual power" when it "occupied itself more and more [restrictively]
with politics."[62] Special-interest "little magazines" promoting one or another avant-garde–ism fare no better. The concern the *New Age* expresses
regarding *Blast*'s eminent publication exemplifies this vein of criticism: "I
hear that a magazine, to be named "Blast," will shortly appear under the
editorship of Mr. Wyndham Lewis to provide a platform for the discussion of Cubism and other aesthetic phenomena," "R. H. C." notes in the
editor's column, "Readers and Writers." "It will, of course, be amusing
for an issue or two, and connoisseurs will purchase early numbers as an

investment for their old age." "[B]ut *will it encourage discussion, the one thing needed?*" he then asks (emphasis added).

My own experience is that effective discussion can take place only in an independent arena. Arguments must meet on common ground. But the conductors of "Blast" will naturally be more concerned to propagate their ideas than to defend them.[63]

The quarrels waged between *New Age* Guild Socialists and all manner of both socialists and modernist avant-gardists can thus be summarized as follows. On the one hand, what Guild Socialists, Arts and Crafts and Clarion movement socialists, and modern avant-gardists value in common is craftsmanship, understood not narrowly as a matter of formal technique but as a vehicle of cultural uplift. Pound's emphasis on the poet's craftsmanship in the third and fourth installments of "The Serious Artist," for example, bears an important resemblance to Penty's distinction between "the technical side of craftsmanship" and its "aesthetic side"; the latter is the means by which a "revival of the arts" shall be a "necessary factor in social salvation."[64] Care for the "aesthetic side" of craftsmanship also serves as a rationale for the linguistic eugenics that runs through both Guild Socialism and the work of many modernist avant-gardists. Recall, for example, Eliot's commitment to purifying the dialect of the tribe or Pound's defense of the public utility of accurate language. And compare these with Orage's praise for writing that deserves to be considered "genuine utterance" because of the way it sounds as well as what it says: "What matters is that when a sentence is completed it is a living organism, as simple as life and at the same time as complex... The manifesto remains a noble piece of English."[65]

On the other hand, Guild Socialists quickly diverge from both Fabian Socialists and modernist avant-gardists in their characterization of the need for a larger sense of history and a more expansive conceptualization of literary tradition. If there are certain surface similarities between, for example, Pound's arguments about the need for a "uniform criticism of excellence" and Guild Socialists' interest in raising aesthetic standards, this does not shelter Pound from the *New Age*'s criticisms of his insufficient knowledge of contemporary English literature – and hence his misguided valorization of French poetry. In fact, Pound's characterization of "an international standard of prose writing"[66] flies directly in the face of Guild Socialists' aesthetic nationalism, as exemplified in Orage's dismissive remarks about Pound's promotion of Japanese Noh drama in a 1915 editorial:

Japan is quite welcome to them. Mr. Pound does his best to make them intelligible and even to link them with his own little cult of imagism; but I understand them quite as little as their modern twig. The plays have atmosphere, and many of the speeches are charming; but head or tail of the whole I cannot make. Mix Maeterlinck with Mr. Pound under the influence of Mr. Yeats, and stir with modern spiritualism, and the result to my mind is that of the 'Noh-dramas.' It is not really encouraging."[67]

If in some regards Pound shares with Guild Socialists a sense of the need for what the *New Age* terms "a common standard, a high culture and a terrible pen,"[68] Pound's commitment to an ideal of world poetry nonetheless differs significantly from *New Age* Guild Socialists' nationalistic, working-class educationalism.

What a "terrible pen" means is no doubt fairly clear from the *New Age* material included here. What the *New Age* editors mean by "a common standard" and "a high culture," however, and what I mean here by working-class educationalism, deserve some discussion before continuing with this inventory of the journal's "quarrells" with both the modernist avant-gardists and other socialists.

"Common" is, crucially, always a politically inflected term for the *New Age*. It does not mean, as it does for Pound, universal. Instead, along with "popular," it bears the full weight of Guild Socialism's critique of the British class system in its characterization of cultural values that are accessible to all. Thus, when *Blast I* describes itself as "popular" and equates popular art with "the art of individuals," the *New Age* is quick to ridicule these assertions by featuring them in "Current Cant" alongside other objectionable sayings in the recent press such as Desmond Mac-Carthy's request, in the *New Statesman,* for a more satisfying theatrical representation of "squalidness," a Supreme Film Company's advertisement for "The Baboon's Vengeance, or the Conscience of the Great Unknown," and the *Daily Herald's* association of women with logic.[69] Scholars such as Marjorie Perloff and Colin MacCabe have argued for the radicalness of avant-garde discourses before the war, but the *New Age* clearly and consistently distinguishes between the work of an avant-garde coterie culture or submarket (before, during, and after the war) and what Raymond Williams has termed the work of "the long revolution."

For example, Rowland Kenney's series of articles for the *New Age* on "Education for the Workers" in the spring of 1914 situates the journal very clearly on a spectrum of working-class educational efforts, and can help us understand the political values informing its trumpeting of both "high culture" and "a common standard." Kenney distinguishes among three kinds of working-class education: technical, civic, and revolutionary. "To say that [a technical education] can make any appreciable difference in the conditions of the masses" is an insult to labour's intelligence, Kenney begins by noting, for "a technical education for the labourer is simply a means of making him into a more profitable machine for his employer."[70] Because the skilled labor market is as overcrowded as the unskilled labor market, a competent craftsman "may tramp from London to Dundee without getting one day's work at his own skilled trade," while "carpenters, metalworkers, skilled workmen of every kind are driven to take jobs as labourers, and no further improvement of their knowledge of their [new] trade will lift them out of the unskilled labour rut (652).[71]

The Workers' Education Association and the Ruskin College movement in Oxford epitomize Kenney's second type of working-class educational effort, whose object is "to give discontented workers an education in politics, economics, and in all sociological matters." That this kind of education becomes a means of "draining off" "what brainy men the labour movement possesses" and "turning... [them] into university slimed prigs" is "one of the most terrible wrongs a man can inflict upon the working classes," Kenney contends. The alleged "non-party, non-sectarian" stance of the Workers' Education Association and the Ruskin College movement's anxiousness "to steer clear of the idea that it is out for the workers as a class" earn both associations Kenney's contempt (652).

"Revolutionary" working-class educators alone garner Kenney's praise, but, notably, their ranks are slim: the *New Age*, the Central Labour College, and "in a less degree, one or two other journals" (which remain unnamed) are working all but single-handedly "to keep the minds of workers clear from the cant and lies that are being so widely disseminated by and in the interests of the profiteering classes." "So far," Kenney writes,

labour has had but a limited consciousness of the fact that its position of inferiority was imposed upon it by its superiors. It has struck out blindly against oppression when the intensity of that oppression has become unbearable, but few of the workers have understood, or have been helped to understand, what they were striking against exactly, or to what end their blows and campaigns were waged. Each struggle has seemed something apart from the general course of their lives; a sudden disaster, some strange phenomenon. In short, revolting labour has been an almost blind and unintelligent force. Now the workers are gradually learning that a battle between themselves and the profiteers is no strange outburst due to some sudden change in their relations, or increase in the price of bacon, but simply an incident in one long campaign that must end either in the overthrow of wagedom or in their own eternal enslavement. And, as we have seen, labour has so far been the losing party in the campaign. The process of enslaving the worker is now going on, and the civic educators are helping it along; the technical educators are, at the very best, doing nothing to prevent or hinder it. (653)

"The Bondage of Wagery: An Open Letter to the Trade Union Congress" on August 28, 1913 offers additional evidence of the *New Age*'s goals as a revolutionary working-class educational forum. Contrasting the "artificial excitement" of contemporary Parliamentary politics with the "thrilling interest" to be inspired by a transition from capitalism to a national guild collectivism, the *New Age* identifies its opposition before asserting its own claims: "There is a coterie of thinkers who now assert that capitalism has finally subdued our population into a servile state." Not only has the *New Age* "combated that view" "intellectually," it has "passionately resented it," and it writes now to the Trade Union Congress in order to urge the latter to understand "the evils" that "flow out" of a capitalist wage system. "[F]ounded as it is upon wagery," modern capitalism is "by no means the last word in social or industrial organization," the *New Age* insists. "Our belief in the principles of democracy remains unshaken," the editorial continues: "[Ou]t of the mass of the working population can be developed genius and character as great as can be found under any aristocratic or autocractic system of life and government."[72]

But how is such "genius and character" to be nurtured? Through exposure to "high culture" and "a common standard," rather than through absorption in the spectacular attractions of a burgeoning commodity culture – a commodity culture with which *New Age* Guild Socialists perceive the modernist avant-garde establishing an all-too-comfortable relationship. *New Age* Guild Socialists insist upon the radical democratization of education. ("But first let us object to our correspondent's suggestion that the average boy will not read the Iliad if he gets the chance. He does not get the chance. He is made to plough through a little of Homer in the Greek; but the English translation of the Iliad still costs twelve shillings, and we dare swear that not one English boy in forty thousand has ever seen it."[73]) At the same time, however, they refuse to endorse art's commodification – whether the culprit is Selfridge's, the department store giant that dabbled in educational politics in the 1910s, or whether it's the end product of what the *New Age* will term the modernist avant-garde's "faddish" "charlatanism."

The *New Age*'s dismissal of a variety of avant-gardists in a March 1915 "Readers and Writers" is a particularly telling example of its attitudes in this regard. "The most serious complaint we can make of our age," this column opens by observing, "is that nothing dies of criticism. Fads arise, absurd theories, charlatans and humbugs of every kind, and are duly criticized here or elsewhere; whereupon they continue as if they had passed the tests with flying colours."[74] Given the obscurity into which the *New Age* itself has fallen, it is impossible for a contemporary reader to read the following remarks unironically. Note, though, how "Readers and Writers" charts the "progress" of the modern avant-gardists' descent into commercial success:

Time, it is true, puts an end to them [fads, absurd theories, charlatans and hum-bugs of every kind]; but for a considerable period, long after they have been failed with contumely, they enjoy public reputation and other marks of public favour. The cubist, the vorticist, and similar freaks of irresponsible 'artists' are a case in point. I venture to say that there is not one sincere vorticist in the world – or ever was. The most simple of them has never even deceived himself; and, as for the public, not a living soul, I believe, has affected to himself to understand or to relish the 'school.' For all that, the movement goes on, impervious to war as well as to criticism; but its end is approaching! A friend of mine has invented an auto-matic cubist-vorticist picture-maker that turns you out a Bomberg "Mud-bath" or a Wadsworth "City" with the turn of a wrist. A frame contains coloured pieces of flat wood which shift themselves into 'arrangements' (as Mr. Pound would have said) expressive of profound emotions! Specimens, I understand, can be seen at the Chenil Gallery at Chelsea. The invention will shortly be placed upon the market. (509)

The editors stop just short in this particular "Readers and Writers" of accusing the modernist avant-garde of going commercial. The "friend" who has figured out how to mass-produce Bombergs and Wadsworths isn't himself identified as an avant-gardist. But the alliance between the avant-garde and what Rowland Kenney had termed the "profiteering classes" is being forged nonetheless, and the *New Age* is adamant that this effort will succeed in accomplishing what criticism and the war have failed to do: namely, end the "irresponsible" avant-gardism of Cubists, Vorticists, and "similar freaks" through their assimilation into commodity culture.

Two points need to be made here in conclusion. First, the *New Age*'s cri-tique of the avant-garde for its cozy relationship with bourgeois consumer culture is part and parcel of its materialist critique of consumer culture itself. That is to say, the *New Age*'s critique of modernity encompasses its critique of the modernist avant-garde: the former drives the latter, not vice versa, even as it powers *New Age* Guild Socialism's antagonism to other socialisms as well. And second, it is impossible to read these fighting words, as we would now term them, without noting their irony. The editors speak with great confidence in the "Readers and Writers" discussed above about the way "time will put an end" to avant-garde fads. Yet, of, course it was Guild Socialism, not the modernist avant-garde, which quickly receded into the backwaters of history, superseded in Orage's own life first by an interest in Freudian psychoanalysis and then by Gurdjieffian mysticism in the early 1920's. Always a minority culture within British socialism, Guild Socialism quickly lost its visibility as a venue of open debate about politics *and* the arts. It was roundly trumped in the political arena by a version of Labour Party Parliamentarianism that solidified not only the rarification of the aesthetic sphere that Guild Socialism had resisted so fiercely but also the professionalization of intellectuality and literary study we've seen the Joyce–Pound–Eliot nexus of modernism promote as it secured its own safe housing in the modern academy.

NOTES

1. C. H. Bechhöfer, "More Contemporaries," *New Age* 15, 13 (July 30, 1914), 308.
2. L'Hibou, *New Age* 17, 12 (July 15, 1915), 258.
3. Michael Levenson, "Introduction," *The Cambridge Companion to Modernism* (Cambridge University Press, 1999), p. 1.
4. Sam Hynes, *Further Speculations* (Minneapolis: University of Minnesota Press, 1955); T. S. Eliot (ed.), *Literary Essays of Ezra Pound*; Baechler, Litz, and Longenbach (eds.), *Ezra Pound's Poetry and Prose: Contributions to Periodicals*. See also *The Collected Writings of T. E. Hulme*, ed. Karen Csengeri (Oxford: Clarendon Press, 1994).
5. For a useful discussion of this watchword of the *New Age*, see Wallace Martin, *The New Age Under Orage: Chapters in English Cultural History* (Manchester University Press; New York: Barnes & Noble, 1967), pp. 40–1.
6. Tom Steele, *Alfred Orage and the Leeds Art Club 1893–1923* (Brookfield, V.T.: Scolar Press, 1990), p. 15.
7. This is Wallace Martin's approach in *The New Age Under Orage*.
8. Steele, *Alfred Orage and the Leeds Art Club*, p. 15; Martin, *The New Age Under Orage*, p. xi.
9. "To Our Readers," *New Age* 2, 6 (25 April 1908), 503.
10. "Press Cuttings," quoting the Bristol *Venture*, *New Age* 17, 19 (September 9, 1915), 464.
11. "R. H. C.," "Readers and Writers," *New Age* 13, 14 (July 31, 1913), 393.
12. *Ibid.*, *New Age* 16, 3 (November 19, 1914), 69.

13. *Ibid., New Age* 15, 10 (July 9, 1914), 229.

14. *Ibid., New Age* 17, 13 (July 29, 1915), 309.

15. A. J. Penty, "Art and Plutocracy," *New Age* 15, 1 (May 7, 1914), 10; Penty, "Aestheticism and History," *New Age,* 14, 22 (April 2, 1914), 683–4.

16. North, *Reading 1922*, p. 11.

17. "R. H. C.," "Readers and Writers," *New Age* 16, 3 (November 19, 1914), 69.

18. T. W. Pateman, "A Post-Impressionist Parable," *New Age* 14, 9 (January 1, 1914), 282.

19. F. T. Marinetti, "Geometric and Mechanical Splendour in Words at Liberty," trans. Arundel del Ré, *New Age* 15, 1 (May 7, 1914), 16–17.

20. George A., "FUTURISTICS A LA MARINETTI," *New Age* 15, 2 (May 14, 1914), 45.

21. Charles Brookfarmer, "Futile-ism. Or, All Cackle and No Osses," *New Age* 15, 7 (June 18, 1914), 154.

22. T. E. Hulme, "Contemporary Drawings," *New Age* 14, 22 (April 2, 1914), 688. Hulme does go on to stack the deck a bit in favor of modern art in his next sentence when he hints at his antagonism toward conservative art critics that will soon be played out over responses to Jacob Epstein's work in the pages of the *New Age* (as will be discussed further below). Nonetheless, his initial invitation to *New Age* readers is uncharacteristically gracious in its acknowledgement of readers' right to decide for themselves what they think about modern art.

23. Many of "Tom T." [Jan de Junosza Rosciszewski]'s cartoons for the *New Age* are reproduced in Martin's *The New Age Under Orage*, and those at issue here will also be available shortly on the Modernist Journal Website. See "Tom T.," "Anthony Ludovici," *New Age* 14, 14 (February 4, 1914), 448; "Tom T.," "Roger Fry," *New Age* 14, 26 (April 30, 1914), 828; see also Will Dyson, "Progress," *New Age* 14, 12 (January 22, 1914), 376.

24. Hulme, "Mr. Epstein and the Critics," *New Age* 14, 8 (December 25, 1913), 251–3.

25. Arthur E. Hight, "Art," *New Age* 14, 10 (January 8, 1914), 319.

26. Douglas Fox Pitt, "Mr. Epstein and His Work," *New Age* 14, 10 (January 8, 1914), 319.

27. J.A.M.A., "Letter to the Editor," *New Age* 14, 12 (January 22, 1914), 382.

28. Arthur Rose, "Letter to the Editor," *New Age* 14, 12 (January 22, 1914), 382.

29. Wyndham Lewis, "Letter to the Editor," *New Age* 14, 10 (January 8, 1914), 319. See also his letter to the editor on April 2, 1914, in which he describes Walter Sickert as "the scandal of the neighborhood" thirty years ago, and a man who now "sits at his open front door and invents little squibs and contrivances to discomfort the young brigands he hears tales of, and of whose exploits he is rather jealous" (*New Age* 14, 22 (April 2, 1914,) 703].

30. "R. H. C.," "Readers and Writers," *New Age* 15, 10 (July 9, 1914), 229.

31. *Ibid., New Age* 15, 11 (July 16, 1914), 253. Subsequent references to this essay will be cited parenthetically in the text. Rebecca West is consistently

reviewed poisonously in the *New Age*. See *ibid*. 13, 9 (June 26, 1913) on the *New Freewoman* in general ("a great deal of cackle, but mostly lively cackle") and the characterization of West's "clever travel sketch," as being "marred . . . by some immature atheisms of the very dogmatic sort." "Indulgence in such senseless and insensitive audacities must not be prolonged if this writer wishes to be read by any but a clique," the reviewer suggests in closing (p. 237). See also "Current Cant," *New Age* 14, 5 (December 3, 1914), which holds up for ridicule West's statement in a recent issue of *The New Republic* that "There is now no criticism in England" (p. 115).

32. Ezra Pound, "Affirmations II," *New Age* 16, 11 (January 14, 1915), 277.

33. Pound, "Letter to the Editor," *New Age* 16, 14 (February 4, 1915), 391.

34. Steele, *Alfred Orage and the Leeds Art Club*, p. 39.

35. "Alice Morning" [Beatrice Hastings], "Impressions of Paris," *New Age* 16, 12 (January 21, 1915), 308–9.

36. John Riddle, "Letter to the Editor," *New Age* 16, 12 (January 21, 1915), 327; Herman Scheffauer, "Letter to the Editor," *New Age* 16, 15 (February 11, 1915), 415; John Duncan, "Letter to the Editor," *New Age* 16, 15 (February 11, 1915), 415.

37. D. Lawrence, "Letter to the Editor," *New Age* 16, 16 (February 18, 1915), 438.

38. "Current Cant," *New Age* 13, 27 (October 30, 1913), 780.

39. T. K. L. [Beatrice Hastings], "All Except Anything," *New Age* 13, 25 (October 16, 1913), 733. See also "The Way Back to America," *New Age* 13, 21 (September 18, 1913), 604–5; "The Clear Tongue plus Pindarism," *New Age* 13, 22 (September 25, 1913), 636–7; "Humanitism and the New Form," *New Age* 13, 23 (October 2, 1913), 669–70); "Aristophanes or Tailharde?," *New Age* 13, 24 (October 9, 1913), 702–3.

40. Beatrice Hastings notes in her autobiography that Orage wrote very few of the "Readers and Writers" columns and that she herself "had entire charge of, and responsibility for, the literary direction of the paper, from reading and selection of MSS to the last detail of spacing and position" between 1907 and 1914 (*The Old 'New Age' Orage – and Others* [London: Blue Moon Press, 1936], p. 3.) I note this problem of attribution but also set it aside for further consideration elsewhere.

41. "R. H. C.," "Readers and Writers," *New Age* 15, 19 (September 10, 1914), 449. Subsequent references to this essay will be cited parenthetically in the text.

42. *Ibid.*, *New Age* 17, 14 (August 5, 1915), 332.

43. This particular "Readers and Writers" opens by noting that "Mr. James Douglas has half accused THE NEW AGE of inventing Mr. Ezra Pound" (*New Age* 17, 14 [August 5, 1915], 332).

44. "R. H. C.," "Readers and Writers," *New Age* 14, 2 (November 13, 1913), 51.

45. See "Mr. and Mrs. Sidney Webb," *New Age* (April 10, 1913); "Tom T." [Jan de Junosza Rosciszewski], "Mr. George Bernard Shaw," *New Age* 14, 19 (March 12, 1914), 608; "Tom T.," "Mr. G. Bernard Shaw," *New Age* (June 5,

1915), 160; and "Tom T.," "Mr. H. G. Wells," *New Age* (May 29, 1913), 128. As noted above, many of these are reprinted in Wallace Martin's *The New Age Under A. R. Orage*, and will also be available soon on the MJP website.

46. Martin, *The New Age Under Orage*, pp. 202, 206.
47. As quoted in Martin, *The New Age Under Orage*, p. 209.
48. "Press Cuttings," *New Age* 17, 19 (September 9, 1915), 464.
49. Ivor Brown, "Towards National Guilds," *New Age* 17, 3 (May 20, 1914), 54.
50. Penty, "The Restoration of the Guild System VI," *New Age* 13, 18 (August 28, 1913), 511.
51. Penty, "The Restoration of the Guild System VII," *New Age* 13, 19 (September 4, 1913), 545.
52. Ramiro de Maeztu, "Not Happiness, But–," *New Age* 17, 10 (July 8, 1915), 224.
53. For further discussion by de Maeztu of aestheticism's inappropriate association of beauty with luxury, see "On Art and Luxury," *New Age* 16, 24 (April 15, 1915): 640–2.
54. I'd like to thank Margaret Stetz for this insight into his mis-characterization of aestheticism's exclusivity.
55. See Jonathan Freedman for a very different view of the way in which aestheticism is "always already" politicized, *Professions of Taste: Henry James, British Aestheticism, and Commodity Culture.*
56. "R. H. C.," "Readers and Writers," *New Age* 17, 6 (June 10, 1915), 133. The editors' remarks here are inspired by the first quarterly issue of the *Gypsy* featuring the work of Jacob Epstein and others, which the *New Age* views as retro-aestheticism. "Really it is an astonishing revenant from 1892," "Readers and Writers" suggests. "How those old ghosts do walk to be sure! They are, however, a little faded from their detention among the earth-bound shades. Mr. Odle is Beardsley without genius; and the writers are either dead, decadent or desirous of soon becoming one or the other." The *Gypsy* in this regard is a "challenge" to the *New Age*: "The war should have completed our work rather than have made it, as it now appears, all to be done over again. However, no cause is better to spend one's life in. Have at them!" (p. 133).
57. "R. H. C.," "Readers and Writers," *New Age* 15, 10 (July 9, 1914), 229.
58. See Shusterman, "Wilde and Eliot," p. 142, on the "skeletons of influence" in Eliot's closet; "social pariah" is his phrasing as well. For further discussion of the *New Age*'s borrowings from Wilde, see my "Oscar Wilde's Legacies to *Clarion* and *New Age* Socialist Aestheticism," in Joseph Bristow (ed.), *Oscar Wilde in Context* (forthcoming, University of Toronto Press). On the erasure of Wilde's contributions to socialist debate, see Christopher Hitchens, "Style and Socialism," in Regenia Gagnier (ed.), *Critical Essays on Oscar Wilde* (New York: G. K. Hall, 1991), pp. 88–90.
59. "The Death of an Idea," *New Age* 18, 11 (July 10, 1913), 287; "R. H. C.," "Readers and Writers," *New Age* 16, 13 (January 28, 1915), 346.

60. *New Age* 16, 13 (January 28, 1915), 346. On *Blast*'s association with *Yellow Book* decadence, see *New Age* 15, 10 (July 9, 1914), 229. On Tagore see also "Present-Day Criticism," *New Age* 12, 25 (April 24, 1913), 608, where he is described as a bengali Yeats: "wordy, pathetically sensuous, self-complacent, careless of the better example of better men." In December of 1913, the *New Age* will note with relief that "the indecent debauch is now over or nearly over, and one by one the victims of Mr. Yeats' frenzy [in promoting Tagore] will awake to discover that their discovery was illusory" [*New Age* 14, 7 (December 18, 1913), 209].

61. "Journals Insurgent," *New Age* 13, 15 (August 7, 1913), 414, 415. Subsequent references to this essay will be cited parenthetically in the text.

62. See, for example, "Retrospect," *New Age* 14, 1 (Nov. 6, 1913), 8. In this unsigned editorial reviewing the previous twenty-five years of socialism, the *Clarion* is accused of having "thoroughly imbibed the doctrine of State Socialism." Here and elsewhere, the complaint is also that the *Clarion* provides no opportunity "for 'living' discussion or controversy" because Robert Blatchford remains caught up in 1890s socialist paradigms (Geo. Brimelow, letter to the editor, *New Age* 13, 26 [23 October, 1913], 773).

63. R. H. C.," "Readers and Writers," *New Age* 14, 10 (January 8, 1914), 307.

64. Penty, "Aestheticism and History," *New Age* 14, 22 (April 2, 1914), 684. See also "Art and Revolution," *New Age* 14, 26 (March 19, 1914), 617; and "Art and Plutocracy," *New Age* 15, 1 (May 7, 1914), 10.

65. "R. H. C.," "Readers and Writers," *New Age* 13, 26 (October 23, 1913), 762.

66. Pound, "Affirmations VI," *New Age* 16, 15 (February 11, 1915), 410.

67. "R. H. C.," "Readers and Writers," *New Age* 17, 12 (July 22, 1915), 282.

68. *Ibid.*, *New Age* 14, 6 (December 11, 1913), 176.

69. "Current Cant," *New Age* 15, 12 (July 23, 1914), 268.

70. Perloff, *The Futurist Moment: Avant-Garde, Avant Guerre, and the Language of Rupture*; Colin MacCabe, *James Joyce and the Revolution of the Word* (New York: Barnes and Noble, 1979); Raymond Williams, *The Long Revolution* (Westport: Greenwood Press, 1975).

71. Rowland Kenney, "Education for the Workers," *New Age* 14, 21 (March 26, 1914), 652–3. Subsequent references to this essay will be made parenthetically in the text.

72. "The Bond of Wagery: An Open Letter to the Trade Union Congress," *New Age* 13, 18 (August 28, 1913), 505.

73. "R. H. C.," "Readers and Writers," *New Age* 13, 14 (July 31, 1913), 393.

74. *Ibid.*, *New Age* 16, 19 (March 11, 1915), 509.

Conclusion: modernism and English studies in history

> The arts, literature, poesy, are a science, just as chemistry is a science... The arts give us a great percentage of the lasting and unassailable data regarding the nature of man, of immaterial man, of man considered as a thinking and sentient creature.
>
> Ezra Pound, "The Serious Artist"[1]

> In the early 1920s it was desperately unclear why English was worth studying at all; by the early 1930s it had become a question of why it was worth wasting your time on anything else. English was not only a subject worth studying, but *the* supremely civilizing pursuit, the spiritual essence of the social formation. Far from constituting some amateur or impressionistic enterprise, English was an arena in which the most fundamental questions of human existence – what it meant to be a person, to engage in significant relationship with others, to live from the vital centre of the most essential values – were thrown into vivid relief and made the object of the most intensive scrutiny.
>
> Terry Eagleton, "The Rise of English"[2]

I begin with these epigraphs in order to remind my readers of the backdrop of disciplinary restructuring that has framed this historical recontextualization of the Joyce–Pound–Eliot strand of literary modernism as I review the main objectives of this study. Fascinating work has been done recently on 1922, the *ano mirabilis* of literary modernism, that challenges us to think more expansively about popular as well as high culture modernisms. In contrast to that kind of synchronically "thick description" of literary modernism, however, I have chosen to work diachronically in this book: I have tried to position "the men of 1914" within a cultural debate about the value of the arts, and the mission of English language and literature studies in particular, that began at least as early as 1880 in Britain. This debate animates not only T. H. Huxley's claims in 1880 that the "modern" university's curriculum should be centered on training in science rather than the classics and Matthew Arnold's counter-argument

in defense of humanistic studies as a "scientific" enterprise in "Literature and Science" (1883). It also informs Beatrice Potter's decision *not*
to be a novelist every bit as much as it powers Ezra Pound's defense of
"scientific" artists in "The Serious Artist" (1913). And D. H. Lawrence's
defense, in 1920, of a particular kind of high-art novel's cultural capital
in a world increasingly dominated by visually oriented mass media. And
T. S. Eliot's and Guild Socialists' careful ghosting of Oscar Wilde and
the Victorian *fin de siècle* from, respectively, either an "English" literary
tradition or a socialist campaign for social change.

My province thus has been turn-of-the-twentieth-century studies, not
modernist studies *per se*. Such a field, through its historical delimitation alone, calls into question the temporal and evaluative divide the
Joyce–Pound–Eliot strand of modernism and its most influential academic promoters constructed between themselves and the nineteenth
century. Moreover, it challenges the divide scholars of modernism continue to make between the pre- and the postwar period, which has been
reinforced by recent work on the "long nineteenth century" (1780–1914)
as well. Perhaps most importantly, turn-of-the-twentieth-century studies
provides the most useful historical frame of reference for thinking about
the panoply of changes in the public sphere that has been addressed
here because of its bearing upon the rise of English studies and literary
modernism's "access[ion] to cultural legitimacy":[3] namely, the consolidation of modern disciplinary distinctions, the emergence and decline
of, respectively, new and residual aesthetic forms such as film and music
hall theater, and the debates about literature's role in culture generated
by middlebrow feminists and Guild Socialists in their efforts to carve
out alternatives to both a bourgeois public sphere and the modernist
submarket of literary production.

In very obvious ways this study is informed by feminist scholarship
on modernism and other work in the new modernist studies that has
"disclose[d] territories previously forgotten or unknown" in "the all too
familiar terrain" of "*fin-de-siècle*, Edwardian, and Modernist literature."[4]
In less obvious ways, perhaps, it is also informed by the work of sociolo-
gists of science and cultural theorists such as Bruno Latour as well as by
that of literary scholars who, inspired by Latour, are challenging us to rethink the "hitherto unexamined relations between [literary] modernism
and science."[5] In foregrounding the pressures of "scientific" professionalism attending upon and contributing to the Joyce–Pound–Eliot strand
of modernism's defense of "experimental writing," I have sought to show
how Pound's and Eliot's signature rhetoric about the scientific precision

of poetic observation, for example, can best be understood by taking account of the culture of professionalism driving the consolidation of modern disciplinary boundaries at the end of the nineteenth century. Modernism's defense, however contradictory, of a pristine and sacralized high art against the threatening pollution of mass culture needs to be recognized, I have tried to suggest, as one component of a very complex network of great divides separating "literature" from non-literary writing, "science" from commonplace ideas, and "progressive" from "degenerate" evolutionary trends in human history. Once we recognize the extent to which literature functioned as an "open field"[6] at the turn of the century – a varied, highly unstable, and fiercely contested discursive territory – it becomes possible to see similarity where the "men of 1914" map only difference: among the repertoire of cultural forms that ethnographic *poseurs* such as Beatrice Potter share with "scientific" artists, for example. It becomes possible as well to find nuance, depth, and subtlety where modernists chart only an absence – as in the case of Netta Syrett's quiet but nonetheless devastating critiques of avant-garde "blasting and bombadiering." And it becomes possible to recognize a wealth of evidence in the archives of a "modernist" journal such as the *New Age* recording Guild Socialists' fierce "quarrells" with the modernist avant-garde on any number of grounds.

A distinction has often been made between a pre-World War I "avant-garde" and postwar "modernism" on the basis of the latter's cozy relationship with bourgeois institutions such as museums and the academy. My purpose in coining the phrase "modernist avant-garde" and in looking, in the first two chapters of this study, for example, at modernists' envy of scientific authority and English studies' retreat from any sort of avant-garde valuing of scandalous sexuality in the wake of Oscar Wilde's trials, has been to call into question commonly held views of the avant-garde's radicalness and to expose instead its deep investments, *before* as well as after the war, in securing majority approval for its minority cultural values. What Michael North has termed the new modernist studies' "return to the scene of the modern," shouldn't simply ignore the modernist avant-garde's exclusionary moves and anxious territorialism, I have argued. To reproduce modernism's negative evaluations, silences, and outright erasures of other readings of modernity is simply to reinscribe a modernist mapping of turn-of-the-twentieth-century British literary and cultural history. Such a mapping, as I have tried to show here, is exactly that: *a* mapping not *the* mapping of either the literary field or of "modern" British culture.

That the modernists' mapping of "modern" culture and the literary field has been tremendously influential is undeniable. The rise of English studies not only coincided with the historical avant-garde's transformation into modernism, a culturally sanctioned and institutionally based phenomenon. It was facilitated *by* literary modernism – facilitated, that is, not only by the promotion of modernist "masterworks" as valid objects of critical study but also by the standardization of key modernist categories of literary critical analysis ("the literary," "art," "the artist"). But a "return to the scene of the modern" in our own turn of the century needn't renaturalize a modernist mapping of either the period or the literary field. To read canonical modernist texts, as I have done here, as places of narrow intensity on the great spectrum of the publishing industry at the turn of the twentieth century is to read them better, I would maintain, particularly insofar as this gives us a means of recognizing how they intersect with, borrow from, and react against other cultural enterprises of their time. Additionally and perhaps equally importantly, to read them with one eye focused on the "privileges and powers *of the subject position* we've inherited from modernist intellectuals" is to read our own moment in history, our own disciplinary practices, both more responsibly and more intelligently.[7]

NOTES

1. Pound, "The Serious Artist," *Ezra Pound: Poetry and Prose: Contributions to Periodicals, Volume One*, p. 186.
2. Eagleton, "The Rise of English," p. 31.
3. Levenson, *A Genealogy of Modernism*, p. 213.
4. Kaplan and Simpson, *Seeing Double: Revisioning Edwardian and Modernist Literature* (New York: St. Martin's Press, 1996), p. xx.
5. Squier, "Invisible Assistants or Lab Partners?," p. 301.
6. Beer, *Open Fields: Science in Cultural Encounter* (Oxford: Clarendon Press, 1996).
7. Jacobs, "Feminist Criticism/Cultural Studies/Modernist Texts: A Manifesto for the '90s," p. 276, emphasis in original.

Select bibliography

Allen, Robert, *Vaudeville and Film, 1895–1915: A Study in Media Interaction*, New York: Arno Press, 1977.

Altieri, Charles, "Can Modernism Have a Future?," *Modernism/Modernity* 7, 1 (January 2000), 127–43.

Apter, Emily, "Ethnographic Travesties: Colonial Realism, French Feminism, and the Case of Elissa Rhais," in Gyan Prakash (ed.), *After Colonialism: Imperial Histories and Post-colonial Displacements*, Princeton University Press, 1995, 299–325.

Ardis, Ann L., *New Women, New Novels: Feminism and Early Modernism*, New Brunswick: Rutgers University Press, 1990.

Armstrong, Timothy, *Modernism, Technology, and the Body: A Cultural Study*, Cambridge University Press, 1998.

Baechler, Lea, A. Walton Litz, and James Longenbach (eds.), *Ezra Pound's Poetry and Prose: Contributions to Periodicals*, New York and London: Garland, 1991.

Baldick, Chris, *The Social Mission of English Criticism, 1848–1932*, Oxford University Press, 1983.

Barkan, Elazar and Ronald Bush (eds.), *Prehistories of the Future: The Primitivist Project and the Culture of Modernism*, Stanford University Press, 1995.

Batsleer, Janet, Tony Davies, Rebecca O'Rourke, and Chris Weedon (eds.), *Rewriting English: Cultural Politics of Gender and Class*, London and New York: Methuen, 1985.

Beer, Gillian, *Open Fields: Science in Cultural Encounter*, Oxford: Clarendon Press, 1996.

Chinitz, David, "T. S. Eliot and the Cultural Divide," *PMLA*, 110, 2 (1995), 236–47.

Clark, Suzanne, *Sentimental Modernism: Women Writers and the Revolution of the Word*, Bloomington and Indianapolis: Indiana University Press, 1991.

Clark, T. J., *Farewell to an Idea: Episodes from a History of Modernism*, New Haven, C.T.: Yale University Press, 1999.

Clarke, Bruce, *Dora Marsden and Early Modernism: Gender, Individualism, Science*, Ann Arbor: University of Michigan Press, 1996.

Cockburn, Claude, *Bestseller: The Books that Everyone Read 1900–1939*, London: Sidgwick and Jackson, 1972.

Collini, Stefan, *Public Moralists: Political Thought and Intellectual Life in Britain, 1850–1930*, Oxford: Clarendon Press, 1991.

Colls, Robert, and Philip Dodd (eds.), *Englishness: Politics and Culture 1880–1920*, London: Croom Helm, 1986.

Combes, Annie E., *Reinventing Africa: Museums, Material Culture, and Popular Imagination in Late Victorian and Edwardian England*, New Haven, C.T.: Yale University Press, 1994.

Coyle, Michael, *Ezra Pound, Popular Genres, and the Discourse of Culture*, University Park: Pennsylvania State University Press, 1995.

Crawford, T. Hugh, *Modernism, Medicine and William Carlos Williams*, Norman: University of Oklahoma Press, 1993.

Cross, Nigel, *The Common Writer: Life in Nineteenth-Century New Grub Street*, Cambridge University Press, 1985.

Dettmar, Kevin J. H., and Stephen Watt (eds.), *Marketing Modernism: Self-Promotion, Canonization, Rereading*, Ann Arbor: University of Michigan Press, 1996.

DiBattista, Marie (ed.), *High and Low Moderns: Literature and Culture, 1889–1939*, Oxford University Press, 1996.

Di Leonardo, Micaela, *Exotics at Home: Anthropology, Others, American Modernity*, University of Chicago Press, 1998.

Dowling, Linda, *Hellenism and Homosexuality in Victorian Oxford*, Ithaca: Cornell University Press, 1994).

Doyle, Brian, *English and Englishness*, London and New York: Routledge, 1989.

Eagleton, Terry, "The Rise of English Studies," *Literary Theory: An Introduction*, Minneapolis: University of Minnesota Press, 1983, 17–53.

Easthope, Antony, *Literary into Cultural Studies*, London and New York: Routledge, 1991.

Eliot, T. S. (ed.), *Literary Essays of Ezra Pound*, New York: New Directions, [1918] 1935.

Eliot, T. S. (ed.), *Selected Essays of T. S. Eliot*, New York: Harcourt, Brace & World, [1932] 1964.

Eliot, Valerie (ed.), *The Letters of T. S. Eliot*, London: Faber and Faber, 1988.

Elliott, Bridget and Jo-Ann Wallace (eds.), *Women Artists and Writers: Modernist (Im)positionings*, New York and London: Routledge, 1994.

Felski, Rita, *Beyond Feminist Aesthetics: Feminist Literature and Social Change*, Cambridge, M.A.: Harvard University Press, 1989.

Felski, Rita, *The Gender of Modernity*, Cambridge, M.A. and London: Harvard University Press, 1995.

Foldy, Michael S., *The Trials of Oscar Wilde: Deviance, Morality, and Late-Victorian Society*, New Haven, C.T.: Yale University Press, 1997.

Freedman, Jonathan, *Professions of Taste: Henry James, British Aestheticism, and Commodity Culture*, Stanford University Press, 1990.

Gagnier, Regenia, *Idylls of the Marketplace: Oscar Wilde and the Victorian Public*, Stanford University Press, 1986.

Gagnier, Regenia, *Subjectivities: A History of Self-Representation in Britain, 1832–1920*, Oxford University Press, 1991.

Goodson, Ivor and Peter Medway (eds.), *Bringing English to Order: The History and Politics of a School Subject*, New York, London, Philadelphia: Faber Press, 1990), 47–86.

Guillory, John, *Cultural Capital: The Problem of Literary Canon Formation*, University of Chicago Press, 1993.

Huyssen, Andreas, *After the Great Divide: Modernism, Mass Culture, Postmodernism*, Bloomington and Indianapolis: Indiana University Press, 1986.

Hynes, Samuel, *The Edwardian Turn of Mind*, Princeton University Press, 1968.

Jacobs, Deborah, "Feminist Criticism/Cultural Studies/Modernist Texts: A Manifesto for the '90s," in Lisa Rado (ed.), *Rereading Modernism: New Directions in Feminist Criticism*, New York and London: Garland, 1994, 273–98.

Joseph, Michael, *The Commercial Side of Literature*, London: Hutchinson, 1925.

Kaplan, Carola M. and Anne B. Simpson (eds.), *Seeing Double: Revisioning Edwardian and Modernist Literature*, New York: St. Martin's Press, 1996.

Katz, Tamar, *Impressionist Subjects: Gender, Interiority, and Modernist Fiction in England*, Champagne-Urbana: University of Illinois Press, 2000.

Keating, Peter, *The Haunted Study: A Social History of the English Novel 1875–1914*, London: Secker and Warburg, 1989.

Kelly, Joseph, *Our Joyce: From Outcast to Icon*, Austin: University of Texas Press, 1998.

Kemp, Sandra, Charlotte Mitchell, and David Trotter (eds.), *Edwardian Fiction: An Oxford Companion*, Oxford University Press, 1997.

Kenner, Hugh, *The Pound Era*, Berkeley and Los Angeles: University of California Press, 1971.

Koestenbaum, Wayne, *Double Talk: The Erotics of Male Literary Collaboration*, New York: Routledge, 1989.

Laity, Cassandra, *H. D. and the Victorian Fin-de-Siècle*, Cambridge University Press, 1996.

Lawrence, D. H., *The Collected Letters of D. H. Lawrence*, ed. Harry T. Moore, New York: Viking Press, 1962, 2 vols.

Ledger, Sally and Scott McCracken, (eds.), *Cultural Politics at the Fin de Siècle*, Cambridge University Press, 1995.

Lepenies, Wolf, *Between Literature and Science: The Rise of Sociology*, trans. R. J. Hollingdale, Cambridge University Press, 1988.

Levenson, Michael H., *A Genealogy of Modernism: A Study of English Literary Doctrine 1909–1922*, Cambridge University Press, 1984.

Levenson, Michael H. (ed.), *The Cambridge Companion to Modernism*, Cambridge University Press, 1999.

Levine, Lawrence, *Highbrow/Lowbrow: The Emergence of Cultural Hierarchy in America*, Cambridge, M.A.: Harvard University Press, 1984.

Lewis, Wyndham, *Blasting and Bombardiering*, 2nd edition, Berkeley and Los Angeles: University of California Press, 1967.

MacKenzie, Norman (ed.), *The Letters of Sidney and Beatrice Webb*, Cambridge University Press, 1978.

McAleer, Joseph, *Popular Reading and Publishing in Britain 1914–50*, Oxford: Clarendon Press, 1992.

McDonald, Gail, *Learning To Be Modern: Pound, Eliot, and the American University*, Oxford University Press, 1993.

McDonald, Peter D., *British Literary Culture and Publishing Practice 1880–1914*, Cambridge University Press, 1997.

Martin, Wallace, *The New Age Under Orage: Chapters in English Cultural History*, Manchester University Press; New York: Barnes & Noble, 1967.

Mix, Katherine Lyon, *A Study in Yellow: The Yellow Book and Its Contributors*, Lawrence: University of Kansas Press, 1960.

Morgan, Robin, "The Englishness of English Teaching," in Goodson and Medway (eds.), *Bringing English to Order*, 187–241.

Nelson, James, *Early Nineties: A View from the Bodley Head*, Cambridge, M.A.: Harvard University Press, 1971.

Nicholls, Peter, *Modernisms: A Literary Guide*, London: Macmillan, 1995.

Nord, Deborah Epstein, *Walking the Victorian Streets: Women, Representation, and the City*, Ithaca: Cornell University Press, 1995.

Nord, Deborah Epstein, *The Apprenticeship of Beatrice Webb*, Amherst: University of Massachusetts Press, 1985.

Norrie, Ian, *Mumby: Publishing and Bookselling in the Twentieth Century*, 6th edn, London: Bell and Hyman, 1982.

North, Michael, *Reading 1922: A Return to the Scene of the Modern*, Oxford University Press, 1999.

Parkes, Adam, *Modernism and the Theater of Censorship*, New York: Oxford University Press, 1996.

Perloff, Marjorie, *The Futurist Moment: Avant-garde, Avant Guerre, and the Language of Rupture*, University of Chicago Press, 1986.

Perloff, Marjorie, *Radical Artifice: Writing in the Age of Media*, University of Chicago Press, 1991.

Pound, Omar and A. Walter Litz (eds.), *Ezra Pound and Dorothy Shakespear: Their Letters 1909–1914*, New York: New Directions, 1984.

Rado, Lisa (ed.), *Modernism, Gender and Culture: A Cultural Studies Approach*, New York: Garland, 1997.

Rado, Lisa (ed.), *Rereading Modernism: New Directions in Feminist Criticism*, New York and London: Garland, 1994.

Rainey, Lawrence, *Institutions of Modernism: Literary Elites and Public Culture*, New Haven, C.T.: Yale University Press, 1998.

Robbins, Bruce, *Intellectuals: Aesthetics, Politics, and Academics*, Minneapolis: University of Minnesota Press, 1990.

Robbins, Bruce, *Secular Vocations: Intellectuals, Professionalism, Culture*, London and New York: Verso, 1993.

Schaffer, Talia, *The Forgotten Female Aesthetes: Literary Culture in Late-Victorian England*, Charlottesville and London: University Press of Virginia, 2000.

Schaffer, Talia and Kathy Alexis Psomiades (eds.), *Women and British Aestheticism*, Charlottesville and London: University Press of Virginia, 1999.

Schenck, Celeste, "Exiled by Genre: Modernism, Canonicity, and the Politics of Exclusion," in Mary Lynn Broe and Angela Ingram (eds.), *Women's Writing in Exile*, Chapel Hill and London: University of North Carolina Press, 1989, 225–50.

Scott, Bonnie Kime, *Refiguring Modernism: The Women of 1928*, Bloomington and Indianapolis: Indiana University Press, 1995, 2 vols.

Sedgwick, Eve Kosofsky, *Epistemology of the Closet*, Berkeley: University of California Press, 1990.

Squier, Susan, "Invisible Assistants or Lab Partners? Female Modernism and the Culture(s) of Modern Science," in Rado, *Rereading Modernism: New Directions in Feminist Criticism*, 299–320.

Steele, Tom, *Alfred Orage and the Leeds Art Club 1893–1923*, Brookfield, V.T.: Scolar Press, 1990.

Stetz, Margaret D., "'Life's Half-Profits': Writers and Their Readers in Fiction of the 1890s," in Lawrence Lockridge, John Maynard, and Donald Stone (eds.), *Nineteenth-Century Lives* (Cambridge University Press, 1989), 169–87.

Stetz, Margaret D., "The Bi-Social Oscar Wilde and 'Modern' Women," *Nineteenth-Century Literature*, 55, 4 (March 2001), 515–37.

Stetz, Margaret D. and Mark Samuels Lasner, *England in the 1890s: Literary Publishing at the Bodley Head*, Washington, D.C.: Georgetown University Press, 1990.

Stetz, Margaret D. and Mark Samuels Lasner, *The Yellow Book: A Centenary Exhibition*, Cambridge, M.A.: Houghton Library, 1994.

Stokes, John, *In the Nineties*, University of Chicago Press, 1989.

Strychacz, Thomas, *Modernism, Mass Culture, and Professionalism*, Cambridge University Press, 1993.

Suleiman, Susan, *Subversive Intent: Gender, Politics, and the Avant-Garde*, Cambridge, M.A.: Harvard University Press, 1990.

Trodd, Anthea, *Women's Writing in English: Britain 1900–1945*, London and New York: Longman, 1998.

Viswanathan, Guari, *Masks of Conquest: Literary Studies and British Rule in India*, New York: Columbia University Press, 1989.

Walkowitz, Judith, *City of Dreadful Delight: Narratives of Sexual Danger in Late-Victorian London*, University of Chicago Press, 1992.

Webb, Beatrice, *The Diary of Beatrice Webb, Volume I, 1873–1892*, ed. Norman and Jean, MacKenzie, London: Virago, 1982.

Webb, Beatrice, *The Diary of Beatrice Webb, Volume II*, ed. Norman and Jean, MacKenzie, London: Virago, 1984.

Webb, Beatrice, *My Apprenticeship*, London: Cambridge University Press, 1979.

Wexler, Joyce Piell, *Who Paid for Modernism? Art, Money, and the Fiction of Conrad, Joyce, and Lawrence*, Fayetteville: University of Arkansas Press, 1997.

White, Allon, *The Uses of Obscurity: The Fiction of Early Modernism*, New York: Routledge and Kegan Paul, 1981.

Williams, Raymond, *The Politics of Modernism: Against the New Conformists*, London and New York: Verso, 1989.

Willison, Ian, Warwick Gould, and Warren Chernaik (eds.), *Modernist Writers and the Marketplace*, London: Macmillan; New York: St. Martin's, 1996.

Witemeyer, Hugh, *The Future of Modernism*, Ann Arbor: University of Michigan Press, 1997.

Wolff, Janet, *Feminine Sentences: Essays on Women and Culture*, Berkeley: University of California Press, 1990.

Woolf, Virginia, *Collected Essays of Virginia Woolf*, London: Hogarth Press, 1967.

Woolf, Virginia, *The Letters of Virginia Woolf*, ed. Nigel Nicholson and Joanne Trautmann, New York: Harcourt Brace Jovanovich, 1975, 6 vols.

Woolf, Virginia, *The Voyage Out*, New York: Signet Classic, 1991.

Index